Arthur James Johnes

On the Causes which have Produces dissent from the established Church in the Prinicipality of Wales

Arthur James Johnes

On the Causes which have Produces dissent from the established Church in the Prinicipality of Wales

ISBN/EAN: 9783337162283

Printed in Europe, USA, Canada, Australia, Japan

Cover: Foto ©ninafisch / pixelio.de

More available books at **www.hansebooks.com**

JOHNES

ON THE CAUSES WHICH HAVE PRODUCED

DISSENT

FROM

THE ESTABLISHED CHURCH,

IN THE

PRINCIPALITY OF WALES.

REPRINT, WITH ADDITIONAL PREFACE.

LONDON:
HOULSTON AND SONS, 65, PATERNOSTER ROW;
LLANIDLOES: JOHN PRYSE.
MDCCCLXX.

GARTHMYL, MONTGOMERYSHIRE,

April 6, 1870.

For a long time I have been urgently pressed by my neighbour, Mr. Pryse, Bookseller, of Llanidloes, to permit him to republish the accompanying volume. Hitherto I had refused my consent—from a reluctance to risk a repetition of the controversies in which I was involved by its first appearance—and by a regard to other calls on my time—which in themselves, overtax such energies as I still possess. Circumstances have, however, induced me now to grant his request. I think it an act of justice to announce, that he has undertaken the publication at his own risk; and I trust that he will receive from the Public that support which he anticipates and merits.

The work is now out of print, and the last copy in my possession was a few months since, presented by me to the Prime Minister, Mr. Gladstone, by whom its receipt was acknowledged in the subjoined Letter, and who has since selected an eminent Welsh clergyman to fill the Bishopric of St. Asaph, an appointment, which will be gratefully received both by Churchmen and Dissenters in the Principality. That appointment will also secure to that eminent Statesman, the honour of having been the first to break through the systematic exclusion of Welshmen from the Welsh Sees, an abuse introduced by the corrupt Governments of the last century, and a fertile source in the affairs of the Church in Wales, of jobbing and mal-administration—which form a striking contrast with the conduct of the native Bishops selected by Queen Elizabeth, and her immediate successors (See pages 94 to 111 inclusive).

I have deemed it inexpedient to publish a new Edition. The present volume is a reprint of the Second Edition, which appeared in 1832.

It is now about forty years ago since I reluctantly consented—at the urgent request of an excellent friend now no more—a clergyman of the Church of England, the Reverend Thomas Richards, of Llangyniew, in this county—to embark on the task of preparing "An Essay on the Causes of Dissent in Wales," as a candidate for a prize, that had been offered for the best Essay on that subject, by the Royal Cambrian Institution of London. That prize was awarded to me in May, 1831, by the Judge, the highest authority on Welsh Literature—Dr. W. O. Pughe—who pronounced it to contain a true account of the Causes of Dissent in Wales; and recommended its publication at the expense of the Society. The First Edition appeared soon afterwards.

In the following year, 1832, a Second Edition was published, with copious Historical and Statistical details, which, notwithstanding various attempts made through the Press to impugn their correctness, were eventually accepted by unprejudiced men, whether Churchmen or Dissenters, as truthful and accurate.

Had I leisure for the task, I do not think I could advantageously re-examine or alter those details. Nor do I think it advisable to remodel or change passages expressive of impressions entertained by me in my twenty third year, on questions such as the voluntary system and its effects—the question how far, and under what circumstances is separation from an Established Church justifiable—and other similar topics, on which wide differences prevail among men of honest and enlightened minds.

During the long period of my life that has elapsed since the first publication of this volume, some Bishops who have presided over Welsh Sees, have laboured industriously to redress the abuses of patronage, for which their predecessors were responsible. Time has also enhanced my opinion of the benefits, that Dissenting bodies have conferred on Wales,—benefits fully described in this volume.

I have chosen, however, to reprint the Essay unaltered. Churchmen and Dissenters alike, especially the few survivors of those who aided me with their advice and information at the time of its first appearance, will, I believe, prefer to see it unchanged, although its contents may not, in all their details, have met with their full concurrence. Many will, I anticipate, agree with me in thinking it undesirable on light grounds to destroy the identity of a publication, of which the usefulness and interest must depend on the truths it contains, and not on the individual impressions entertained in early youth by its Author.

As the compiler of a work of more labour and research, I may without pride or presumption indulge the expectation, that this Volume, on account of the facts it contains, may reach the hands of distant generations of my countrymen. The eloquent Member for Merthyr Tydvil, Mr. Richard, published some years ago, an able answer to various charges that had been made against the peasantry of Wales. I venture to think, that, all men of just and enlightened minds, who may read this Essay, in future times or in our own, will rise from its perusal with the conviction, that those who stand in need of vindication are the unprincipled and corrupt rulers in Church and State, of whom the people of that country have so long been the victims. I consider it necessary for their good to preserve unimpaired this picture of the extent to which they have been wronged during the age in which we live and in former times. I may direct the attention of those who desire information on the subject, to a recently published History of Wales, that combines in an eminent degree the merit of extensive research, with clearness and condensation in narrative and in reasoning.*

I can well recollect a remark that was once made in his place in Parliament, by an industrious patriot, to whom his country owes a

---

* A *History of Wales*, by Jane Williams; London, Longmans and Co.

lasting debt of gratitude, the late Mr. Joseph Hume, that the backward condition of the population in many districts might, in his opinion, be attributed to the non-residence of the clergy.

There was a time when the name of "Englishman" was a by-word and a reproach. (See Lord Macaulay's *History of England*, with reference to the period succeeding the Norman Conquest). In all ages of the world, the oppressor has invariably cast on a misgoverned race the responsibility for the consequences of injuries inflicted by himself. Thus tyranny and injustice have always obtained a plausible excuse in the eyes of the ignorant and superficial, that tends to perpetuate their reign. This is true of the treatment that the Celtic populations of this kingdom have experienced at the hands of the English Government. I believe that the laws of the Turks against the Greeks have never been more cruel and intolerant than those in existence against the Irish Catholics in the last century, which have been gradually repealed. The absurd theory, that had been broached by some speculative writers, as to an alleged natural inferiority in the Irish, Welsh, and other Celtic nations has doubtless contributed to subject them to misrule. That theory, if an ignorant assumption deserves to be dignified with the name, is in direct contradiction to the proofs of the gifted character of the Celtic Race, furnished in modern times by the experience of schools and from other sources. For a recent example I may refer to the facts contained in the Report that appeared in June last, of the Bangor Normal College for training teachers for British Schools in Wales. Equally inconsistent with the truth of that assumption is the genius for poetry and music, which has ever been displayed by the Celtic nations under the most unfavourable circumstances, and during the darkest ages.

Within a few miles from this place, the Principality ceases, and the English border land begins. It forms no distant part of the landscape, which daily meets my eye. It is a region which unites the beauties of England and Wales,—verdant pastures with picturesque mountains, enchanting valleys, and rich woodland scenery. The inhabitants of this district (West Shropshire), speak the English language exclusively. None of the faults, which have been ascribed to their neighbours in the Principality, have ever been imputed to them. And it cannot be denied that for intelligence and good conduct they stand high in the scale among the people of the English counties. But there is every reason to believe that they are by blood and descent Cambro-Britons, though in language they are English. Such is the conclusion of writers of high authority who have deeply investigated the subject, on which several valuable Essays have lately been written in competition for a prize offered by the Cambrian Eisteddfod, for the best Essay "On the Origin of the English Nation with reference to the question how far that nation is descended from the Ancient Britons?" A friend, who has peculiar means of observation, has stated that the characteristics of the people in West Shropshire, and in the adjoining Welsh districts in Montgomeryshire are the same; and that in both instances (as compared to the country farther east), he finds intelligence and courtesy in the adults, and ability and vivacity in the children. These Celtic traits are thus alluded to in a very interesting volume.*

"All the Highlanders are so amusing and really pleasant and instructive to talk to—women as well as men—and the latter so gentlemanlike." Page 118. Again at page 132, the following note occurs:—"We were always in the habit of conversing with the Highlanders—with whom one comes so much in contact in the Highlands. The Prince highly appreciated the good-breeding,

* *Leaves from our Journal of Life in the Highlands*; London: Smith, Elder & Co. This volume has been admirably translated by *Idrysyn*, the Rev. J. Jones, Vicar of Llandysilio, and published in the Welsh language; Caermarthen: Morgan & Davies. Though it relates chiefly to the Scottish Highlands, it presents glimpses of all the Celtic provinces in the British dominions, Ireland, Cornwall, Wales, and the Isle of Man.

simplicity, and intelligence, which make it so pleasant and even instructive to talk to them." See also p. 42. The Highlanders of Scotland have been especial objects of attack by those shallow pretenders to philosophy, who have maintained that the Celt is incapable of civilization, and naturally inferior to the followers of the founders of the Anglo-Saxon dominion, Hengist and Horsa. They have had their share of persecution, of which the massacre of Glencoe is an example that will never be effaced from the pages of History. As many, perhaps most, of my readers may be uninformed on the subject, it may be expedient for me to state, that the common origin of the Irish, Welsh, Highland Scotch, and of the inhabitants of the Isle of Man, of Cornwall, and of Brittany or Armorica, can be demonstrated clearly by the evidence of language. The dialects of the Highlanders and the Irish differ very slightly, and the affinity of both to the Welsh is plain and manifest. The language of the Isle of Man is an abbreviated Gaelic, bearing to that dialect a relation similar to that which the French does to the Latin. The Cornish, which though extinct as a living language, has been preserved in literary remains, differs little from the Welsh, and the Armorican is much more nearly related to the Welsh and Cornish than it is to the Gaelic.[*] During the time of the long war with Napoleon a party of French prisoners were stationed at Montgomery, about 3 miles from this place. Their intelligence and their pleasing and amiable manners made them general favourites, and they were hospitably received in the houses of the neighbouring gentry. They employed themselves commonly in teaching music, dancing, &c. Among them were some Bretons. The author of these pages at

[*] Among other works see Llwyd's *Archælogia* that appeared in the last century; and a Cornish Dictionary published a few years ago by the Rev. Mr. Williams, Rhyd y Croesau, near Oswestry; Llandovery : Roderic ; London : Trübner & Co. ; also a work by the Author of this Essay, entitled *Philological Proofs of the Original Unity of the Human Race* ; London : John Russell Smith : in which evidence is adduced that the differences between the various Celtic dialects are the results of time and of causes now in operation.

that time in his childhood, has been told by his mother (the wife of the late Dr. Johnes, of Garthmyl, a Physician), that she could understand them when speaking in the Breton language. Doubtless, however, it would not have been possible for her to carry on conversation with them, and she must have been influenced by the resemblance to the Welsh of individual Breton words. My late friend, the Rev. Thomas Price, in his valuable *Tour in Brittany*, states that the Welsh and Bretons can not discourse together. Comparatively slight differences in grammar and in accent suffice to make kindred nations unintelligible to each other; but the words in the Welsh and Breton vocabularies are obviously the same, and the acquisition of a knowledge of the Welsh Language would be an easy task to a Breton, and *vice versa*. A celebrated writer, distinguished both by scientific attainments and by learning, has shown that at the dawn of history the Celtic Race occupied a vast section of Europe, including the British Islands, France, the Rhine, the whole of Switzerland,* a portion of South Western Germany, and the North of Italy. The researches of Wilhelm Humboldt, followed by the investigations of the writer just alluded to, have also proved that Spain at the same period was divided between tribes of Celts and of Iberians or Basques, intermingled through that Peninsula. It may be inferred that the French nation is descended from Celtic ancestors, as the old Gaulish was spoken long after the establishment of the Franks in that country, viz., down to the eighth century, nearly until the time of Charlemagne.† The character of the Gauls as described by the Roman writers, bears a marked resemblance to that of the modern French, who possess so high a rank in the scale of civilization. The same character is observable in the Celts of the British Isles, especially in the Irish, who have retained the

* Dr. Prichard on the *Eastern Origin of the Celtic Nations*.

† Kerdanet's *History of the Language of the Gauls and Armoricans*, translated by David Lewis, Esq., in the *Cambrian Quarterly Magazine*.

Catholic Religion, which has a tendency to preserve the impulsiveness and susceptibility that belong to the Celtic family. One of the most interesting topics which have been discussed by the authors of the Essays above alluded to, is the extent to which a fresh infusion of Celtic blood, especially among the higher classes, was the result of the Norman Conquest, as the Conqueror's army was to a great extent composed of Bretons, and the Norman portion of it consisted of soldiers partly descended from Celtic ancestors. For a long series of years the Eisteddfod (which is another name for the Literary Association of Wales), has offered prizes on topics of the highest interest, which it has thrown open to all the world, while it has selected its judges impartially from the greatest authorities in Europe, who would consent to undertake the task.* A portion of the English Press has mistaken the proceedings of this Association which it has habitually represented as manifestations of reaction and barbarism. With what justice can be judged of by the preceding explanations. Oppression of its Celtic subjects has been the standing danger of the British Empire. The task of redressing the wrongs of different branches of the Celtic race has appropriately devolved on the same Statesman.

As this work—now and hereafter—may in many instances, be studied by readers to whom it may be unknown, I think it expedient to mention the interesting circumstance, that Mr. Gladstone is closely connected with the Principality, Mrs. Gladstone being a sister of Sir Stephen Glynne, of Hawarden Castle, Flintshire, the representative of one of the chief families of Wales, I

---

* The subject of the Prize above alluded to was suggested by the Author of this volume. Several years elapsed before a decision was pronounced, as on two occasions the Prize was not awarded to either of the competitors. On the third occasion it was given to Dr. Beddoe, Secretary of the Anthropological Society. On the first occasion the judges were Prince Lucien Buonaparte, a highly distinguished Celtic Scholar, the Rev. Basil Jones, a gentleman of great literary attainments, and the Author of this volume, who unfeignedly shrank from the duty. On the second and third occasions the late Lord Strangford, whose wonderful accomplishments are well known, kindly consented to act alone as judge.

may add that the Prime Minister himself commonly spends his vacations in that country, which has afforded him an opportunity of receiving the representations of its inhabitants in favour of the appointment of a Welsh Bishop to the vacant See of St. Asaph, representations to which he has given a most patient and respectful hearing, and with which he has lately complied.

ARTHUR JAMES JOHNES.

[COPY.]

10, *Downing Street, Whitehall, Jan.* 1, 1870.
Sir,—

Mr. Gladstone desires me to return his sincere thanks for your kindness in sending him your "Essay on the Causes of Dissent in Wales," which he will peruse with much interest.

I am, Sir,

Yr. Obdt. Servant,

W. B. GURDON.
A. J. Johnes, Esq.

AN ESSAY

ON THE

CAUSES WHICH HAVE PRODUCED

DISSENT

FROM

THE ESTABLISHED CHURCH,

IN THE

Principality of Wales,

BY

ARTHUR JAMES JOHNES, OF GARTHMYL, ESQ.,

One of Her Majesty's Judges of the County Courts of Record;

TO WHOM THE ROYAL MEDAL WAS AWARDED AT AN EISTEDDVOD OF THE LONDON CAMBRIAN INSTITUTION, HELD IN MAY, 1831.

REPRINTED FROM THE LAST EDITION.

"For honourable priesthood is like a shower from Heaven, it causes blessings every where; but a pitiful, a disheartened, a discouraged clergy, waters the ground with a water pot here and there, a little good, and for a little while, but every evil man can destroy all that work whenever he pleases." — *Bishop Jeremy Taylor.*

LLANIDLOES:
PRINTED AND PUBLISHED BY JOHN PRYSE.

1870.

TO THE COUNCIL OF THE ROYAL CAMBRIAN INSTITUTION.

GENTLEMEN,—

Permit me to thank you for the honour you have conferred upon me. I now hasten to lay before you the Second Edition of my "Essay on the Causes of Dissent," enlarged with such historical facts as seem calculated to place its positions in a more unequivocal light.

It may naturally suggest itself to many of my readers, that the subject of the following Essay might have been more satisfactorily discussed by a member of another profession. I am of that opinion myself; and it was only when I found that those gentlemen who were best qualified to do it justice were restrained by motives of delicacy from interfering, that, I became a Candidate for the Prize you have awarded me; no one would have rejoiced more than myself had that Prize fallen into other hands. For myself I can claim no other qualifications for the task, than an anxiety to detect, and impartially to point out the sources of the present impopularity of the Church in Wales; the humble claim to impartiality I may fairly assert for labours on which you have set the seal of your approbation.

I remain,

GENTLEMEN,

Your humble servant,

ARTHUR JAMES JOHNES.

Garthmyl, Montgomeryshire, May, 1832.

PREFACE TO THE SECOND EDITION.

THE only object of the Author of this little volume is to exhibit a faithful delineation of those abuses which have alienated so large a mass of the people of Wales from the communion of the Church of England. In undertaking this task, he was actuated by no other feelings than those of regard to the interests of the country to which he belongs, and of the church of which he is a member. Encouraged by the reception experienced by his first edition,—by the kind and indulgent attention extended to him by those who must have the security of our national Church most peculiarly at heart,—he was led to renew his investigations, under the assurance that his humble labours would be received in the spirit by which they were directed, and that in denouncing the profanation of the temple, he should run no risk of being suspected of any want of reverence for the sacred edifice itself.

Convinced that her privileges are for the benefit of the community, he is no advocate for throwing the Establishment on the suffrages and contributions of the people. From the days of the sophists of Athens, down to those of the Mendicant orders in the Romish Church, experience is but little in favour of ethical teachers, dependent on the breath of popular favour. Instructors thus circumstanced, have generally been found prone to sacrifice truth to novelty—to modify the severe doctrines of morality to the varying passions, the prejudices, or the morbid ingenuity of their audience.

The operation of a similar influence is but too strongly apparent in the religious economy of the Dissenters of our own times; ethical novelty was never more industriously pursued in the schools of ancient Athens, than it is in our days in the chapels of our modern separatists. It is too often assumed, that a dependence on his flock is a security for the zeal and efficiency of the minister; but I need only refer to the account given in the opening pages of this work, of the feeble condition to which the primitive Welsh Dissenters had been reduced just before the breaking out of Methodism, for a proof, that occasional lethargy is no peculiarity of endowed Churches. From all that I can learn of the state of Dissenting congregations at that time, I have been led to believe, that the dependence of their ministers on voluntary contribution had an effect precisely the reverse of that which is sometimes ascribed to it; for, instead of making them anxious for the instruction of the people generally, it made them indifferent to all except a few opulent adherents, by whom they were maintained. But evils of a darker cast may easily be traced to the same influence; the abject dependence of the minister on his flock engenders habits of temporizing and insincerity in the former, which extend themselves, by the force of example, to the latter; and the rancorous divisions to which their system of popular suffrage continually gives rise, have often the effect of leading men far more widely astray from a Christian spirit than the indolence or even immorality of individual ministers of the Church of England.

Abstractedly speaking, the system of voluntary contribution has a semblance of justice, which fixed endowments do not possess; yet, I am fully convinced, that it is more oppressive in practice, as it transfers the burden from the rich to the poor, and imposes a peculiar weight on the best disposed members of the community. The statutes of mortmain are a standing proof, that even a Popish nation deemed it against public policy, to leave the pious generosity of individuals uncontrolled; and abundant instances may be pointed out in our times, of individuals who have been reduced by this feeling to a state of pauperism or bankruptcy. It is also well worthy of remark, that the system to which I have alluded does not, in the end, secure even the popularity of the clergy; long before the reformation, the Mendicant orders had become far more odious than the regular clergy,—and we shall find from Chaucer, that their exactions on the charity of the people were regarded with an aversion far deeper than that which has ever been expressed towards the fixed possessions of their wealthier brethren. In point of fact, the whole argument in favour of voluntary contributions will be found to owe its force to the confusion of two distinct questions,—that of contribution and that of patronage,—the sources of Church revenues, and the influence by which they are controlled. Whether the income of the clergy be derived from the bounty of the people, or from landed endowments, if the appropriation of the fund be confided to improper trustees, the same grievances must arise; if, on the other hand, the present fixed endowments of the Church were placed under a proper system of patronage, we should have exactly the same security for their proper appropriation, that we can possess in the case of any other species of property whatever.

Convinced, then, that a reform of administration is the real desideratum, and not a wild spoliation of the endowments of the Establishment,—the author entered upon the following investigation, —an investigation that has involved but little either of pleasure or of profit; its fruits, indeed, are at length condensed into a small space, —but the same, alas! cannot be affirmed of the hours which have been devoted to its fulfilment. Nevertheless, should the following pages contribute, in any degree, to ensure to his native country those advantages—literary and religious—which she is so fully entitled to enjoy, it will leave him without any just grounds of regret. With the Principality of Wales he is connected by no other ties than those of birth and affection; in her future prospects he has no wordly interest,—and it will, in all probability, be his fate to spend the remainder of his days far remote from her mountains. In entering an indignant protest against that sordid system of which her noblest interests have, for centuries, been the sport, he is conscious of no other motives than those sentiments of love and respect—which he has ever entertained—and which he shall never cease to cherish, towards her kind-hearted, intelligent, and virtuous people.

CONTENTS.

CHAPTER I.

Brief History of the Origin of Dissent in Wales.—Independents.—Methodists.—The Methodism of Wales of earlier date than the commencement of Dissent in England under Whitefield and Wesley.—Vicar Pritchard.—Griffith Jones.—Howel Harris.—Daniel Rowland.—The Williamses.—Thomas Charles.
Page 7—49.

CHAPTER II.

CAUSES OF DISSENT IN WALES.—The unpopularity of the Episcopal Clergy ascribable to two causes:—1. Their want of sympathy with the feelings and tastes of the people.—2. Their neglect of the Language of the people.—Both those causes themselves the effects of an English Hierarchy. Page 50—93.

CHAPTER III.

THE TWO ERAS.—The influence of the native Welsh Bishops compared with that of their English successors:—1. On Church Patronage.—2. On religious and general education.
Page 94—110.

CHAPTER IV.

Primary and derivative causes of Dissent in Wales distinguished.—Ecclesiastical misgovernment the sole cause of its predominance.
Page 111—140.

CHAPTER V.—CONCLUSION.

Progressive Spoliation by the English Government, of the literary and religious endowments of Wales. Page 141—158.

APPENDIX I.

Number of Churches.—Progressive increase of the number of Dissenting Chapels.—Peculiarities of the different Sects in Wales.
Page 159—162.

APPENDIX II.

The state of the Church and Church Revenues of South Wales.
Page 163—179.

A statement of the value of the Benefices and Dignities in North Wales. Page 180—212.

Summary of the state of Patronage in South Wales. Page 213.

The amount of Church property (in North Wales) belonging to Sinecurists, Absentees, Clergymen ignorant of the Welsh language, Bishops and their Relatives—compared with the amount enjoyed by the general body of the Clergy. Page 217.

INDEX TO SEVERAL SUBJECTS DISCUSSED IN THE FOLLOWING PAGES.

	PAGE.
Absenteeism.—Its effects	66, 151
Bishoprics (Welsh).—Their immense possessions—accumulated within the last two centuries—and from what sources	217
Cathedrals.—Their immense wealth, an innovation	120, 123
The Clergy unpopular in districts appropriated to Cathedrals, Colleges, &c.	68, 69
Clergy.—Their want of zeal and seriousness considered the leading cause of Dissent by Griffith Jones.—Bishop Burnett's opinion on the subject	59, 71
Commendam.—A power generally abused	131
Curates (Stipendiary).—A system prohibited in Popish times	130
Inefficiency of recent legislative measures in removing its evils	125
Education (History of in Wales).—G. Jones's schools	18—31
Thomas Charles's exertions in the diffusion of education	44—47
English schools—their bad effects on children ignorant of the English language	62, 90
Scriptures (Welsh versions of)	100
Welsh Magazines—their number	63, 102
Leases (Ecclesiastical).—Their evils	123, 129
Queen Anne's Bounty (History of)	
The origin of the fund—its diminution—the gross abuses in its application	190, 185, 191
Sinecures.—Their origin—imaginary benefits—effects	199
Vicars (Origin of).—Their residence held indispensible in Romish times	130
Welsh Language.—Its probable duration, a question irrelevant to the present enquiry	91

VALUATION OF THE BENIFICES OF NORTH WALES.

EXTRACTED FROM

The Report of the Ecclesiastical Commissioners appointed by His Majesty, dated the 16th June, 1835.

IN prefixing these Returns to the following pages, I have not been actuated by any wish to vindicate my own character (which I am content to leave in abler hands), but by the anxiety that the state of the Welsh Church should be judged of by a more authoritative test than the assertions of an individual. The desired criterion is now before the public; and, after a careful examination, I feel no hesitation in stating, that the Returns made to the Commissioners present as unfavourable a picture of the abuses of the Welsh Church as the representations originally published in this volume! I do not mean to affirm that there is a perfect coincidence between my estimates and the Returns—no one acquainted with the fluctuating value of tithes can expect such a result—but, in the great majority of cases the approximation is as close as the nature of this kind of property admits; and, in those few instances in which discrepancies of some magnitude occur, it will be found that the valuations contained in the Report are quite as favourable to my general conclusions as the estimates on which those conclusions were originally founded.* It will clearly appear that I have neither exaggerated the wealth of the Church, nor the proportion

* It is to be regretted that the Commissioners have thought proper to sanction the glaring abuse of filling the Welsh Sees with persons ignorant of the Welsh language, by proposing to unite the Diocese of Llandaff, a purely Welsh district, with the English See of Bristol!

of its revenues enjoyed by the higher orders of the Clergy! If these results are capable of proof, the details are unimportant.

To prevent misconstruction, I feel it necessary to add a few remarks. In stating that the Report confirms the valuations in this volume, I beg to confine that observation to the livings of the parochial clergy; for, with regard to the benefices of the Dignified Clergy, the Commissioners have not yet given to the public that information on which alone a fair comparison can be formed! The amount of their annual incomes are indeed stated, and the names of the parishes from which they issue; but this is no criterion whatever of the benefit they actually reap from these sources, as it often, nay, commonly, happens that the tithes are leased,—when the annual rent is a mere trifle, though the fines paid for a renewal invariably prove a source of considerable emolument! Many of these leases have been granted under circumstances which constitute something very like a direct fraud on the Church. To enable the public to form a judgment on this subject, it is essential that the following details should be obtained :—1. The actual value of all tithes and other property attached to Bishoprics, Prebends, &c. 2. The annual rent reserved, and the fines which have been paid, as far back as can be ascertained, and the dates of the leases. This information, it is to be hoped, will be procured by the future researches of the Commission!

I take this opportunity of congratulating my countrymen on the success that has hitherto attended the able and generous efforts that have been made in Parliament to obtain a reform in the Welsh Bishoprics. It is hardly to be believed that any Government will much longer venture to uphold, against the united voice of the press* and the public, the scandalous practice of filling the Welsh Sees with Prelates ignorant of the language of their flocks!

* The *Chronicle*, the *Times*, and the *Herald*, the three leading daily journals, which are at once both the guides and indicators of national opinion, have repeatedly denounced this corruption. The Author begs to express his gratitude to the first journal for courtesy to himself personally on many trying occasions.

ANGLESEA.	Gross Amount	Deductions.
Aberffraw	967	79
Amlwch	222	
Bodedern	104	
Bodewryd	70	
Bodwrog†	105	
Heneglwys	448	65
Holyhead	167	
Llanbadric	191	22
Llanbeulan	921	128
Llanddona	87	
Llandegfan	336	
Llanddeusant	679	64
Llanddyfnan	...	...
Llandyfrydog	526	69
Llaneilian	400	
Llaneugrad	170	35
Llanfachreth	610	53
Llanfaethle	685	70
Llanfair-pwllgwyngill	243	20
Llanfechell	400	100
Llanfihangel ysceifiog	97	
Llangadwaladr	282	37
Llangefni	525	79
Llangeinwen	801	137
Llangristiolus	125	
Llangoed	104	
Llangwillog	90	
Llanidan	340	48
Llanrhyddlad	600	70
Llansadwrn	415	34
Llantrisant	1016	101
Llanvaes	180	
Newborough	240	26
Penmynydd	86	
Penrhos	75	
Rhoscolyn	330	70
Talyllyn	65	
Trefdraeth	558	93

CARNARVON.

Bangor Diocese.

Aber	412	30
Aberdaron	82	
Abererch	96	
Bangor	1006	128
Beddgelert	90	
Bettws y coed	101	
Bettws garmon	93	

* These are certain deductions which occur regularly.
† I take this opportunity of correcting an error in my Tables at the end, in which Mr. P. B. Williams is stated to be the incumbent of Bodwrog. This benefice is not held by him, but by Mr. H. Griffith.

CARNARVON--continued	Gross Amount	Deductions.
Bodfaen	223	25
Bryncroes	167	
Capel curig	89	
Ceidio	85	
Clynnog	179	21
Conway	181	60
Cricineth	379	30
Dolwyddelan	156	
Dwygyfylchi	126	
Edern	386	86
Gyffin	115	
Llanaelhaiarn	245	20
Llanbedr	365	76
Llanberis	189	
Llanbeblig	375	45
Llanbedrog	500	115
Llandegai	114	
Llandeiniolen	344	39
Llandudno	96	
Llandwrog	400	86
Llanengan	427	29
Llanfairfechan	333	28
Llanfihangel y pennant	160	33
Llangelynin	241	29
Llangian	...	
Llangybi	500	50
Llangwnadle	50	
Llaniestyn	671	76
Llanllechid	542	71
Llanllyfni	268	28
Llannor	151	
Llanrug	191	25
Llanwynda	280	10
Llanystumdwy	550	
Mellteyrn	200	22
Nefyn	89	
Penmachno	92	
Penmorfa	300	
Rhiw	100	
Ann's St	222	
Trefriw	180	12
Tydweiliog	80	

St. Asaph Diocese.

Eglwysrhos	81	
Llysvaen	250	

DENBIGHSHIRE.

Bangor Diocese.

Clocaenog	348	56
Derwen	420	
Efenechtyd	200	
Jesus Chapel	63	
Llanbedr dyffryn clwyd	426	86

DENBIGHSHIRE—continued.	Gross Amount	Deductions	DENBIGHSHIRE—continued.	Gross Amount	Deductions
Llandyrnog	...	...	Chester Diocese.		
Llanelidan	300	48			
Llanfair dyffryn clwyd..	357	96	Holt	101	
Llanfwrog	526	97	Iscoed		
Llangwyfan	288	32			
Llangynhafal	460	53			
Llanrydd and Ruthin ...	509	246			
Llanrhaiadr yn kimmerch	752	143	FLINTSHIRE.		
Llanychan	200	30	St. Asaph Diocese.		
Llanynynys	475	100			
St. Asaph Diocese.			Bodfari	326	30
			Caerwys	361	76
Abergele	400		Cilcain, or Kilken, (vicar)	224	7
Bryneglwys	90		Sinecure Rector	253	
Bettws	395	62	Cwm	251	33
Cerrig y druidion	492	32	Dyserth	113	
Chirk	570	104	Eastyn, alias Hope (vicar)	215	
Denbigh	445		Sinecure Rector	215	
Erbistock	271	31	Flint	225	
Eglwysfach	260	40	Gwaunysgor	193	15
Foelas	200		Halkin	318	6
Gresford	715		Holywell	290	40
Gwytherin	133		Llanasa	300	
Henllan	165		Meliden	90	
Kegidock, or St. George's	160	24	Mold	361	6
Llanarmon dyffryn ceiriog.	157	24	Nannerch	299	7
Llanarmon mynydd mawr.	67		Nercwis	92	
Llanarmon yn Yale (vicar)	332	50	Newmarket	90	
Sinecure Rector	435	90	Northop	413	
Llanddoget	212	25	Rhuddlan	266	
Llanddulas	110		St. Asaph	183	
Llandegla	115	20	Tremeirchion	240	
Llandisilio	112		Tryddyn, in Mold	78	
Llandrillo yn rhos	347		Whitford	417	58
Llanelian	249		Ysceifiog	655	
Llanfairtalhaiarn	84		Chester Diocese.		
Llanferes	319				
Llanfihangel	188	43	Bangor—Monachorum with Overton	1,200	
Llangadwaladar	55				
Llanyblodwel	284		Hanmer	428	
Llangedwin	90		Hawarden, with Buckley Broughton	3,286	442
Llangerniew	310	35			
Llangollen	381	31	Threapwood	87	
Llangwm	177	34	Worthenbury	395	33
Llanrhaiadr yn mochnant.	612	92			
Llanrwst	951	231			
Llansannan	191	28			
Llansaintffraid glyn ceiriog	190	66	MERIONETHSHIRE.		
Llansantffraid	240		St. Asaph Diocese.		
Llansilin	307				
Marchwiail	765	57	Bettws gwerfyl goch	125	
Nantglyn	245	23	Corwen	376	
Ruabon	638	50	Gwyddelwern	138	
St. German's	110		Llandderfel	305	45
Trevor Chapel, Llangollen.	87		Llandrillo	215	18
Wrexham	749		Llanfawr	304	
Yspytty	122		Llangar	179	19

MERIONETHSHIRE—continued.	Gross Amount.	Deductions.	MONTGOMERY-SHIRE—continued.	Gross Amount.	Deductions.
Llansantffraid	98		Llanfyllin	588	100
Llanuwchllyn	113		Llangadfan	349	50
Llanycil	256		Llangyniew	400	64
Mallwyd	325	70	Llangynog	143	17 ✓
Bangor Diocese.			Llanllugan	49	
			Llanllwchaiarn	404	49
Dolgellau	505	65	Llanmerewig	155	12
Festiniog, with M'twrog	284	30	Llansaintffraid (vicar)	198	
Llanaber, with B'mouth	256	43	Sinecure Rector	...*	...
Llandanwg, with Ll'bedr	203	9	Llanwrin	340	68
Llanegryn	82		Llanwyddelan	240	64
Llanelltyd	62		Llanwddyn	100	
Llanfachreth	100	8	Machynlleth	320	90
Llanfair	195	30	Manafon	286	59
Llanfihangel y pennant	46		Meifod	654	66
Llanfihangel y traethau	107		Newtown	510	104
Llanfrothen	81		Penegoes	300	
Llangelynin	398	53	Pennant	200	15
Talyllyn	84		Tregynon	87	
Towyn	242	18	Trinity Ch'l, in Ll'drinio	56	
Trawsfynydd	180		Welshpool	319	46
			Bangor Diocese.		
			Carno	100	
MONTGOMERY-SHIRE.			Llandinam	290	20
			Llangurig	241	29
St. Asaph Diocese.			Llanidloes	180	29
			Llanwnog	100	53
Aberhafesp	304	59	Penystrowed	120	25
Berriew	450	94	Trefeglwys	143	40
Bettws	454	43			
Castle caereinion	672	97	*St. David's Diocese.*		
Cemmaes	350	62			
Darowen	131	52	Kerry	300	
Garthbeibio	94	8	Mochtre	86	
Guilsfield	417	57			
Hirnant	160	25	*Hereford Diocese.*		
Llanbrynmair	425	95			
Llandrinio	213	11	Buttington	107	
✓ Llandysilio	133		Churchstoke	151	
Llandyssil	440	67	Crigion	108	
Llanerful	367	59	Forden	119	
Llanfair caereinion	380	42	Hyssington	173	12
Llanfechan	600	70	Montgomery	393	46
Llanfihangel yn ngwynfa	370	36	Snead	90	

BISHOPRICS OF WALES.

St. Asaph	7,408†	1,107	St. David's‡	2,490	593
Bangor	6,580	2,116	Llandaff	1,008	84

* The amount is not given in the Returns.

† In this volume set down at 9,026. The difference arises from the advantageous leases granted by former Bishops. It is stated that the revenues of St. Asaph and Bangor have declined since this estimate was taken.

‡ The same remark applies. The only mode in which the property of these Sees can be cleared of their incumbrances, is by rendering it imperative on each new Bishop, at the time of his promotion, to abstain from renewing existing leases. Such a condition would be no injustice, if imposed previously to the promotion.

The revenues of the Cathedrals and Collegiate Churches, Prebendaries, Sinecurists, &c., appear to correspond pretty generally with the statements of this volume.

It will be borne in mind, that this work relates chiefly to North Wales. I must protest, however, against the inference, that the administration of the Church is purer in South Wales. I appeal to the Returns for a direct proof of the contrary; pluralities and absenteeism appear to prevail there, even to a greater extent; and these abuses are the more inexcusable, as the extreme poverty of the Church renders it the bounden duty of its patrons to exercise strict economy in the application of its revenues. The scandalous system of leases also prevails there to a grievous extent! It is discreditable to Bishop Burgess (a prelate otherwise estimable), that he should have granted a variety of leases on the very eve of his translation from St. David's to Salisbury! In one case (stated in this work) he appears to have resorted to an expedient but little consistent with the dignity of his station—I allude to the circumstance of his having, when Bishop of St. David's leased the tithes of a Welsh parish to a friend, by whom he caused the lease to be afterwards assigned to himself, when Bishop of Salisbury! This lease he still retains!!

The state of patronage in South Wales may form a subject of future inquiry.

CHAPTER I.

BRIEF HISTORY OF THE ORIGIN OF DISSENT IN WALES.—INDEPENDENTS.—METHODISTS.—THE METHODISM OF WALES OF EARLIER DATE THAN THE COMMENCEMENT OF DISSENT IN ENGLAND UNDER WHITEFIELD AND WESLEY.—VICAR PRITCHARD.—GRIFFITH JONES.—HOWEL HARRIS.—DANIEL ROWLAND.—THE WILLIAMSES.—THOMAS CHARLES.

"To confess the truth, he expects that the fate of this little work will be similar to that of the Roman army which first landed in Britain, and were forced to complain to their friends abroad—'The Britons drive us to the sea, and the sea drives us back to the Britons.' So will it fare with this little pamphlet. * * * * If it meet with any favourable reception from either party, it will be upon this ground, that it has given the other party its portion with impartiality, and has spoken the plain truth to both parties without any ill will to either of them.—May peace and piety be the portion of all parties."

The Welsh Looking Glass, or Thoughts on the State of Religion in North Wales, published in 1812.

To the Members of the Royal Cambrian Institution.

GENTLEMEN,

THE present state of religious opinion in the Principality may not be without its interest even to a superficial enquirer; but to those who unite a patriotic love of Wales with a deep reverence for the benevolent precepts of Christianity, her religious divisions must be a subject of frequent and painful meditation.

The Welsh have long been proverbial for their attachment to ancient usages, and for habits of cheerful respect towards their superiors. The general disposition of the people is evidently that of obedience to existing authorities. Whence, then, it will be asked, their present alienation from that most sacred of ancient usages—

the religion of their forefathers? Whence this general spirit of defection from the ecclesiastical rulers of the land? How has it come to pass that in almost every district of the Principality the Dissenting Chapels are in a treble proportion to the Churches of the Establishment? Whence is it that even in this Metropolis, the Welsh language has been preached for years in no fewer than six Dissenting* places of worship; whilst as yet not even a prospect has been afforded of a similar institution on the principles of the Church of England?

The facts which constitute the history of Dissent† in Wales, are so little known, that before entering into an abstract dissertation on its causes, I feel it necessary to give a brief narrative of its rise and progress: many of the causes will thus naturally develope themselves; others will form the subject of the next Chapter.

The following singular account is preserved of the commencement of Dissent in Wales.‡ In the reign of James I. a clergyman of the name of Wroth was Vicar of Llanvaches, in Monmouthshire. Being of a joyous temper, and, like most of his countrymen, passionately fond of music, he was sometimes carried beyond the bounds of propriety by this enthusiasm. On one occasion, a gentleman with whom he was on terms of intimacy, having presented him with a new harp, fixed a day on which, in company with some friends, he would visit him and hear him perform upon it. The day appointed came, and Wroth was anxiously expecting his visitor, when a messenger appeared to inform him that his friend was no more! This incident affected him so deeply, that, repenting the levity of his youth, from a gay clerical Troubadour he

* In London there are six Welsh Dissenting Chapels, viz. three belonging to the Calvinistic Methodists, one to the Independents, one to the Wesleyans, and one to the Baptists.

† In the following pages, the term Dissent is used in the enlarged sense of a separation on any ground from the Establishment.

‡ *Trysorva*, p. 155.

became all at once a sad but zealous divine. With these impressions, he determined to commence preaching to his congregation, a practice then almost unknown in the Churches of the Principality. As a preacher, he soon distinguished himself so much, that the Welsh peasantry flocked from all the neighbouring counties to hear him. His audience, being frequently too numerous for his church to contain—on such occasions he was in the habit of addressing them in the church-yard. It is said that Sir Lewis Mansel of Margam, a man illustrious for his exalted religious and patriotic zeal, was often one of his congregation.

The irregularity alluded to at last exposed him to the censure of his Diocesan, who, on one occasion, asked him in anger, how he could vindicate his infringement of the rules of the Church? To this reprimand, Wroth replied by appealing, with tears in his eyes, to the religious ignorance which prevailed throughout the country, and to the necessity of employing every means to dissipate it: by which answer, the Bishop is said to have been deeply affected. Eventually, however, by refusing to read the "Book of Sports," and by the general tenor of his conduct, he rendered himself so obnoxious to the dignitaries of the Church, that he was deprived of his benefice. After his expulsion, he continued to preach in secret to his old followers, and at last he formed from amongst them a regular Dissenting congregation, on the Independent model. From Llanvaches, the opinions of its pastor soon spread themselves into the remotest corners of Wales: during his life, this village was regarded as the rallying point of the Welsh Nonconformists. Wroth, nevertheless, seems to have cherished to the last some feeling of affection towards the Church, of which he had once been a minister; for, on his death, which occurred in 1640, he was buried, at his own request, under the threshold of the Church of Llanvaches.

During the civil wars, which broke out soon afterwards, the Independents were not only tolerated, but predominant. In Cromwell's time, an attempt was made to get rid of every thing like an Establishment, and to substitute a few itinerant ministers in its place. The modicum of preachers proposed to be given by this plan of œconomical piety was six to a county; it was lost in the House of Commons by a majority of two voices. It was felt, however, that the bright thought was too precious to be discarded without an experiment; and, accordingly, it was partly carried into effect in Wales under Hugh Peters and Vavasor Powel,* and a confiscation of Church property in that country ensued, to an enormous amount; for, unhappily, under all the various forms of civil and ecclesiastical polity which have prevailed in England, the Welsh Church has been treated as a fair field for experiments, no less injurious to the general cause of religion than to Wales.

In the times of the Stewarts, Dissent from the Episcopal Church became once more an object of persecution; but the Ministers of the Welsh Nonconformists still continued to traverse the wild hills of the Principality, braving all dangers for the sake of their few and scattered followers. Their congregations still occasionally met, but it was in fear and trembling, generally at midnight, or in woods and caverns, amid the gloomy recesses of the mountains.

At the revolution, these Dissenters exhausted their strength by controversies amongst themselves on the rite of baptism; on which subject a difference of opinion had long existed amongst them, though persecution had prevented them from making it a ground of disunion. Till the breaking out of Methodism, their cause continued to decline.

In the year 1736, there were only six Dissenting Chapels in all North Wales. In this year an incident occurred which forms an interesting link between the history of the early Welsh Dissenters (the followers of Wroth) and that of the Methodists, connecting together the darkening prospects of the former and the first symptoms of that more powerful impulse which was communicated by the latter. One Sunday, Mr. Lewis Rees, a Dissenting Minister from South Wales, and father of the celebrated author of the Cyclopædia, visited Pwllheli, a town in the promontory of Lleyn, in Caernarvonshire, and one of the few places in which the Independents still possessed

* Southey's Life of Wesley, note at the end of first volume.

a chapel. After the service, the congregation, collecting around him, complained bitterly, that their numbers were rapidly diminishing, that the few who yet remained were for the most part poor, and that every thing looked gloomy to their cause. To which the Minister replied, "The dawn of true religion is again breaking in South Wales,—a great man named Howel Harris has recently risen up, who goes about instructing the people in the truths of the Gospel." Nor was he mistaken, either in his anticipation that Dissent was on the eve of bursting forth with tenfold vigour in Wales, nor in the man from whom he expected this result; the first elements of Methodism were already at work; Howel Harris was its founder, and one of its most distinguished champions. Properly speaking, the history of Methodism is the history of Dissent in Wales; before entering, however, upon this interesting subject, it will be necessary to give a cursory view of the state of the Church in Wales at the time of its origin, as hardly a doubt can be entertained that the predisposing causes to Methodism were to be found in the inefficiency of the Establishment.

The following is a translation of an Account of the State of Religion in Wales about the middle of the Eighteenth Century. It was taken from the mouth of a very old Welsh Methodist, and published in 1799, in the *Trysorva*, a Welsh Periodical, edited by the Rev. Thomas Charles, of Bala; and I have high authority for asserting that the descriptions it affords are in no respect exaggerated.

"In those days," says the narrator, "the land was dark indeed!
" Hardly any of the lower ranks could read at all. The morals of
" the country were very corrupt; and in this respect there was no
" difference between gentle and simple, layman and clergyman.
" Gluttony, drunkenness, and licentiousness prevailed through the
" whole country. Nor were the operations of the Church at all
" calculated to repress these evils. From the pulpit the name of the
" Redeemer was hardly ever heard; nor was much mention made of
" the natural sinfulness of man, nor of the influence of the Spirit.
" On Sunday mornings, the poor were more constant in their attend-
" ance at church than the gentry; but the Sunday evenings were

"spent by all in idle amusements. Every Sabbath, there was what
"was called 'A chwareu-gamp,' a sort of sport in which all the young
"men of the neighbourhood had a trial of strength, and the people
"assembled from the surrounding country to see their feats. On
"Saturday night, particularly in the summer, the young men and
"maids held what they called 'Singing eves' (nosweithiau canu);
"that is, they met together and diverted themselves by singing in
"turns to the harp, till the dawn of the Sabbath. In this town
"they used to employ the Sundays in dancing and singing to the
"harp, and in playing tennis against the town-hall. In every corner
"of the town some sport or other went on, till the light of the
"Sabbath-day had faded away. In the summer 'Interludes' (a kind
"of rustic drama), were performed, gentlemen and peasants sharing
"the diversion together. A set of vagabonds called the 'Bobl
"gerdded' (walking people), used to traverse the country, begging
"with impunity, to the disgrace of the law of the land."

Such, then, was the state of Welsh society and the Welsh Church in the middle of the last century; and it is a singular instance of the impression left by the vice and levity of this period, that the sounds of our national instrument are still associated, in the minds of many, with the extravagances of which it was formerly an accompaniment, though, apart from adventitious associations, its simple and pensive tones are certainly far more congenial with devotional feeling, than with levity or with joy. I have frequently heard, that the late Mr. Charles, of Bala, was so much under the sway of these recollections, that it was quite painful to him to remain in a room in which any one was playing upon the harp.*

At first sight nothing would appear more improbable than that Methodism should find proselytes among a people so gay and thoughtless as the Welsh of that period; or that the joyous group which assembled at Bala on a Sunday evening, should become, as was shortly afterwards the case, a leading congregation of modern Puritans. But the religion of the Welsh and their fondness for

---

* See a View of the State of Religion in the Diocese of St. David's, by Erasmus Sanders, D.D. London, 1721. See also the Works of Dr. Clarke (the Traveller), for an Account of the Clergy he met with in Wales.

national music arose from the same cause, an earnest and imaginative frame of mind. A disposition to melancholy, disguised by external gaiety of manner, is characteristic of all Celtic nations.

> "As a beam o'er the face of the waters may glow,
> Tho' the stream runs in darkness and coldness below."

With all their social sprightliness, the Welsh were then a superstitious and consequently a gloomy race. The influence of the Church had confessedly done little to civilize the people; they still retained many habits apparently derived from Paganism, and not a few of the practices of Popery. Their funerals, like those of the Irish, were scenes of riot and wassail. When the Methodists first came into North Wales, the peasantry expressed their horror of them and their opinions by the truly Popish gesture of crossing their foreheads; they also paid great veneration to a tale called "Breuddwyd Mair" (Mary's dream), obviously a Popish legend.*
Children were taught, even within my recollection, to repeat a rhyme like the following, as soon as they had been put into bed at night :—

> "There are four corners to my bed,
> And four Angels there are spread;
> Matthew, Mark, Luke, and John;
> God bless the bed that I lie on."

Some of their customs and notions were extremely fanciful. On the Sunday after a funeral each relative of the deceased knelt on his grave, exclaiming "Nevoedd iddo" (literally, Heaven to him); that is, "may he soon reach Heaven." This is plainly a relict of the Popish custom of praying the soul out of purgatory. If children died before their parents, the parents regarded them as so many candles to light them to Paradise. When Wesley came into Wales, he found the ignorance of the people so great, that he pronounced them "as little versed in the principles of Christianity as a Creek or Cherokee Indian." To this declaration he adds the striking ex-

---

* *Trysorva*, vol. ii. p. 516. *Drych yr Amseroedd.* See also the late learned and excellent Peter Roberts's *Cambrian Superstitions*.

pression that, notwithstanding their superstition and ignorance, the people "were ripe for the Gospel," and most enthusiastically anxious to avail themselves of every opportunity of instruction,—an interesting proof, that the necessary tendency of the corruptions of the Welsh Church to produce the consequences which have since ensued, was sufficiently obvious even to the cursory view of a stranger.

It is quite clear, then, to those who lived whilst Methodism was yet in its infancy in Wales, that the country was about to become the scene of a great religious change. There was evidently a movement in the minds of the people—a longing for the extension of their spiritual advantages, which would ultimately lead them out from the Establishment, unless provided with food from within. In such a state of popular feeling towards existing institutions, whether civil or ecclesiastical, it often happens that the most trivial deviation from ordinary routine, becomes the basis of a series of innovations, and serves to impart an impetus and a direction to the dormant elements of disunion. It is only by keeping these considerations steadily in view, that we can clearly comprehend the early history of Methodism in Wales, and avoid the confused ideas that are sometimes entertained as to the conduct of those with whom it commenced, and the exact date of its commencement. The real truth is, that the separation of the Welsh Methodists from the Church took place by insensible degrees. The first symptom was an unusual and somewhat irregular zeal in a certain body of Clergy in the Church itself; and these first faint traces of irregularity, (which, probably, at the time excited little notice), gradually, and in the course of generations, widened into a broad line of demarcation. It was in this manner that the breaking out of Methodism was undoubtedly hastened by the exertions of two eminent divines, whose only intention was to infuse new vigour into the Established Church,—I mean the Rev. Rhees Pritchard and the Rev. Griffith Jones.

The former, who is familiarly known to his countrymen under the name of "Vicar Pritchard," was vicar of the parish of Llanddyvri, in Caermarthenshire, in the time of James the First and

Charles the First. Of the particulars of his life, little is known, except that whilst he stood high in the estimation of his countrymen as a preacher he was at the same time an object of peculiar favour with the ruling powers of the day,—honours which his countrymen in recent times have rarely seen enjoyed by the same individual. Though, like Wroth, he is said to have attracted numerous congregations, and to have occasionally preached in his church-yard, still he had the good fortune to be made Chaplain to the Earl of Essex,—received from James I. the living of Llanedi, and eventually became Chancellor of the Diocese of St. David's. As a proof of his charitable disposition, and of his anxiety to enlighten his countrymen, we are informed that he gave a donation of twenty pounds a year, charged upon land, to establish a School in his parish of Llanddyvri, and also a house for the Schoolmaster. This endowment (no insignificant one in those days), went on prosperously for some time, but on the death of the founder's son, —Thomas Manwaring, son of Dr. Manwaring, Bishop of St. David's, who had married "the Vicar's" granddaughter, took possession of the land belonging to the school, undertaking to pay the Schoolmaster himself; which he did for a year or two, and then withheld from it all support. His biographer adds, that in 1682, the land was still in the possession of the Manwaring family,—and that the School-house had been swept away by an inundation of the river Tywi!

But, the veneration still felt in Wales for the memory of "Vicar Pritchard" is mainly attributable to a small volume of Poems, which are not a little remarkable, as a summary of Christian doctrine and duty, at once simple, poetical, and concise. No book, except the Bible, has been there so much and so enthusiastically studied; its author may justly be styled the Watts of his native country; and, notwithstanding the unhappy divisions that have since his day distracted her, the undiminished popularity of his little book proves that there is even yet no schism in the Principality as far as the "Divine Poems" of "Vicar Pritchard" are concerned.

I can hardly hope, that the following imperfect translations will convey any thing like a just conception of his bardic merits, though they may perhaps afford some slight idea of the peculiarities of his style:—

GWEDDI VOREUOL.—MORNING PRAYER.

At dawn when first thy slumber flies,
Raise to the Lord of Hosts thine eyes;
To him who watched, and gave, and blest,
Thy hours of helplessness and rest.

Oh! give the first fruits of thy heart,
The first fruits of thy mind and tongue;—
For, second thoughts are not the part
Of Him to whom all hearts belong!

The red-breast, ere his little bill
He moistens in the morning dow,
Carols to Him who saved from ill
His tiny couch the darkness through.

Alas! that man should wake, more dead
To all the blessings God has shed,
Than the wild birds which morn and eve
His gifts with hymns of praise receive!

CYNGHOR I'R MILWR.—COUNSEL TO A SOLDIER.

Before thou wendest to the fray,
(For king and country)—Soldier! pray
The Lord of Hosts to give thee heart,
And strength to act a warrior's part.

In danger, prayer shall more avail
To him who shares the deadly strife,
Than mail to guard when foes assail,
Or brand to take the foeman's life.—

His hands when Moses heavenward spread,
More of the Gentile warriors fell,—
Than by the sword of Joshua bled,
And all the bands of Israel.—

Then let thy hand be in the fray,
But with thy heart, O Soldier, pray:
Pray,—and thou yet shalt find in fight,
That prayer is more than mortal might!

After the poet's death, his works were collected and published by Steven Hughes, a worthy Nonconformist, who zealously disseminated them through Caermarthenshire and the adjacent parts of South Wales. In almost every cottage where the Scriptures were to be found, the Vicar's little volume occupied a place beside them: it became a class-book in every school, and its most striking passages passed into proverbs among the peasantry. Hence, at the beginning of the last century, a spirit had sprung up in certain districts of South Wales, that formed a strong contrast to the general ignorance which at that time pervaded the Principality. The effect of poetry on minds left unoccupied by other reading, has in all ages been remarked: thus, we are told that the great Bishop Bull, when Bishop of St. David's, was so much struck with the impression made on the minds of the people by the writings of "Vicar Pritchard," that he expressed a wish to be buried in the same grave with him!

Griffith Jones was born at Kilrhedin, also in the county of Caermarthen.* Even in his boyhood, he evinced a strong sense of religion, which has sometimes, though erroneously, been thought incompatible with the unformed views and elastic spirits of our earlier years. Like Bishop Heber, he might justly be termed a "religious child:" whilst yet a boy at Caermarthen School, he was in the habit of retiring from the pastimes of his playfellows for the purpose of secret prayer. In the year 1709, he was ordained by Bishop Bull; on which occasion he experienced marks of peculiar kindness and approbation from that illustrious prelate, the recollection of which continued ever after a source of gratitude and delight to him. In 1711, he was presented to the living of Llandeilo Abercowyn, and in 1716, Llanddowror was added to it by the patron, Sir John Phillips of Picton Castle, in Pembrokeshire, with whom he was connected by marriage.

His constitution was naturally delicate, and he describes himself as having been in early youth so much afflicted with asthma, that he could not walk across a room without pain and difficulty; but his was a mind which seemed capable of imparting a portion

* *Trysorva*, vol. ii. p. 1.   † *Trysorva*, vol. ii. p. 9.

of its own energy, even to his debilitated frame; as he advanced in life, this infirmity, in a great measure, forsook him; and of this we have ample proof in the various labours he accomplished.

The fame of Griffith Jones chiefly rests on an institution he devised for the diffusion of education in Wales, still known under the name of the "Welsh Circulating Schools."* The main feature of this plan is the instruction of the people by means of itinerant schoolmasters; it was first suggested to him by the following train of circumstances:—On the Saturday previous to Sacrament Sunday, it was his practice to assemble his flock together, and read to them the service of the Church. At the conclusion of the second lesson, he would ask, in a mild and familiar tone, if any one present wished an explanation of any part of the chapter they had just heard; and on a difficult verse being mentioned, he would expound it in plain and simple language, adapted to the capacities of his hearers. On the day following, before admitting communicants to the Sacrament, he used to examine them on their ideas of Christian doctrines and as to their general moral conduct. On these occasions, his church was generally crowded; numbers came from the neighbouring districts, and it frequently happened that twenty or thirty persons were publicly examined by him before receiving the communion. But he found that those who were likely to derive most benefit from this plan of instruction—men who had grown up in ignorance were deterred from attending by a consciousness of their inability to answer the questions that might be put to them. To remedy this, he made a practice of fixing the Saturday before the Sacrament Sunday,—for the distribution among the poor of the bread purchased by the money collected at the previous Sacrament. Having by this means brought them together, he arranged them in

* Minute as the following detail may appear, no part of it can be omitted in justice to the main object of this Essay, for every one of the rules established by Griffith Jones for the management of his parish, have been adopted (with some slight modifications) by the Methodists as a body; even the Welsh Catechism written and employed by him is a favourite class-book with them.

a class, and proceeded to ask them a few easy questions, with an affability and kindness of manner that immediately removed all embarrassment and reserve; and pursuant to an arrangement he had previously made, these questions were answered by some of the more advanced scholars. In a little time the humbler classes became willing and constant attendants at the altar. And for the purpose of still further grounding his flock in religious knowledge, he was in the habit of requesting them to commit to memory every month a certain portion of the Bible. Thus it became a regular custom among his poor parishoners, to repeat each a verse of Scripture on receiving the bread purchased with the Sacrament money.

This system of examination had the effect of affording him a very clear insight into the notions and attainments of the peasantry, the result of which was an opinion that preaching was calculated to convey only vague and imperfect views to the minds of the poorer classes, unless combined with catechising and other methods of instruction. Following up these impressions, he was led to consider the incalculable benefit that would result, were a well-organized system of schools extended over the whole surface of his native country. These were the steps by which he arrived at the first conception of that noble machinery which he soon afterwards set in motion. At first, it would seem, that he looked upon his plan rather in the light of a favourite day-dream, than as a project which had the slightest chance of success. Nevertheless, he had too much "moral chivalry" to despair,—too much of that imaginative love of enterprise, without which no great impression has ever been made on the people with whom he had to deal. Accordingly, a beginning was made. In the year 1730, the first school was founded, with the Sacrament money of the parish of Llanddowror; and it answered so well, that a second was established shortly afterwards; and this again was attended with such admirable effects, that several benevolent individuals, both in Wales and England, were induced to support the scheme with a liberality that enabled their founder to realize his fondest anticipations. The Society for promoting Christian Knowledge voted him a very generous donation of Bibles and other books. Thus supported, the schools continued rapidly to increase; from an account published in August, 1741, that is, about ten years after their commencement, it appears, that the number of schools in existence during the past year had amounted to 128, and the number of persons instructed in them to 7595. The plan on which Griffith Jones proceeded was simply this; he first engaged a body of schoolmasters, and then distributed them in different directions over the country. The duty of these men was to teach the people to read the Scriptures in the Welsh language, to catechise them, to instruct them in psalmody, and to promote their religious advancement by every means in their power. They were sent, in the first instance, to the nearest town or village where their assistance had been requested; and then, having taught all who were desirous of instruction, they were to pass on to the next district where a similar feeling had been manifested. In the course of time, they were to revisit the localities whence they had at first started, and resume the work of education anew on the youth who had sprung up in their absence; and thus making a continual circuit of the whole country, to present to every generation as it arose the means of knowledge, and the incentives to virtuous principle.

Originality of design was very judiciously made to harmonize with the discipline of the Church. The schoolmasters were not allowed to interfere with the authority of the clergy; nor, in fact, were they sent to any parish without either the request or approbation of the resident minister; nor allowed to instruct in another parish without having previously obtained a testimonial of good conduct from the clergyman of that which they had last left.

A more vivid idea may be formed of the effects of these schools, by the following extracts; for the length of which I need hardly apologize, considering the light which they will be found to throw on the subject under investigation—the circumstances which gave rise to Dissent in the Principality.

It will appear from the following extracts, that the schoolmasters were in the habit of spending their evenings in instructing, at their own homes, those families who could not come to them in the day-time:—

*Letters to Griffith Jones, on the subject of the Schools,
illustrating,—*

1. THE EFFECT OF THE SCHOOLS IN REVIVING RELIGION IN THE CHURCH.

*Extract of a letter from the Rev. P. Thomas, Curate of Gelligaer,
Glamorganshire.*

"1. Our churches in general in this neighbourhood are now near as full again of auditors, as they used to be before those Welsh Charity Schools circulated about the country. Their ministers endeavoured before, both by fair and rough means, to bring the people under the droppings of the sanctuary, but all in vain; yet now (blessed be God) our solemn assemblies are thronged: and what is more to be taken notice of, there is a visible change for the better in the lives and behaviour of the people; which induces me to hope, that God pours down his blessing in great abundance upon this new way (if I may so call it) of reviving religion among us. As by learning to read they are taught to see their master's will with their own eyes, as well as to hear it with the ear, it is hoped that the advantage they receive by both senses, will doubly encrease their love and affections to God and his holy ways.

"2. We have now a monthly communion about us here in several parish churches, where within very few years past, it could hardly be administered so often as thrice a year, for want of persons to receive it: but (thanks be to God) I hear there are near six score monthly communicants in one of these parishes at present, viz. Eglwys Helen; where not long since they wanted a convenient number to minister the blessed sacrament on one of the three solemn feasts in the year. I am also informed that the communicants increase monthly at Bedwas, Mynydd-yslwyn, and Bedwelltey, in Monmouthshire, and in several other parishes distant from me, where the schools have been for one or two quarters: and if you had been able to afford them the continuance of the schools for a longer time, it is thought that by the blessing of God the effect would have been proportionable; as we find it has been in other places, where they have been for three or four quarters.

"3. It was difficult for the poor to find fit persons, according to the excellent institution of our church, to stand godfathers and godmothers to their children when they brought them to be baptized; as few made conscience of receiving the Lord's Supper, indeed very few could give a tolerable account of it, nor of the creed and ten commandments, nor of the very plainest principles of Christian religion.

"4. The Welsh schools have been means, under God, to reform the profanation of the Sabbath-day; which the generality of the common people formally spent in tippling, gaming, &c., notwithstanding all the good laws in force against it. Many of them at present are as fervent for the sanctification of it, as before they were in profaning it; for as *then* they assembled together for their plays and diversions without much interruption, neighbours associate *now* on the Lord's-day evening to read their Bibles or other good books, and to repeat what they remember of the instructions given them from the pulpit in the morning; singing psalms and praying with their families, which before they were taught to read they neither did nor could do. They gratefully own the light and reformation they are now blessed with, to be owing (next under God) to the charitable supporters of these schools; which they acknowledge to be the most beneficial charity that ever could be offered towards promoting religion among the poor and ignorant, praying God to continue and prosper, and abundantly to reward the authors of it."

Extract of a Letter from the Rev. Jenkin Jones, Curate of Llanbadock, Monmouthshire.

"It is with a great deal of pleasure I acquaint you that I find much benefit by your charity in my neighbourhood already. Instead of five or six communicants generally in Llanbadock twice or thrice in a year, I have now thirty monthly, and expect daily increase. May the Almighty reward you plentifully, and shower down his blessing in a manifold manner upon you and your adherents, for your good wishes to our country. Such an universal charity, I am confident, must originally proceed from the great and good God of the universe."

The following opens upon us a beautiful glimpse of one of those scenes of simple piety, which marked the progress of these schools throughout the country:—

Extract of a Letter from the Rev. John Kenrick, Minister of Llangernyw, in Denbighshire.

"When I wrote my last to you, I was not aware of your receiving, much less of your publishing the several certificates, in relation to the circulating Welsh Charity Schools, or I would have put mine in the same form: I am now therefore to assure you (and I do it with great truth), that the said school, removed by your indulgence from this village, on *May* last, to the upper end of the parish, was extremely agreeable, so beyond expression acceptable to the poor inhabitants in that part of the parish, which we call the Blanau of Llangernyw, as that they immediately flocked to him in numbers; had during the summer quarter about forty boys and girls. Some of whom I have heard read the Bible perfectly well; and to my very great satisfaction have five or six young lads, that seldom fail attending morning and evening service on *Sundays;* and make all the responses audibly and distinctly: and so diligent, yea so indefatigable is the old man, the teacher amongst them, that I never once surprised him as doing nothing, or absent from his charge and employment, and the poor innocents all around him give the mind a very pleasing sensation: one time, of many, I came upon them at prayers, in the litany; which all from the biggest to the least, answered devoutly; and was, methought, a lovely scene or sight."

---

2. THE EFFECTS OF THE SCHOOLS IN SUPPLYING THE DEFICIENCIES OF THE CHURCH

The following exhibits a picture, for which an original may be found in most counties of Wales:—

Vindication of a Schoolmaster, in a Letter from the Parishioners of Llanvihangel-rhos-y Corn, Caermarthenshire.

"We whose names are hereunto subscribed, being the inhabitants of the parish of Llanvihangel-rhos-y-Corn, and other adjacent neighbours, do hereby humbly acknowledge ourselves very much indebted and obliged to our benefactors, for the much esteemed favour and loving-kindness of bestowing on us and many others (though unworthy) a Welsh Charity School, to teach our poor children and other ignorant people to read the word of God in their native language; for which your great charity and mercy towards us, we return our most humble and hearty thanks, and pray God to bless and reward you, which we hope he will do, out of that abundant mercy which inclined you to be merciful to our poor ignorant country. And we beg leave to certify, that the master has been very painful and diligent in teaching his scholars not only to read, but likewise to instruct them in the *Church Catechism*, explainig and confirming the doctrines of it by Scripture proofs, by the help of such authors as have wrote upon the Catechism; that his scholars might understand the first rudiments of the Christian religion, and learn to practise their duty towards God and man. And whereas we are informed, that his diligence has been represented by some (who care not for these things) as if he had taken more upon him than became a schoolmaster, we think it our duty to certify that there was no cause or foundation for it but what we shall freely testify, viz. That the master, when invited to lodge over night with some or other of his scholars in their houses, did use to examine them in the Church Catechism, by the help of his book, in the long winter nights, and sometimes read a chapter, or part of a chapter, in the Bible, bidding them to mind and take notice of the plainest and most observable things and the practical duties contained therein; concluding with singing of a psalm and prayer, and that only in a private house, at the request of the householder and his family, and not otherwise; which all hereabout, *as well as we, know to be very necessary for us of this neighbourhood: our lately deceased Vicar (we are sorry to say it) taking little care of us, having neither sermon nor service for several*

Sundays together in the winter time; he living remotely from us, and having three churches to serve, besides a fourth he employed a curate in. And therefore the master of the Welsh Charity School has been very useful, and much desired to instruct us and many others of our mean rank and capacity, about our misery as fallen by sin, and concerning our recovery by redeeming grace, through Christ Jesus. As the truth of all here asserted is known by every one of us, in testimony thereof we have hereunto voluntarily subscribed our names, this 7th day of July, A.D. 1741."

Griffith Jones seems to have been in his day the most popular and indefatigable preacher in the Principality. He was, in consequence, often solicited by his clerical brethren with applications to preach in their pulpits, with which he was in the habit of complying, by making a kind of tour through the neighbouring districts of South Wales, and preaching in the churches as he passed. Like Wroth and Vicar Pritchard, he would sometimes forsake the pulpit for the tomb-stone or the green sward, when he found the church too small for his audience.

He generally managed to make these excursions during the Easter and Whitsun-week, as he had a greater chance, at these seasons, of falling in with some of those scenes of pugnacious uproar, and drunken frolic, which were at that time so much in vogue in his native country, and which it was always his object to discourage.

When he met with one of these rustic carnivals, he would attempt to disperse it with all the arguments he could employ; and we are told by an individual who frequently accompanied him on these occasions, that though the beginning of his address was generally received with looks of anger and churlish disdain, its conclusion was always marked by symptoms of strong emotion, and by an expression of reverence and awe, from the whole assembled multitude. The great number of persons whose conversion (and I use the word in the sense of a change, not of opinion, but of conduct—a fundamental moral revolution of the motives of the heart), is traceable to him, furnishes a strong additional proof, that there was something peculiarly impressive in the eloquence of Griffith Jones. His biographer has very forcibly described the distinctive excellence of his pulpit oratory, by saying, it was "gavaelgar ar y gydwybod," that is, it possessed a "*grasp on the conscience;*" and he adds, that the commencement of his discourses was generally familiar and unadorned; but that as he went on, his spirit seemed to kindle and burn, "gwresogi a thaniaw," with his subject. Indeed, his merits as a preacher seem to have been held in high estimation beyond the limits of his native country; for, it is an interesting incident in his history, that at one period of his life, he received an invitation from the Society for the Propagation of the Gospel in Foreign Parts, to become one of their missionaries. Ultimately, as we have seen, he decided that his path of duty lay in the humble land of his birth.

After accomplishing a variety of labours, which might have seemed quite incompatible with his delicate health,—and establishing his favourite schools in almost every parish of Wales,—this excellent man breathed his last in the month of April, 1761, leaving behind him, in the religious regeneration and the religious gratitude of a nation of mountaineers, a memorial, which will be envied most by those who are at once the greatest and the humblest of mankind, and which will endure when the ostentatious monuments of wordly power shall melt away "like the baseless fabric of a vision."

In 1761, the year of Mr. Jones's decease, that is about thirty years after the first experiment had been tried with "the Sacrament money of the parish of Llanddowror,"* the number of schools, which had been established at different times and in various places† in Wales, amounted to 3495; and the number of

* Last Letter of Griffith Jones, at the end of the third volume of *Welsh Piety.*

† It should not be forgotten, that a School rarely or never continued in the same place for more than half a year at a time.—*Welsh Piety*, first number, p. 56.

scholars who had been educated in them amounted to 158,237. This was certainly a degree of success which the most sanguine friends of the institution could hardly have anticipated; we can only justly appreciate its real extent, when we recollect that the population of Wales during this period continued on an average between 4 and 500,000. It should also be kept in mind, that the number of scholars just given applies merely to those who frequented the schools in the day time; Griffith Jones informs us, that those who received tuition by the night visits of the schoolmasters were twice as numerous* a class as the regular day-scholars. Nor are these details in any respect a matter of vague conjecture, as one of the duties of the schoolmasters was to keep† a minute account of the names, dispositions, and progress of their pupils. Two-thirds of the regular day-scholars were adults;‡ and many instances are recorded of old men who "for age were obliged to wear spectacles," coming to the schools for the purpose of learning to read;§ and this interesting feature of humble literary zeal is well known to have presented itself frequently in more recent times, when schools of a similar character were founded in North Wales, by Mr. Charles, of Bala, and his coadjutors. Many old persons came, and bursting into tears, lamented "that they had not had an opportunity of learning forty of fifty years sooner;"|| and several blind persons constantly attended during the hours of tuition, and by dint of attention to what was going on, learned by heart several chapters of the Bible. Servants were in the habit of hiring labourers "to serve in their room," to enable them to frequent the schools,—and afterwards of spending the long winter-nights in imparting their little stock of lore to their fellow-servants; in one word, every incident in the history of these schools contributes to prove that the ignorance of the Welsh of that time was ascribable to a total want of the means of knowledge, and not to any indisposition in the people to employ them when offered.

* *Welsh Piety*, first number, p. 65.

† Griffith Jones's Letter, in *Welsh Piety*, first number, p. 3.

‡ Ditto, p. 65.   § Ditto, p. 26. || Ditto, p. 5, 6.

It may now be asked with what degree of propriety the rise of Dissent in Wales can be connected with the name of Griffith Jones —a man whose whole life was spent in exertions to render the Establishment impregnable against Dissent on the one hand, and the more fearful encroachments of sin, ignorance, and superstition, on the other? One answer only can be given; it is a melancholy truth—a truth, nevertheless, but too well sanctioned by experience, that a few pious ministers are the weakness, and not the strength of an Establishment, when the majority of its ministers are sunk in indifference to their sacred duties! The zeal of the few only serves to cast into darker shade the apathy of the many; and, by raising the moral sentiment of the people, to make them more sensitively intolerant of the abuses that surround them. It is upon this principle only, that we can explain whence it was, that Methodism broke out first, and most extensively, in that division of Wales where the Poems of Rhees Pritchard and the schools of Griffith Jones had exerted the most powerful influence. And hence it was, that so many of those clergymen who had been connected with the latter became eventually the missionaries of Methodism;* and it may also be remarked, that the irregularities of the Methodist clergy, which led in the end to systematic itinerancy, appear to have begun by the practice of preaching from church to church, which they seem to have adopted in imitation of Griffith Jones's "Easter and Whitsun" circuits.

In tracing the effects of Griffith Jones's schools, in the plain and unsophisticated narratives of the clergymen who corresponded with him, we are irresistibly led to three conclusions :—

 1st. That before the rise of Methodism in Wales, the churches were as little attended by the great mass of the people as now.

 2nd. That indifference to all religion prevailed as widely then as Dissent in the present day.

* Daniel Rowland first imbibed serious views of religion from Griffith Jones : see Life of Rowland, in the *Goleuad Cymru*, for 1S_6.—Howel Davies, another Methodist clergyman, was his pupil : see Griffith Jones's Life, in the *Trysorva*.

3rd. That if the influential members of the Church had evinced the same zeal for the religious education of the people as was shewn by Griffith Jones and his coadjutors, the Welsh peasantry would have continued to look to the Church for instruction, instead of seeking it from the Methodists.

Now, notwithstanding the zealous support afforded to him by a large portion of the clergy, there can be no difficulty in affirming that he must have met with quite as much opposition from another portion of his brethren; in those days many of the higher classes were systematically opposed to the education of the poor; a few of the Welsh clergy (though, I trust, but a few), are so, even yet. He unequivocally intimates, in one of his letters, that the Bishops of Wales had not even countenanced* his measures. Alluding to the various discouragements and vexatious calumnies to which he had been exposed, he adds, with much feeling and eloquence, "The temple-work, it seems, must be carried on still with a weapon of defence in one hand, as well as with a building instrument in the other!"

The more attentively we consider the plan of the "Circulating Schools," the more strongly shall we feel inclined to admire it. Had the scanty funds by which they were propelled been expended in a given number of local endowments, it needs hardly be remarked, how insignificant in comparison would have been the effects produced! Nor was economy the only excellence of the machinery of the system; it was eminently efficient and elastic. Continual change of place and scene preserved the activity and zeal of the schoolmaster, and increased at once his professional tact and his general intelligence; whilst the necessity of maintaining a character for diligence and piety, in a succession of strange neighbourhoods, formed a stimulus and a discipline very unlike that to which his stationary village brethren are generally subjected. It

* *Welsh Piety*, for 1741, p. 29.—This neglect will appear the more extraordinary, when we consider, that the "Society for Promoting Christian Knowledge,"—a society conducted under the auspices of the rulers of the Church of England, had given the schools their sanction and support.

may also be remarked, that the influence of one of these wandering preceptors must have been greatly augmented by the same circumstances which imposed on him a higher degree of energy and self-restraint; a strange face would naturally have its attractions in the schoolroom—just as it now has in the pulpit, and the consciousness that his was but a mere "angel visit"—that school and schoolmaster would pass away with the long social nights of winter,* furnished his pupils with a powerful motive to a close and speedy attention to study. And when, after the lapse of years, the schoolmaster returned to the scene of his early labours, he would be welcomed back with all the fondness felt for an honoured guest—an old long-absent friend!

No one who is familiar with the habits of the Welsh peasantry can fail to perceive how nicely all these arrangements were calculated to make the engine of education float as it were with the tide of their every-day manners and fancies. Accordingly, its salutary tendency became every day more visible throughout the country; the brutal fights which at one time disgraced it, gave way to scenes of moral beauty and religious tenderness, very like those which travellers have witnessed amongst the romantic mountains of the Protestant Vaudois,—children employed in the work of mutual religious instruction, —a spirit of decency and devotion extending itself amongst people of all ages and ranks; in one word, the course of each of these little Nomade Gymnasia was traceable through the sequestered glens it had visited, by the softened manners and the improved feelings which it had left behind on the whole population.

It is truly painful to reflect, that this noble moral revolution should have tended at last to a schism from a Church which, in its

* *Welsh Piety*, first number, p. 5.—"The inconveniency of the days being shorter than in summer is no disadvantage to the design; for they (i. e. servants and labourers) commonly use to be together for four or five hours in the night; and several labourers, whom the pressing necessities of their poor families will not admit to attend the schools by day, do, in some places, constantly resort to them at night."

general spirit and ordinary administration, may justly be held the purest and most tolerant in the world! Yet, such was the result. After Mr. Jones's death, the schools were superintended and chiefly supported by a Mrs. Bevan, of Laugharne, in Caermarthenshire, who left a legacy of £10,000 to them. But, unhappily, on the death of this benevolent lady, about the year 1780, her will was litigated, and her bounty remained hung up in the Court of Chancery till 1811; in that year the legacy, with an immense arrear, of interest, was awarded to the schools, which have since continued their operations. But, in the mean time, the means of knowledge had been withdrawn; that splendid instrument of education, which had risen like a dream—like a dream had passed away; there was a void—and the Methodists supplied it! Schools on a similar model, as we shal' hereafter prove, were established in the interval, by Mr. Charles, of Bala: and before the year 1811, the whole country had learnt to regard the Methodists and Dissenters as the instructors of the people. This brief memoir of Griffith Jones may be concluded with his warning to his brethren on this very subject. It is a striking instance of foresight and sagacity, and an interesting specimen of his peculiar style:—

"The poor have now in many places a stirring among them, they thirst for knowledge, and *if they have it not in the Church, they will turn about and apply to some other.* To refuse the necessary means of instruction, would tempt them to look upon it as a step towards reducing them again under the yoke of bondage, which their forefathers have been some time subject to in former days,—or as the foreboding of threatening Popish darkness."*

We are now arrived at the period when Methodism began to assume a positive and tangible shape in the Principality. Before entering at large into its history, it is necessary to observe, that the Welsh Methodists are a body distinct, both in origin and doctrine, from the Wesleyans, the sect to whom that appellation is generally applied in England. The latter, it is well known, are Arminians; but the for-

* *Welsh Piety* for 1740 and 1741, p. 34.

mer profess Calvinistic opinions. It is, indeed, usually supposed, that the Methodism of Wales was merely a result of that general religious impulse first communicated by Wesley and Whitefield; and that its first propagators were followers and disciples of those two celebrated men. We are, however, in possession of the clearest evidence, that this is an erroneous opinion. It is true, indeed, that both Wesley and Whitefield did occasionally visit the Principality, and that a good deal of friendly intercourse was carried on between them and the patriarchs of Welsh Methodism: but it is an interesting fact, that religious societies had been formed in Wales, by Howel Harris, some time before the fame of either of the two English Preachers had extended itself very widely; indeed, before Whitefield had even received deacon's orders.

Yet, separated as the Welsh Calvinistic Methodists are, by language, doctrine, and origin, from the first followers of Wesley, both were originally regular members of the Establishment; and there is a striking analogy between the phases through which both parties arrived at the point of an unequivocal secession from it. The following brief summary of the stages by which this result was attained is equally applicable to both denominations:—The first step was the adoption of the practice of preaching in the open air, and other irregularities. The second was lay preaching. The third, the formation of religious societies amongst those who were in the habit of listening to itinerant preachers. As each society grew numerous, the necessity was felt for some place of assembly larger than an ordinary dwelling-house: this led to the fourth stage, the erection of chapels. The fifth was the admission of laymen to the functions of the ministry, by which the schism from the Church was completed.

Any one who has read Mr. Southey's Life of Wesley will perceive directly that there is a strict analogy between the steps by which Wesley and his followers became Dissenters and the different phases of Welsh Methodism. The Wesleyans, however, passed through these stages with much greater rapidity; for though Wesley did not begin to preach in the open air till long after the first Welsh Methodists, his followers became decided schismatics in his life time, and by his own consent and instrumentality; whereas the Welsh Methodists clung enthusiastically to the Church till the year 1810, at which period the original founders of their body were in the grave.

The following comparison of dates may serve to put the subject in a clearer point of view :—

WELSH METHODISTS.	ENGLISH METHODISTS.
1735* — Field preaching by Howel Harris.	1739.—First field preaching in England by Whitefield.—Southey's Life of Wesley, vol. i. p. 230.
1736.—Formation, by Howel Harris, of religious societies, which afterwards seceded from the Church	1739. — Formation of classes or societies by John Wesley.—Idem, vol. i. p. 391.
1810. — Ordination of laymen, by Welsh Methodist clergymen.	1784.—Wesley ordained Dr. Coke.

When we consider the deep ignorance of the plainest doctrines of Christianity, and the general laxity of morals which prevailed in the middle of the last century, throughout the Principality, it may naturally suggest itself, that a man of unusual ardent religious feelings could have looked abroad without sensations similar to those of a missionary in a heathen land! Such was the origin of the preaching of Howel Harris, which was, undoubtedly, the commencement of Methodism in Wales.

Howel Harris was born in the year 1714, at Trevecca, in the parish of Talgarth, in Brecknockshire.† Being connected with

* Whitefield was not in deacon's orders till the year 1736.

† Since the publication of the first edition of this Essay, I have met with a curious little tract, which is my principal authority for the following life of Howel Harris. It is entitled, "Hanes Ferr o Fywyd Howel Harris, Yscwier, a dunwyd allan o'i Ysgrifeniadau ef ei hun, Trevecea, 1792:" i.e. "A History of the Life of Howel Harris, Esquire, extracted from his own Manuscripts." There can be little doubt, considering the date and the place of publication, that this little compilation was the work of one of the inmates of of the Monastery of Trevecca, done by authority of the Fraternity.

the patrons of some benefices in his neighbourhood, he was destined by his friends for the Church. He describes himself as having continued till his 21st year, without any very serious views on the subject of his intended profession, though his mind was occasionally visited with strong misgivings. At this period, a circumstance occurred, to which he ascribes the whole tenor of his subsequent life. One Sunday in the year 1735, he went to Talgarth Church; the subject of the sermon was the responsibility incurred by those who neglected a regular attendance at the Sacrament. In noticing the popular objections raised to the performance of this religious duty, the minister proceeded to advert to those who excuse themselves from coming to the communion on the ground of their unworthiness to partake of it. "If," he exclaimed, "you are unfit to visit the table of the Lord, you are unfit to visit the church, you are unfit to live, and unfit to die!"

Harris, who, it should seem, had not been very constant in his attendance at the communion, was forcibly conscience-struck by these expressions; his feeble and half-stifled compunctions burst out into a deep sense of remorse; he determined to relinquish the trifling habits which he had contracted, and to make the service of God from that time forward the key-stone of his conduct. He lost no time in evincing the force of his new resolutions; on his way from church, that very Sunday, meeting with a neighbour with whom he had been at variance, he confessed that he had been in error, and entreated his forgiveness.* He remained for some time in a state of great mental anguish; at last his spirit revived, and he immediately commenced the practice of going about,† exhorting and instructing the poor at their own houses, which formed, for a long time afterwards, the sole occupation of his life. In November, 1735, he went up to Oxford to finish his studies, preparatory to taking orders, but was so much offended at the immorality which prevailed there, that, after keeping one term, he determined to return to his native country. On arriving at home, he resumed his former

* Confirmed in Whitefield's *Journal*, p. 163.   † Ditto, p. 164.

practice of exhorting and preaching. His discourses were generally delivered "in a field; but at other times in a house, from a wall, a table, or anything else."*

About the end of the year 1736, he established religious societies; the following is his own account of this measure :—

"By this time many had become imbued with serious impressions; and I began to establish religious societies. In the formation of these associations, I followed the rules given by Dr. Woodward, in a work written by him on the subject. Previously to this period, no societies of the kind had been founded either in Wales or England. The English Methodists had not become famous as yet, although, as I afterwards learnt, several of them in Oxford were at that time under strong religious influences."†

The date alleged by Harris for the commencement of his societies is confirmed by Whitefield, who, in his Journal for 1739, which year he visited the Principality, affirms that Harris had by that time established thirty of them in South Wales.†

Though at the time he began to organise these societies, Howel Harris had abandoned all thoughts of entering into the Church, there is not the slightest reason to suppose, that he foresaw, that each of these confederacies would become the nucleus of a Dissenting congregation. Indeed, the members of these societies were at first exclusively Churchmen; and the revival of the real spirit of Christianity within the Establishment was his professed object through life, —an object, which he certainly pursued with single-mindedness, good faith, and courage, though not always with discretion. There is an interesting passage in Bishop Burnett's History of his Own Times, which places his conduct on this occasion in a very different light from that in which it has generally been viewed, inasmuch as it renders it probable, that the formation of these societies was rather an imitation of measures which had already met with considerable countenance in the Church, than the introduction of a novelty entirely of his own invention.‡

* Whitefield's *Journal*, p. 164. † Ditto.
‡ A.D. 1702 Vol. iii. 349.

" Such an evil spirit as is now spread among the clergy would be a sad speculation at any time; but in our present circumstances, when we are near so great a crisis, it is a dreadful thing: but a little to balance this, I shall give an account of more promising beginnings and appearances, which, though they are of *an elder date*, yet of late they have been brought into a more regulated form. In King James's reign, the fear of Popery was so strong as well as just, that many in and about London began to meet often together, both for devotion and for their further instruction; things of that kind had formerly been practised only among the Puritans and the Dissenters; but these *were of the Church*, and came to their ministers to be assisted with forms of prayer and other directions: they were chiefly conducted by Dr. Beveridge and Dr. Horneck. Some disliked this, and were afraid it might be the original of new factions and parties; but wiser and better men thought it was not fit nor decent to check a spirit of devotion at such a time: it might have given scandal, and it seemed a discouraging of piety, and might be a mean to drive well-meaning persons over to the Dissenters. After the revolution, these societies grew more numerous; and for a greater encouragement to devotion, they got such collections to be made as maintained many clergymen to read prayers in so many places, and at so many different hours, that devout persons might have that comfort at every hour of the day; there were constant sacraments every Lord's day in many churches: there were both great numbers and greater appearance of devotion at prayers and sacraments, than had been observed in the memory of man."*

In 1732, Whitefield and Howel Harris met for the first time at Cardiff; similarity of character and doctrinal opinion ensured a cordial meeting. The former, in his Journal, points out symptoms in the state of Wales, from which he very justly augurs the subse-

---

* Howel Harris affirms that the effect of his preaching and other measures, was to make each denomination more attentive to their religious duties according to their own peculiar views,—to send the Churchman to the Church, and the Dissenter to the Dissenting Chapel.

quent result. To quote his own language, "People make nothing of coming twenty miles to hear a sermon, and great numbers there are who are not only hearers but doers also of the Word; so that there is a most comfortable prospect of the spreading of the Gospel in Wales. I really believe there are some now living which shall not taste of death till they see *the kingdom of God come with power*."* About the same time, Harris had an interview with John Wesley at Bristol; and, although prepossessed against him, his feelings were entirely changed, after he had heard him preach on the leading doctrines of Christianity; and he acknowledges, with much simplicity, the impression made upon him, when, before they retired to rest, Wesley prayed with much fervour and eloquence, "for Griffith Jones, for myself, and for Wales."†

In the year 1736, Daniel Rowland, Curate of Llangeitho, in Cardiganshire, associated himself with Howel Harris. Before this time, he had been very indifferent to his professional duties; the remarkable change that took place in him was begun by the friendly advice and remonstrances of a pious minister of the Independent persuasion, who had a congregation in his parish, and consummated by one of Griffith Jones's sermons.‡ The former, whose name was Hugh Pugh, was long known in the tradition of the country, by the quaint but expressive title of "Hugh Pugh dinod," or the faultless: it is recorded, that when Rowland's popularity began to increase, and to attract away some part of the congregation of his early Mentor, instead of repining, this excellent old man expressed himself in terms of unfeigned joy, that his advice had prevailed even to the detriment of his own worldly interests.

Both Harris and Rowland occasionally extended their preaching into North Wales—at that time a land of no slight peril to any kind of itinerant preacher; and both of them, on many occasions, ran no small risk of their lives from the fury of the mob. Harris was once nearly stoned to death near Bala. But the kind of persecu-

---

* Whitefield's *Journal*, p. 166.   † *Hanes Ferr.*

‡ *Goleuad Cymru* for 1826.

tion to which the Methodist Preachers were most frequently exposed, consisted of attempts to stifle their voices with drums, speaking trumpets, &c. There is no doubt, that these annoyances were in many instances nothing more than a retaliation for an ill-timed interruption of amusements, perfectly harmless in themselves, and reprehensible only when carried to excess. At the same time, there is no doubt, that the magistrates of the country were frequently betrayed by their prejudices, into acts of oppression. Several of Harris's lay preachers were pressed during the war; and, though they were ultimately released, it was clear that this was merely for the purpose of petty persecution. These unjust measures were not only reprehensible, but unwise; since they tended very much to the progress of those opinions which they were intended to stifle. To answer its end at all—persecution must be carried to its height; by sweeping away every living professor of a creed, its progress may be arrested for ever; and hence the suppression of the Reformation in Italy and in Spain. But all inferior grades of intolerance serve only to give to the persecuted a hold upon the pity and affections of the multitude, more particularly amongst a people by nature open to such impressions. In these violent proceedings, the clergy were sometimes implicated; but they seem on the whole, to have been much more temperate in their conduct than the lay magistrates.

In the year 1743, the Methodists had made great progress in South Wales; they had at this time ten clergymen belonging to them, forty lay preachers, or "advisers," (cynghorwyr,) and one hundred and forty societies. Rowland had three thousand communicants in Cardiganshire, and Howel Davies two thousand in Pembrokeshire.*

The rapidity with which Methodism overran South Wales has been well described by a term frequently used by the old Welsh bards, to indicate the career of a conflagration, over the withered underwood of the mountains ("goddaith").† In 1752, however, its advance was for some time impeded by a breach between Harris and

* *Hanes y Methodistiaid*, p. 21.   † Ditto.

Rowland, which led to the abandonment, by the former, of the active life he had previously led. Endowed with a constitution of such iron hardihood, as to keep pace even with his own ardent and restless spirit, he had been enabled to go through a life of amazing exertion, having, for many years past, travelled about twenty miles, and preached three or four times every day. His journeys generally lay through the rugged mountains of Wales; but he had also itinerated through the English counties of Kent, Essex, Buckingham, Wilts, Somerset, Gloucester, Oxford, Warwick, and Hereford.*

After his variance with Rowland, he adopted the singular resolution of founding a monastic institution on Protestant principles; and accordingly, retiring to his own estate at Trevecca, he erected there an edifice for the reception of such persons as might choose to pass the remainder of their days in such a place of seclusion from the busy scenes of this world! In the year 1754, about one hundred pilgrims had arrived at Trevecca, from different parts of Wales. The course of life pursued by these recluses was very analagous to that of some of the Popish Orders of Monks; they assembled for divine service three times in the course of the twenty-four hours; and their first summons to prayer was before dawn. This last feature of the institution is thus alluded to in a Welsh poem, written by a Methodist bard, to express his regret that Harris had retired from the labours of a public preacher:—

> With him, within Trevecca's walls,
> Prayer—long before the dawn—is found;
> Whilst yet the reign of slumber falls,
> In listless dreams, on all around.
>
> Y mae gweddi cyn y wawr-ddydd,
>   Yn Nhrevecca ganddo fe;
> 'R amser bo trwm-gwsg freuddwydlyd
>   Yn teyrnasu yn llawer lle.†

* *Hanes Ferr*, p. 68. † *Trysorva*, vol. ii.

In the year 1759, a circumstance occurred, which again opened a new career to this singular man, who seemed destined to exhibit in himself the extremes of energy and repose. A dread of a French invasion being at that time prevalent, the Lord Lieutenant of the county of Brecon applied to him to accept a commission in the Militia; after some consultation with his Fraternity, he consented to take an Ensigncy, on condition, however, that he should be at liberty to preach to the Militia and to the people of those towns in which they might be stationed on duty. These terms were readily conceded; and accordingly, he joined the regiment, with twenty-four of the inmates of his Monastery, twelve of whom he supported through the campaign at his own expense. After having been for some time an Ensign, he was promoted to a Captaincy,—and enjoyed what to him must have been a much higher gratification, an opportunity of preaching at will through the remotest districts of England, with the bold yeomanry of his native county for his body guard. This was a proud change indeed, from the time when he could hardly venture to preach a few miles from his own home, without exposing himself to danger!

In this kind of life, he continued three years; and on peace being proclaimed at the end of that period, he and his twenty-four Knights Templars, after having given full proof of their loyalty and patriotism, returned once more to the solitude of Trevecca, from whence he rarely afterwards absented himself.

Harris was always anxious to be considered a firm friend to the Church, as an institution, and used to bring forward many arguments to defend himself from the charge of having encroached on the functions of the clergy. Every Sunday, he attended, with all his brethren, at Talgarth Church, where they were accommodated with a separate gallery, and where the Vicar of the parish was in the habit of administering the Sacrament to them once a month, apart from the rest of the congregation.

In 1768, at the request and expense of Lady Huntingdon, he changed his paternal mansion at Trevecca into a College, for the education of lay preachers, to officiate in her chapels. The tenets of the ministers of Lady Huntingdon's Connection are precisely the same as those of the Welsh Calvinistic Methodists; both profess to regard themselves rather as auxiliaries than rivals of the Establishment. The former, however, read the Church Service in their chapels, and in this respect approximate still nearer to the Church than the latter, who have no set form of prayer. It was Harris's practice to attend at the College once every day, to exhort, and converse with the students; and, with the exception of a few occasional excursions, to preach in the neighbouring counties, this continued to be his only avocation till his decease, which occurred in July 1773. On his death-bed, he repeated the expressions of attachment to the Church of England which he had so often employed; and directed, that his ashes should be entombed underneath the altar of Talgarth Church, the spot where he was first struck with a sense of sin, and of the necessity of a Saviour.

About twenty years ago, an excellent North Welsh clergyman still living, was led, in the course of an excursion through South Wales, to visit the neighbourhood of Trevecca. He found the monastery still in existence—under a new President, who pressed him with much warmth to remain and dine with him and his Fraternity. On this invitation being accepted, his host seemed highly pleased, and the whole household evinced an evident gratification at having a clergyman of the Church of England for their guest. In the course of the evening, the conversation naturally turned on the days of Howel Harris and Daniel Rowland, when the hospitable successor of the former remarked, "The revival of religion began in the Church in those days, and I think it is beginning in the Church now."

The breach between Rowland and Harris was for some time a considerable impediment to the progress of Methodism; nevertheless, it still continued to gain ground as rapidly as ever in Cardiganshire and Caermarthenshire, two counties in which the eloquence of the former was incessantly exerted. Towards the latter end of the last century, Rowland was expelled from his curacy, after having held it for about forty years; during the rest of his life, he preached chiefly at a chapel that had been built for him in the village of Llangeitho. After his expulsion from the Church, this little place came to be looked upon as the very Jerusalem of Methodism. Two thousand communicants were often seen waiting to receive the Sacrament from his hands: individuals of the lower and middle ranks would often walk fifty or even eighty miles to hear him; and the peasantry have been sometime known to embark by sea from the distant coast of Caernarvonshire, for the purpose of attending on his ministry.* On one occasion, a meeting was held at Llangeitho, under his auspices, at which twenty clergymen and sixty-eight lay preachers were present.†

I have frequently heard the early Welsh Methodists described as proverbial for simplicity, humility, and benevolence: since their separation from the Church of England a far lower tone of morality has prevailed amongst this body, which is in some measure ascribable to the inferior grade of preachers entailed upon them by that event. The clergy connected with them were probably the most powerful and efficient preachers at that time belonging to the Welsh Church. One of them, Peter Williams, is illustrious as having published no fewer than three editions of the Bible, with annotations,—and in the last instance with a very considerable pecuniary loss to himself. Another Methodist clergyman, William Williams of Pant-y-Celyn, is highly esteemed as a religious poet; and it is an interesting instance of the high veneration still entertained by the Welsh for the bardic character and bardic lore, that the Methodists date the revival of their cause from the day on which William Williams came with a volume of Hymns to Llangeitho. In fact, the great strength of their preaching lay in its harmony with the feelings of the people; the sermons of Rowland were Christian lessons taught in that metaphorical style in which all Celtic nations delight. A gentleman who had frequently heard Wesley and Whitefield and other great preachers, was in the habit of saying that Rowland far surpassed them all. "His oratory," he would say, "bears most resemblance to that of

* *Drych yr Amseroedd.* † Morgan's *Life of Charles.*

Whitefield; but then there is this striking distinction, that when Whitefield rose in eloquence, he appeared to fail in matter, whereas Rowland seemed to rise *because* he was *overwhelmed* with matter." The following specimen of the peculiar depth and beauty of metaphor which he mingled in his sermons, may not be without its interest; but I should premise, that he rarely preached without walking about for some time alone in silent meditation : on one of these occasions, as he was wandering near a river which ran by his house, it was observed that he frequently stopped, plunged his staff into the stream, and gazed at it with eccentric earnestness, an action which at that time appeared strange and unmeaning. Yet how beautifully was it explained, when on the next sabbath, while preaching on the afflictions of Christians, he burst forth into the following wild but splendid passage :—

"In this world the cross of Christ seems crooked, though in reality it is straight, as the staff seems bent when immersed in the waters. Oh! the waters of affliction have passed over my soul, and the billows of death surround me ! It is the waters of affliction —the afflictions of this life, that obscure to us the ways of Providence; but hereafter what is dark shall be enlightened and what is crooked made straight."

Rowland died in the year 1790 ; on his death-bed he declared himself firmly attached to the Church of England, adding with enthusiasm, "True religion has begun in the Church, and into the Church it will ere long return!" His death occurred on Saturday evening, and when the melancholy tidings were communicated on the morrow to the congregation that had assembled to hear him, they could not be prevailed upon to attend during that day upon the preaching of another minister, but dispersed themselves to their respective homes, with the strongest expressions of grief and dismay.* I have heard it observed, by a gentleman who resided in a neighbouring district of South Wales, that he has the most vivid recollection of the death of

* *Goleuad* for 1823.

Daniel Rowland, though at that time in his childhood; it seemed to agitate the whole country, and the people evidently regarded it in the light of a great public calamity.

Though Methodism was at first extremely unpopular in North Wales, towards the end of the last century, a missionary sprung up, who was destined to carry it into the the wildest recesses of Snowdon. This was the Rev. Thomas Charles: he was a native of Caermarthenshire, but had served a curacy in North Wales. Hereafter, few names will excite such mingled emotions of pride and regret in the hearts of his countrymen. To him we owe much of the very civilization of our land. It was he who, in exchange for the Popish ignorance of the last century, diffused among the North Wales peasantry, those deep, moral, and religious feelings, and that thirst for information which at present characterise them: nor was his influence confined to his own country; he was the founder of institutions which extend over the whole Christian world. "The Bible Society" commenced with him, and two of his countrymen; and, according to Dr. Pole, he is to be considered as the originator of the "Adult schools."

It is melancholy to think, that such a man should have been led to secede from the Church of England, much more so, that he should have been the instrument of wider separation from her. With such a leader, we need not be surprised that the progress of Methodism in North Wales was one of the most rapid of religious changes. When he first joined them, they were a small and persecuted body; at his death, their chapels were to be found in almost every parish in that division of the Principality.

In North Wales, the Methodist clergy were looked upon with great jealousy; and in the year 1783, Charles became so unpopular with a portion of his parishoners, that he chose to resign his curacy; he found it impossible to gain any employment afterwards in the Church in North Wales. This involuntary idleness was a source of great anguish to a conscience like his, morbidly sensitive. Though an admirer, and in some respects, a follower of Rowland, he had scruples against preaching in the Methodist chapels; at the same time, he was distracted by the idea of remaining idle; and this at length drove him to forsake the Church altogether, and to become a preacher in the Methodist Connection. He found them hardly recovered from the effects of the division between Rowland and Harris. He, however, soon infused new life into their cause, by the well-regulated system of co-operation which he established amongst the preachers of the body. He was himself indefatigable, travelling during the most inclement seasons over wild and dreary mountains, and often preaching two or three times in the course of the day.

In the midst of these toils, he began to form circulating schools on the model of those of Griffith Jones. This he accomplished partly through the assistance of English friends and partly by his stipend as a minister, which he devoted entirely to this purpose, relying for his own support on the industry of his wife; he taught most of the first masters of those schools himself. Nor were the people less zealous than their preceptor; the same avidity for instruction which Wesley had remarked in South Wales soon became apparent in the North; and the schools after a time acquired fresh support daily.

The cause of the Methodists was much advanced by their habits of meeting in large bodies for religious purposes. Nothing can be more imposing than such an assemblage in a mountainous region, as is well known to those who may have seen a "sacramental occasion" in the Highlands of Scotland;* to the feelings of the Welsh, it was peculiarly suited, and the effect of such meetings may be judged of from the following anecdotes. Charles having heard that a kind of rural festivity called by the country people "Wakes," was about to take place in his neighbourhood, had a party of children drawn up before the inn, near the scene where the merry making was to be held, where he catechised them on Scripture precepts that seemed directed against such rejoicing;

* See Letters in the *New Monthly Magazine*.

and strange to say, the revel was actually broken up!* At another time he had a similar examination before the principal inn of a town in North Wales, long known as "An immoral and a persecuting place." The result was shortly afterwards the establishment of a school there, containing one hundred children! The success of these bold experiments can only be ascribed to the peculiar character of the Welsh people.

On several occasions, Charles assembled together in the open air, and in a central district, all the children who had been taught in the schools of North Wales, and they amounted to several thousands. The number of readers had so far increased, that in 1799, he established a Welsh religious periodical. In 1803, he established a press at Bala, in order to print books for his schools. He also printed an elaborate work, called "The Welsh Scriptural Dictionary," and a "Scriptural Catechism." The first has gone through two editions, and the latter no less than fifteen. Some time after this, Charles and some Welsh clergymen founded a society for supplying Wales with Bibles. The plan of this afterwards was enlarged into that of the "British and Foreign Bible Society." The prominent part he had taken in the institution of this society was testified in a manner that must have been highly gratifying to him; he was appointed honorary governor for life, at a time when it had obtained much of its present power and popularity.

A very interesting part of Charles's life is an excursion which he made into Ireland, in company with two other gentlemen, at the request of the Hibernian Society, for the purpose of ascertaining the religious state of the country—and the best means of instructing the people, whether through the medium of the English

---

* One of Griffith Jones's Schoolmasters succeeded by means somewhat similar in reforming a place so notorious for swearing, that even the children were guilty of it. Both Charles and Griffith Jones seem often to have infused a new spirit into the adult population, by the affecting exhibition of the amendment they had produced in the simple mind of infancy. Whole districts thus often learnt wisdom out of the mouths of "babes and sucklings."

or Irish language.* He decided in favour of the latter, and his opinion has since been acted upon on a very large scale. He found in the state of the Irish Church, defects analagous to those which paralyze the Church in his native country; the Irish language was cultivated only by the Romish Priests. "Popery," he says, "and the Irish language always go together: when the one is spoken the other prevails." After delivering his opinion as to the necessity of making Irish the medium of instruction, he adds the following interesting remarks:—

" We have not met with any one who could read Irish. There are no elementary books in their language. Circulating Charity Schools might do wonders. Many parts of Wales in Griffith Jones's time were as dark as Ireland."

A short time after his excursion to Ireland, he had the honour of being consulted by a society formed for the diffusion of education in the Highlands of Scotland, as to the best means of promoting this object. He found that in that country also nothing was taught in the schools but English;—the result of his advice was the establishment of Gaelic Schools.

We are now arrived at the period when the Methodists became entirely detached from the Establishment, in consequence of Mr. Charles and other Methodist Clergymen consenting to ordain some of the Lay Preachers. The following is an extract from Charles's Life by a clergyman of the Church of England:†—

" There was one subject which had for years been mooted by some members of the connection, and which had occasionally been pressed on the attention of Mr. Charles. The Methodists had hitherto been considered a part of the Established Church. None but episcopally ordained ministers administered the Lord's Supper among them; and their children were baptized by the minister of the parish in which they lived. But not a few among them were desirous of introducing a different order of things, that is, of having some of the most approved of the lay-preachers ordained after the manner of the Dissenters, or of the English Methodists. Mr. Charles, and, we believe, all the clergy connected with them,

* Morgan's *Life of Charles*, p. 308.   † Ditto.

resisted this proposal for a long time very strongly, and had it not been for some unhappy circumstances, would probably have wholly prevented its final adoption. The most powerful plea which the advocates of this opinion had to urge, was the inadequacy of the small number of clergy among them to supply the demands of the connection. The policy pursued by the bishops tended to increase this difficulty. There were many pious clergy, besides those in actual connection with the Methodists, who occasionally laboured among them and assisted them. And those clergy were on the increase. But the bishops became stricter, and insisted on uniform regularity. This gave great advantage to those who were for introducing a new order of things; and threw Mr. Charles and many others into great embarrassments. Would it not have been wiser in our spiritual rulers to pursue measures calculated to bring back those who have a little deviated from the road, than such as must of necessity have driven them still further? Too much strictness in some things produces often greater evils than too much laxity. It is better to loosen a tight cord than to break it by rendering it tighter. The effect, however, in the present instance, has been to separate from the Church a large and by far the most religious part of the community. It was in 1810 and 1811 that the new system was introduced."

It is well known that Charles and his clerical brethren were urged into this indefensible measure, by the continual importunity of some of the lay preachers, who were ambitious to participate in the privileges of that profession of which they already shared both the popularity and the toil. There is reason to believe, that he afterwards felt cause to regret the step he had thus taken, and that this feeling, operating on a mind naturally sensitive, combined with his incessant labours and reckless exposure to the inclement skies of the bleak hills of Gwynedd, contributed to hasten his decease, which occurred in 1814, while he was yet in the prime of life. Just before his death, no fewer than fourteen thousand Methodists met at the general association at Bala.* Of Thomas

* Morgan's *Life of Charles.*

Charles, of Bala, in his life, different opinions were held, accordingly as men dreaded the evils of schism on one hand, or felt scandalized at the apathy of the Church on the other. Thus, while some looked upon him as guilty of the sin of Jeroboam, others revered him as the good Samaritan, who gave the word of life to his countrymen, while their clergy, like the Jewish priest of old, passed haughtily by on the other side. Yet, amongst those who knew him best, there was but one impression as to the goodness of his general intentions; and perhaps, as men feel more warmly towards Wales, they will think less of his faults, and more of his temptations. Seldom has any country given birth to a man who so eminently combined the talents that guide and enlighten with a guilelessness and a childlike sensibility that seem hardly of this world. Whilst it must be allowed that no necessity of circumstances could justify his assumption to himself of an authority which, as a clergyman of the Church, he had recognized as belonging exclusively to his spiritual superiors, still, it is more important to reflect, whether a system which provoked such a step from such a man can be altogether blameless, or well adapted to the religious wants o. his country.

It must be remembered, that the causes of Dissent, and not its evils, are the subject of this Essay; and I may take this opportunity of remarking, that it is for this reason, that the biography of Harris, of Rowland, and of Charles, have occupied so large a portion of the preceding pages, to the exclusion of men who laboured quite as earnestly, in a less conspicuous sphere, and in stricter conformity to the discipline of the Establishment. At the same time, I confess I should consider it rather an unsatisfactory mode of investigating this subject, were I to stop short at mere secondary causes, without enquiring whether there was not something in the administration of the Church itself, which tended to generate these divisions. The real question is, why has the whole country joined the Methodists and Dissenters? The first blast of the Alpine horn will bring down the avalanche,—but it is from mountains that are covered with the snows of an eternal winter!

CHAPTER II.

CAUSES OF DISSENT IN WALES.

THE UNPOPULARITY OF THE EPISCOPAL CLERGY ASCRIBABLE TO TWO CAUSES:—1. THEIR WANT OF SYMPATHY WITH THE FEELINGS AND TASTES OF THE PEOPLE.—2. THEIR NEGLECT OF THE LANGUAGE OF THE PEOPLE.—BOTH THESE CAUSES THEMSELVES THE EFFECTS OF AN ENGLISH HIERARCHY.

"Our Orators are observed to make use of less gesture or action than those of other countries. Our preachers stand stock still in the pulpit, and will not so much as move a finger, to set off the best sermons in the world. . . . . . I have heard it observed more than once, by those who have seen Italy, that an untravelled Englishman cannot relish all the beauties of Italian pictures, because the postures which are expressed in them are often such as are peculiar to that country. One who has not seen an Italian in the pulpit, will not know what to make of that noble gesture in Raphael's picture of St. Paul preaching at Athens, where the Apostle is represented as lifting up both his arms, and pouring out the thunder of his rhetoric amidst an audience of Pagan Philosophers." *Addison.—Spectator, No.* 405.

"We cannot help thinking, that English Sermons to Welsh Congregations are neither less absurd, nor more edifying, than Welsh Preaching would be in the centre of England, or Latin Service in the Church of Rome. In some respect, a greater severity this than is imposed by the Romish Antichrist, who, notwithstanding his robes are red with the blood of the saints, yet ordains that preaching be in the known tongue, through all his provinces." *Griffith Jones, of Llanddowror.—Welsh Piety for* 1739.

THE unpopularity of the Church in Wales has a deeper cause than is generally imagined. There are certain differences in the characters of nations that resist all attempts at perfect assimilation; these peculiarities probably arose in the first instance from the combined influence of climate and social institutions.

However this may be, there is irresistible evidence, that the character of the first inhabitants of a country generally communicates itself to each new succession of colonists, and often survives every possible change of laws, language, and civilization. The similarity of disposition between the modern Frenchmen and the primitive Gaul has frequently been noticed; and the Anglo-Irish descendants of English emigrants were early remarked as the most Hibernian of Hibernians. The same principle applies to the present population of Wales; the Welsh of the existing era being very much the same people as they were in the time of Giraldus, with the exception of a few favourable traits which are the result of Protestantism and a more tranquil state of society. No one who is tolerably acquainted with both, can help remarking how different, nay, in some points of view, how completely opposite are the Welsh and English character. The Englishman is grave, averse to all superfluity of words and gesture, and so constitutionally jealous of ostentatious virtue, that he is even apt to censure an involuntary burst of real feeling; whilst the Welshman is imaginative, prone to metaphor and action, and fond of excitement of every kind. Abstractedly speaking, there is perhaps no superiority of moral excellence in either character over the other; the Englishman's virtues and vices spring from his reason, those of the Cambrian from his feelings; each temperament has its advantages, and each requires a different kind of moral and religious cultivation. The admirable adaptation of the precepts of Christianity to all ages and countries, can hardly be doubted; yet it may be said, consistently with this admission, that religion itself cannot be impressively taught, and brought home to the heart, without the aid of that indefinable community of feeling which generally exists between men of the same race,—unless the preacher has the instinctive power, as it were, of applying Christian truths, so as best to foster the peculiar virtues of his hearers. Now, it is in this very point, that the Established Church, as at present regulated, is ill suited to the Welsh people: the clergy are all educated in England,—controlled by English Bishops, and their style of preaching is therefore formed on an English fashion. Thus they insensibly lose the key to the feelings of their countrymen. English preachers, in accordance with the taste of their nation, are more staid and formal than those of any people in Europe: they are obviously, therefore, the worst possible models for the young Welsh clergy. The Englishman would regard the eloquence of the Irish bar as flowery nonsense and affectation; at the same time, to the Welsh mountaineer, a sermon delivered in calm and unimpassioned English style, appears unnatural and even hypocritical. At the present moment, the exciting discourses of the Welsh Dissenters are popular, not because the people would, in ordinary circumstances, run into excesses, but from the revulsion of a feeling that should have been wisely directed and not thwarted. The impulse to Dissent is not given by the noise and vociferation too often employed by the Dissenting Minister, but by the want amongst the clergy of even that degree of animation which is a part of the natural habits,—a part, I had almost said, of the language of the country.

In accounting for the spread of Dissent in Wales, in my humble opinion, too much stress has generally been laid on the neglect of the Welsh language, and too little on the peculiarities of the Welsh character. I cannot help thinking, that if the Cambro-British dialect could be annihilated in a day, the want of sympathy between the clergy and their flocks would still continue to alienate the hearts of the people from the Establishment.

Many great and good men* have been advocates for that undercurrent of national feeling that at present prevails in Wales, as in Scotland and Ireland, and many of the greatest English writers of the present day have sanctioned it. It is certainly unwise to wage war with those distinctions which only serve to promote a friendly and genial emulation. The strength of the British empire will be found to depend not on intellectual monotony, but on the varied endowments of the great Celtic and Teutonic families.

An ancient language or usage ought never to stand in the way of civilization; yet the civilization of a people should as far as possible be built on, and blended with, its hereditary and generous associations. If there be one thing more than another for which Wales is indebted to the manly and dignified liberality

* Dr. Johnson was even an advocate for the preservation of the Welsh language, and "proposed a scheme" for effecting that purpose during his excursion in Wales.—See Johnson's *Tour in Wales.*

of Englishmen, it is for having in her case kept these principles fairly in view; we should be ungrateful did we forget what our Llwyd* owed to Sir Isaac Newton, and how much Welsh literature is indebted to Southey, to Mackintosh, to Sharon Turner, and to Heber. It is with the greatest reluctance, then, that I feel myself bound to state a conviction that may at first sight seem to savour of an ungracious national jealousy; yet, after the most anxious and careful consideration of the subject, I feel that I owe it to truth, to state my persuasion that the crying abuse of the Church in Wales, and the fundamental cause of all the defects peculiar to the Church in that country, is the system of conferring her Bishoprics on Englishmen. For the last century not one individual has ruled a Welsh diocese who possessed the faintest knowledge of the language of the people!

No one would protest more strongly than I should against a puerile clamour at an Englishman holding a high office in Wales, merely because he was an Englishman; my objection is founded purely on the broad Protestant principles of the Church of England, on the Protestant principles of all her pious members; thus far would I go and no farther. Novel and even fantastic as the proposition may at first sight appear, I am compelled to say, that if the principle of the Reformation were emancipation from a slavery to mere superstitious sounds, and its object to give religion once more to the hearts and language of the people, I cannot perceive any real distinction between the present Ecclesiastical government of Wales and a recurrence to the worst practices of Popery!

A consideration of the duties attached to the dignity of a Prelate of the English Church, will, I trust, prove that this is no exaggerated view of the subject. They may be divided into two classes:—First, his duty as a Minister; secondly, his duty as an Ecclesiastical Ruler.

And, first, of his responsibility as a Minister and an Evangelist. To the great bulk of the people of Wales, the language of her Bishops is as unintelligible as the Breviary; from the pulpit, therefore, they can do nothing to augment her religious privileges,

* *Cambrian Biography.*

or allay her sectarian differences; whatever may be the depth of their erudition, or the splendour of their eloquence, from the moment they have reconciled themselves to take the charge of a nation of whose language they are entirely ignorant—those high endowments become as the "talent" which was "buried in the earth." It has, indeed, been said that religious instruction is no part of the episcopal functions,—that "it is not in the bond,"— and therefore the people of Wales have no reason to complain! But it needs hardly be remarked, that there never was a period in which the Bishops of England neglected the practice of preaching to the people, and there never was a time in which the salutary influence of this practice on the clergy and the community—was denied. Those who have frequently had opportunities of listening to the present eminent Bishop of London will not readily allow that it is no injury to a people to be deprived of the ministerial labours of their Diocesan. Accordingly, when that prelate was Bishop of Chester, a forcible parallel was drawn between the state of his diocese and that of an adjoining one, in which the Bishop could not even repeat the Lord's prayer in the language of his people!

But, giving this palliation of abuses its full weight—allowing that it is wise and prudent in itself, when the Church is beset on all sides—respectful to the feelings of seven hundred thousand people—to weigh their religious claims in the discriminating scales of the usurer,—and to circumscribe the spirit of an awful responsibility, by the dry letter of the law—allowing all this as far as the preceding topic is concerned,—yet, what are we to say of the mode in which the rite of Confirmation is administered in Wales? It cannot, in this case, be said, that the responsibility rests with the parochial clergy, and attaches but in a slight degree to the Bishop; for, in this instance, a duty arises, attaching primarily, solely, and exclusively, to the Bishop—a duty which cannot be performed in any other language than that of the nation to whom it is administered, without a complete mockery of the very nature of the ordinance, and of every principle of the Church of England. Yet, it is thus administered!

It is quite chimerical to expect that the Church of England will ever be respected by the Welsh, whilst such abuses as these are continually before their eyes; they are enough to give offence to a peasantry little versed in scriptural knowledge— but to a people with whom Dissent is popular and religious controversy familiar, they will ever remain a source of irritation and disgust.

The duties of a Bishop are not like those of a Judge; he is not the mere enforcer of certain rigid technicalities; if his office has no hold on the affections of the people—if they do not, in fact, love as well as bend to his authority, its Christian utility is at an end. But, what has the visitation of an English Bishop in Wales in it, or associated with it, to influence the affections? As for the clergy, they attend indeed—but not to seek advice as from a father and a friend; but with cold formality, as at the levee of some temporal lord, with whom they are bound to hold for a few brief moments an interview of heartless ceremonial! As for the people, they crowd the church it is true—Dissenter and Churchman; but it is in the spirit in which Englishmen abroad go to see a Popish procession; they hardly understand one word that is said; their Bishop's dress, his words, all that he does are a mere topic for idle gossip and guess work—often of sectarian ridicule!

Secondly, of English Bishops, as the Ecclesiastical Rulers of the Dioceses of Wales:—Undoubtedly, this is a consideration of far more importance than even the last. On the conduct, character, views, and attainments of the Bishop, the general spirit of the whole Establishment will depend. If he be a man of piety and patriotism, men of religious and patriotic spirit will be placed in the commanding situations of the Church, and be encouraged to make the Church their profession. If, on the contrary, he be a man of low religious feeling, strict in exacting the mint and cummin of canonical obedience, but slow in rewarding a life of protracted self-denial and holiness,—then will the Church be thronged with men who make a merit of shunning the hypocrisy of the Pharisee by verging upon the vices of the Publican—and its best benefices will become a premium upon a mere cold negative profession of religion. These principles are so obvious, and, indeed, so generally admitted, that I should hardly have deemed it necessary to repeat them here were it not for their application, by analogy, to the present state of the Church in Wales.—On the same ground, that the moral character of its rulers is found to influence the whole Church as an institution, the ignorance of the Bishops of Wales of the language and feelings of the people, will necessarily tend to fill the Welsh Church with men but little versed in that language and those feelings. It is, of course, not too much to say, that these are qualifications without which no man ought to be allowed to enter into the Welsh Church, or remain in it,—that in proportion as they are possessed in combination with piety, ought to be the station of the individual possessing them,—and, consequently, that the first and chief essential to the right exercise of the episcopal sway, is the power of judging of them. Now, on this subject, the English Bishops of Wales can exercise no judgment; they must depend, and invariably do depend, on the opinions of others; in other words, they do not, in fact, perform the first of those duties which nominally devolve upon them! If the object of episcopacy be to preserve Christian unity, and to secure a wise distribution of patronage, then it is quite impossible to look on the present state of the Welsh Church as sound or defensible. An English Bishop, in discharging the duties of a Welsh see, labours under every possible embarrassment. To distribute patronage so as best to provide for the religious wants of the community requires a knowledge of the peculiar talents of the clergy, and of the various local exigencies of a diocese. Now, an English Bishop in Wales has in this respect everything to learn; from his ignorance of the language, he must judge of circumstances at second hand; from his want of sympathy with the temperament of the people, he cannot rightly appreciate even the information he may receive; he never can attain that nice discrimination of their views, feelings, and peculiar sectarianism, which exists almost intuitively in the breast of one of their own countrymen. Hence, the Bishops in Wales generally abandon after a time that line of policy which at first appeared indispensable; and thus it is, that, often with the best possible intentions on their part, their conduct is a series of vacillations; they differ from themselves and from each other; and the parochial clergy, disgusted at being tossed about by discordant doctrines, and at finding their own local knowledge neutralized, sink into apathy, and content themselves by timidly adhering to mere formalities.

Our first civilization was from Rome, and we still regard her modes of thought with too slavish a veneration. A liberal share of classical learning enlarges the mind, and that a few should make it an exclusive pursuit must be beneficial to the general tone of public sentiment. But when the most awful office in the Church of Christ, when the spiritual interests of a people are rendered secondary to the rewarding of mere classical acquirement, it must be admitted, that the veneration for heathen antiquities is carried to a startling extent. Amongst the English Bishops of Wales have been many men eminent for their scholastic and theological erudition; and some individuals, in many respects, an honour to their age and country; yet, it is but too plain, that these endowments have proved but a bitter and illusory boon to Wales, unaccompanied (as they have been) by that knowledge of localities and individuals, which is the growth only of time and experience—without which, great endowments will be of little avail, and with which, mere plain common sense and integrity may suffice to give to an Establishment all the efficiency of which it is capable. It is sometimes alleged, that none but a stranger can sustain the dignity of the Episcopacy; but, on this subject, we may learn a lesson from our courts of justice, where, it is well known, that an advocate, who is raised to the judicial office to-day, never fails, if possessed of judicial knowledge, to maintain his ascendancy over the minds of those who were but yesterday his friends and associates.

Of all the writers, of past or present times, there is, perhaps, not one to whose opinions so much weight is due, as Griffith Jones of Llanddowror; independently of his other qualifications, he lived when the elements of Dissent were beginning to work, and had an opportunity of forming, from personal experience, a knowledge of its causes—which must, to a writer of the present day, be comparatively a matter of speculation. Nothing can be more explicit than the terms in which he ascribes the weakness of the Church, and the growth of sectarianism in Wales, to the inefficiency of her episcopal discipline. The following picture which he has left us could not have been more applicable to the Welsh Church in his days than it is in our own :*—

"To trace the footsteps which lead to Dissention a little higher. Since it is vain to conceal what none are ignorant of, *except those who have it in their power to reform it*. I cannot but lament an imposition of the worst consequence in the world, which our learned and worthy diocesans in this country are liable to, by the misrepresentation that is *often laid before them of several things, especially in matters of ordination*. Their dioceses being large, and lying remote from the scene of important affairs, which require their attendance for a considerable part of the year, and *the common people being of a different language*, and unable to make known their grievances, their lordships *are therefore obliged to credit the testimonies, and to see with the eyes of others*. But, alas! treacherous eyes that wretchedly betray their head! As many report of others, and likewise recommend candidates for the ministry, by no other rule but according as they are affected, or agree together in politics, and other opinions or morals—several well disposed and laborious men in the ministry very loyal and well affected to the present government in Church and State, have suffered not a little in this way. The minds of their superiors being thus rendered unfavourably disposed towards them, some very hopeful persons have met with great difficulties, if not rejection, when they offered themselves for holy orders, *and others observing these discouragements have been driven to seek imposition of hands in another community*, whereby Dissenters have gained some popular and useful ministers, and the people have followed them; whilst too many others, unworthy the sacred function, got admittance into it, by the interest and recommendations of those, who care not what indignity *they reflect thereby upon venerable characters*."

"Among other necessary qualifications in a steward of the

* 1741. *Welsh Piety*, vol. i.

mysteries of God and holy things, no doubt but the grace of God and a holy disposition are the chief, and should therefore most carefully be enquired into; *for if an unfit pilot be appointed to conduct a ship, who will be charged with the damage it sustains by his disqualification?* It is well known that ministers thus unqualified, whatever other accomplishments they may have, will neither labour heartily themselves in a cause they don't love, nor forbear looking with an evil eye on their fellow servants, whose diligence is their reproach. If they have art and interest enough to engross and abuse the ear of a superior order, such as endeavour to be more industrious, in order to save both themselves and those that hear them, must expect no better treatment, than they would certainly *deserve*, if they lived the idle and corrupt lives of their accusers. As the work of the ministry, almost all of it, in this country devolves generally on the lowest class of the clergy, curates and meanly beneficed ministers, many of them (I bear them witness), would bestir themselves to labour more abundantly in the ministry if they *durst;* but a zeal (however right and regular), which yet exposes them to ill-natured reflections and resentments, is too frightful a thing to venture upon. For nothing would be more heinously provoking than this to some patrons, and others who love to live undisturbed, and at their ease, which tends not a little to the decay of religion in general, and of the interest of the Church of *England* in particular. It is no secret, several profane profligates have confessed their infidelity and sensual liberties, to be owing to the very bad opinion they took up of some clergymen, who they concluded had no more of the christian faith in reality than they; otherwise they would have *preached* and *practised* in a much better manner. The inferior and better disposed people make no such ill use of a corrupt ministry. *They only turn to those who will condescend to explain sacred things to their capacities*, and with becoming zeal and earnestness to apply them to their consciences. Many of the poor laity, because they are wont to employ the trustiest people in all their temporal concerns, can no more commit their souls to the care of a manifestly weak and wicked minister, than they would be clients of an unskilful and unfaithful lawyer; or than they would in a dangerous fever, trust their lives in the hands of a foolish, faithless physician. These sincere souls, rather than part with the Established Church, desire to receive the blessed sacrament (at least sometimes) in another parish. The Dissenters may well be angry with this; for if it was not complied with in very many places, *Meeting-houses* would have been much fuller in *Wales*. *Many Dissenters have been made by scrupling this indulgence.* A few months would produce thousands more, *if strictness of conformity in this respect should be pushed on, to the length some desire.*"*

He then proceeds to say that the Dissenting spirit then growing up was in some measure ascribable to the mode in which it was treated by some of the clergy. "When they happen to come to their Churches and see them empty, they will not fail to rail and declaim most terribly against those whom they *force* to Dissent from them, till they *fix* their aversion and increase their number. For when they pour out dreadful anathemas, moderate people are frightened away, and are sometimes heard to whisper, '*We will not hear this man again;*' whilst many profane and immoral persons are suffered to sooth themselves with *false hopes* under the specious pretence of being *good Churchmen*. This is not *surmising* what *may be*, but is matter of fact."

When the main-spring is not right, the whole machinery must necessarily go wrong. I do not, of course, mean to affirm, that the English spirit of the Welsh Bishops operates as a positive discouragement to preaching and instruction in the Welsh language; but it withdraws from these practices that encouragement which it is the object of their office to afford. Even, should they feel desirous of rewarding merit of this kind, they cannot do it satisfactorily, as they cannot detect or appreciate it; much less can they prevent the more worldly and narrow-minded part of the inferior clergy from entertaining the notion, that a neglect of their native

---

* This is an allusion to the Methodists, and shows clearly that if they had not occupied the ground, the Independents and other Dissenters would have done so.

language is likely to recommend them to the favour of their English Diocesan! Selfish and mercenary men there will be in all Establishments; but the evil is, that selfishness, in this case, invariably takes a peculiarly pernicious turn. Such men will reflect, that however impressive a sermon in their native tongue may be to a native congregation, the understanding and the feelings of their English Bishop are alike unconscious of its merits, and they preach English as often as they can. I quote the sentiments of the Rev. W. Jenkin Rees, the patriotic rector of Cascob, on this point.* "The use of two languages, instead of one, is stated to be productive, in a religious point of view, of no inconsiderable evil to the country, as in consequence of both being used in some places of divine service, those who do not understand the English are induced to leave the church and become frequenters of the meetinghouses. The evil here adverted to certainly exists, but does not arise from the cause alleged by the objector; and is owing rather to the English part of the congregation not understanding Welsh, than the Welsh not understanding the English. In the parish adverted to, the majority of the inhabitants for the most part scarcely understand anything but Welsh; yet, the minister frequently, out of courtesy and compliance to a few English families of consideration who are resident, gives part of the service in the language they understand, hoping to induce them thereby to become a part of his congregation. The ultimate consequence, however, in many instances, is, that the poorer people hearing in church what they do not comprehend, several betake themselves to other places of worship, where the service is altogether in their own tongue, and some by degrees think in their simplicity, that the church *is intended-ed rather for the gentry than for themselves*, and that they do nothing wrong in attending where they hear what is most suitable to their understandings."

The same spirit which served prematurely to Anglify the

* An Address delivered at a Meeting at Brecon, Dec. 5th, 1821, by the Rev. W. J. Rees, M.A., on the Formation of the Cambrian Society in Gwent.

language of the pulpit, extended itself to the system of education, and served in precisely the same manner to alienate the people from the Church, and to attach them to the Dissenters. In the days of Griffith Jones, the schools connected with the Church were very few, and those few, for the most part, framed on the principle of teaching reading and the English language at one and the same time. That the Welsh peasant should learn English is certainly very desirable; he should not, however, be taught to consider his ancient dialect as a disgrace, but rather to regard the acquisition of another as a means of more effectually serving his country; nevertheless, this was certainly not the spirit of the schools attached to the Church, and it is the well known character of the Welshman, that though he will yield all to kindness, he will adhere doggedly even to an absurdity, when combated by arguments which are an insult to his patriotic feelings. To offer him the opportunity of mastering a language which is the key to a new field of enterprize and industry, is one thing; to refuse him instruction in his own, is another. This last course is at once tyrannical and contumelious, and a sacrifice of the means to the end; for the English language can possess no peculiar value to him over that of his native mountains, except as the organ of superior intelligence. Now, it requires but little reflection to discover, that to attempt to teach a child a foreign language, and to read at the same time, is imposing on him a complication of difficulties, which, though easily overcome when taken singly, are almost insuperable when united; the effects of this plan was not to teach the children English, but to disgust them with every sort of instruction. One of Griffith Jones's correspondents thus expresses himself:—

"I can say, from my own experience, that several being superficially taught to read English in their youth, have, for want of understanding the language in which they read, taken such an aversion to it ever after, that they in time forgot their very alphabet."

Both Griffith Jones and Charles, of Bala, pursued a wiser system; they first taught the children to read in Welsh, and then relied on the taste for knowledge acquired by means of that language as an inducement to learn English; and the latter has stated, that, so successful was this plan, that twenty persons had learned English through the impulse given at his schools, for one who was acquainted with it before their establishment. Hence, it has come to pass, that the Welsh peasantry, although in the last century completely immersed in ignorance, are at present possessed of advantages enjoyed by few parts of England. As before observed, Griffith Jones's schools were allowed to fall into disuse after his death, and their place was supplied by the Methodists and Dissenters. Some individual clergymen have very generously established schools at their own expense; but the clergy, as a body, are far less industrious than the Dissenters, in educating the people. The Bishops have done very little towards this object, and are liable in this, as in other instances, to be misled by their anxiety to abolish the Welsh dialect. In this respect, their conduct stands contrasted with that of the native Welsh Bishops, who, living before the Revolution, and in a time of comparative darkness, were generally the founders of some endowment for the education of their countrymen, the translators of the Scriptures, and, in fact, prepared the way for all the religious light which the Principality at present enjoys.*

Since the time of Charles, the press has been a powerful engine in the hands of the Dissenters. Charles's Magazine in the Welsh language was the means of exciting the emulation of the different Dissenting denominations in Wales, and thus gave rise to no less than eight others, which still circulate amongst the peasantry of Wales. They belong to different sects, and defend sectarian opinions; some of them have been the means of spreading a good deal of valuable miscellaneous knowledge; and a singular proof that all attempts to destroy the Welsh language by arbitrary means have only tended to perpetuate it, may be found in the fact that the Welsh of these magazines is less mixed with English than that which appears in books written a century ago. Words have actually been coined from Welsh roots to express the modern sciences, such as geography, &c. The influence of sectarian periodicals has been

* Peter's *Hanes*.

increased by another circumstance; those learned men whose cultivation of our ancient literature has gained so much honour for the Principality, not only in England, but on the continent, and in America, were so much neglected by the gentry of Wales, as to call down severe censures from an able writer in the Quarterly Review. This, of course, gave them a leaning to the side of democracy and Dissent; many of them contributed very able antiquarian dissertations to these periodicals, and thus gave an additional attraction to the opinions of which they are the organs. In more recent times, a magazine has been established on a similar plan by some clergymen of the Church: it is written in a good spirit, and has been the means of propagating much useful knowledge. It is not, however, supported by the Bishops or the influential members of the Church.

The Welsh are social and fond of music; and in the last century their great delight was to meet for the purpose of gratifying these dispositions. Since they have become a more reading and a more religious people, "the singing eves"— the habit of dancing all night to the harp—has been superceded by frequent religious meetings, and by the cultivation of psalmody; and it may be added that sacred music now forms a part of the contents of their various periodicals. In most of the Churches of Wales, the musical arrangements are very bad; the instruments in use are generally of no very harmonious description; and in this respect, the Dissenters possess a manifest superiority, for though they discard instrumental music altogether, their singing is generally sweet and impressive.

Hitherto I have adverted only to the bad effects of the present system on the clergy generally; I now come to a more serious evil, —the temptation it affords to the appointment of men entirely unfit for the duty of a Welsh parish. So long as Englishmen have been in possession of the episcopal patronage in Wales, has this evil uniformly prevailed; it may, to all intents and purposes, be considered a regular part,—a uniform consequence of the system!

Should an English Bishop be guilty of nepotism in England,

the duty may still be efficiently performed; but in Wales, every relation of a Bishop is in language a foreigner; and his uncouth attempts to officiate in his church in a tongue unintelligible to himself, can be felt by his congregation as nothing better than a profanation of the worship of God. Now, were I to affirm that the English Bishops of Wales have been more fastidious in the distribution of their patronage, than their brethren of England, I should contradict the indignant assertions of almost every intelligent writer on Welsh subjects. No where has the Church of England been more disgraced by a selfish disposition of patronage. On putting to a gentleman, upon whose accuracy I can rely, the following question, "What proportion of the collective income of the Welsh Church is held by Englishmen?" I received the following answer:—"Four bishoprics, a great portion of the deaneries, prebends, and sinecure rectories, and many if not most of the canonries." During the reign of the houses of Tudor and Stewart, several Welshmen were mitred; but not one since the accession of the house of Brunswick. The consequence was, that the prelates brought into their respective dioceses, their sons, nephews, and cousins to the ninth degree of consanguinity; the next consequence was a change of service (on the borders) from Welsh to English; and a third and important consequence was, the desertion of the Church. Dissenting places of worship were erected in every direction. I have lately, in a journey of thirty miles, passed by ten churches and double that number of chapels, most of them bearing Scripture names, such as Beulah, Rehoboth, Horeb, Hermon, Salem, Ebenezer, &c. Not only on the borders, but also in the centre, and at the western extremities of Wales, have Englishmen been collated to benefices, whose services, if served at all, should be entirely in Welsh. The strangers, as a make shift, underwent a lecture or two in the Welsh language, *in order to be able to read in.* But the voice of the strangers, instead of collecting a flock, scattered the sheep; and now, in many places, were Paul himself to preach in any of those churches, he would have a congregation for the first Sunday, **afterwards they would bid him adieu!"**

Perhaps the worst effect of time-honoured abuse is its tendency to perpetuate and extend itself over the minds even of the best of men; good and wise men will try to reconcile themselves to think lightly of—evils which they have no hope to see removed,— and thus the moral sentiment of man becomes degraded by a familiarity with corruption—as the eye becomes habituated to darkness. It may, however, without difficulty, be affirmed, that, were the present state of the episcopal office in Wales a thing of imagination, and not of fact and of history—it would excite but one feeling amongst all who respect the principles of Christianity, and the rights of a free people.

The system was in some degree introduced during the profligate reign of Charles the Second; but it was mainly consummated by King William. Thus, the revolution, which brought liberty and toleration to other portions of the kingdom, was to Wales, on the contrary, a source of religious degradation. The mischief has not been so conspicuous in the individual abuses themselves, as in its effect on her whole ecclesiastical establishment. Since all the higher emoluments have been bestowed on strangers, Welshmen of high endowments have naturally considered it humiliating to enter into the Church; the working clergy, therefore, are, for the most part, an inferior "caste." The Bishop of Ferns defends inequalities in Church preferment, as the means of securing a higher class of men than would enter the profession, were there nothing to excite emulation: this is very just, but these means are not employed in Wales in exciting emulation amongst the clergy *generally*, as the best preferments are *uniformly* given to strangers.

As before observed, appointments of this kind have at all times been common since the introduction of English Episcopacy; the grievance was, however, carried to its height just at the time when Methodism was making its appearance; and it is not too much to affirm, that the corruptions of the Church have progressed rather than diminished, with the progressive advance of Dissent. Of the pertinacity with which the abuse alluded to has been practised and defended, a striking instance will be found in the records of this society (the Cymmrodorion),

I allude to the case of Dr. Bowles, who was expelled from the living of Trevdraeth, by the spirited exertions of our predecessors in this institution:—

"In the year 1766, Dr. Bowles, an Englishman, unacquainted with Welsh, was presented by the Bishop of Bangor to the living of Trevdraeth, in Anglesey. In 1773, the churchwardens, aided by the Cymmrodorion Society, brought an action in the Court of Arches, to deprive him of it, on the ground of his incapacity to do the duty in Welsh, &c. In the arguments in this cause, after the advocates of the churchwardens had proved that by the canon, the statute law, &c., he ought to be deprived, the advocates of the defendant, Dr. Bowles, expressed themselves thus:—'Though the doctor does not understand the language, he is in possession, and cannot be turned out. *Wales is a conquered country;* it is proper to introduce the English language, and it is the duty of the Bishops to endeavour to promote Englishmen, in order to introduce the language. It has always been the policy of the legislature to introduce the English language into Wales.' Vide the depositions, arguments, and judgment in this cause, p. 59. The Judge of the Court—'It is proper that the Bishops in Wales should take such order for the cure of souls as to appoint pastors that are acquainted with the language of the country. It is the primitive law of the Church, and is the law at this time. I am of opinion that a want of knowledge of the Welsh language is *a good cause of refusal* in the Bishop, and that he ought to refuse him if he be incompetent. The inhabitants of Wales have great reason to complain of such presentations.'"*

What this exemplary man and his learned advocate may mean by denominating the Welsh emphatically "A conquered people," I cannot divine; unless it be that they remained unconquered by the Normans after the latter had triumphed in every other British district, viz., in England, Scotland,† and Ireland, or, that

---

* See a pamphlet entitled "*Considerations on the Illegality of preferring to Welsh Benefices, Clergymen ignorant of Welsh,*" by J. Jones, A.M., Fellow of Queen's College, Oxon.

† See Chalmer's *Caledonia.*

the people of Wales never submitted peaceably to the English yoke, until they gained at Bosworth, the liberties of Englishmen and the Crown of England for a descendant of their ancient kings. These abstruse points I leave to the learned; my objection to the appointment of Dr. Bowles does not rest on his historical blunders; and I grieve to say, that instances of the kind are as common now as in his time. I am myself acquainted with the case of a divine, who, at the mature age of 50, was advanced to a Welsh living, without knowing a syllable of the language: he accomplished the duty by receiving a Saturday night's lesson from his clerk, on the Sunday's service! Would an actor venture upon a stage thus prepared for his part? How disgusting, then, this trifling with sacred things! It operates upon the people as a perfect excommunication; they are virtually deprived of the benefit of an Established Church.

To incumbents placed in circumstances such as these, every act of professional duty must suggest reflections not easily combated or suppressed! Hence it is, that the English incumbents of benefices in Wales, are often absentees from that country. This is a source of various evils to the Establishment. A clergyman who lives on his benifice has the strongest interest in the good opinion of his flock; upon their good feeling will depend many of the everyday comforts of life,—and the degree of respect and kindness extended to him by the society of his neighbourhood, will generally be a mere echo of their report. On the other hand, an absentee, living, as we may suppose, in some of the midland counties of England, can be little affected, in any way, by the ill-feeling of his Welsh parishoners, or the bad opinion of a few Welsh squires; though looked upon as an oppressor in Wales, in the neighbourhood in which he is resident, he may bask in the broad sunshine of popularity. A resident clergyman may regulate the exaction of tithes, according to the claims of charity and right feeling; an absentee must leave the care of his revenues to a kind of middleman, who cannot, if he would, act in a similar spirit. Independently of the evil of absenteeism—strangers to a country are generally less considerate in their conduct, less moderate in their demands, and it is a remark, I have often had an opportunity of making, that those clergymen who are natives of the country are almost always beloved, as kind-hearted and benevolent country gentlemen, even when, from want of professional zeal, they are not much looked up to as clergymen.

Nor does the evil rest here; the ignorance of the language, and the rapacity of the higher orders of the Church, entail unmerited odium on the native clergy. The funds of Dissenting bodies are perhaps as frequently the subject of litigation as the tithes of the Church. Yet, with the former, each individual bears the odium of his own wrong; while the working clergy, who are often worse paid than Dissenting ministers (from the Church being regarded as a sort of unity,) are looked upon and treated as parties to the oppressive acts of their superiors, over which they have no control, and by which they are often, in fact, sufferers. The evil is thus simply stated by one who no doubt has most undeservedly felt its effects. "Lay patronage and lay impropriations have done great injury to the Church. The patrons have ties of kindred and bonds of friendship more in view than the interests of religion, in the disposal of preferments; and impropriators in general are more strict in the valuation and letting of their tithes, so as to bring an odium not only upon themselves and their agents, but also upon the clergy as a body, though many of them let their tithes at half, or less than that of the value of titheable articles. Dissenting ministers have greatly the advantage in this respect over the clergy of the Establishment; the former being paid by voluntary contributions, the latter, by what is considered by the majority of their parishoners an extortion. This is one of the causes that have had a fatal effect in dissolving the bonds of Church unity, not only in Wales, but also in England, though perhaps in a less degree in the latter than the former. Many of the best livings in Wales are either lay impropriations, or the perquisites of dignitaries in the several cathedrals. The vicarial tithes only are enjoyed by the operative resident clergy; and the full exaction of tithes, in such parishes, by such impropriators or the lessees of such dignitaries who are non-resident, has the effect of creating a coolness between the parishioners of such places and their resident vicars, who have little or nothing to do with the tithe grievances complained of. These coolnesses between parishioners and their pastors have been the causes of Dissent in thousands of instances, where opportunities of Dissent were at hand."

It is very common to affirm, that the great cause of Dissent in Wales, is the distance of some places from any parish church. Unfortunately, however, for this apology (for, such, in fact, it is), the chapels always abound most in the villages and towns, and in the immediate vicinity of the churches. If this were the cause of Dissent, it is rather a singular anomaly, that the chapels should be most numerous, in proportion to the population, in the vicinity of the episcopal residence,—that there should be seven of them in the parish of St. Asaph, and nine in the adjoining parish of Henllan. These facts point, in a manner not to be mistaken, at its real source,—an Establishment fast losing all public confidence and respect. But, granting that the want of churches, in certain districts, has given rise to the erection of chapels, whence is it that churches have not been built and endowed? Have the superfluous revenues of the Establishment been applied to that purpose in any one instance? So far is this from being the case, that every one of the many sinecure rectories in the diocese of St. Asaph, are at this moment divided between three classes of persons:—1. Individuals resident in remote parts of England. 2. Clergymen resident in Wales, but performing no kind of clerical duty. 3. Persons indebted to their connection with the Bishops of Wales for a most unconscionable and unjust share of her Church revenues! There can be no doubt that the population has outstripped the Church; but this is ascribable, not to the scantiness of her revenues, but to the misapplication of them. Nothing can be more revolting than the mode in which deaneries, prebends, and sinecure rectories, are given to absentees, when, from increased population, every economy should be practised in the Church revenues. The Rev. W. J. Rees has declared that our poorer countrymen look upon the Church as never intended for them, but meant only for the rich: it would be strange indeed, if they thought otherwise, for the churches in Wales will seldom hold half the population; all the pews are generally engrossed by the gentry and rich farmers, and the only chance for the poor is to be elbowed about in the aisles. In the town and parish of Newtown, in Montgomeryshire, the population is 6,000; the church will hold only 600, and there are no free seats. Strange to say, I have heard the Welsh gentry censured for this state of things; they, it is said, ought to build chapels of ease. My own opinion is, that if the Church did her duty, they would do theirs. Were the gentry of Wales deficient in attachment to the National Church, no men would deserve less blame for it: in England, the very highest aristocracy are connected by ties of kindred with her ministers, and their religious feelings are bound up with all the charities of life; but in Wales, the clergy are, for the most part, strangers, or men in a humble rank of life; and when the gentry of the Principality have dedicated their children to the Church, it has been to see them placed in galling subordination to adventurers!

The English character is, on the whole, a noble one; but it has its defects, and those are coldness of manner and a want of affability to the humbler ranks of society. Of course, the clergy must, in some degree, partake of the foibles of their nation; and though true it is, abstractedly speaking, that these faults are of little weight in the moral balance, when combined with sterling integrity and worth, yet, it must be remembered, that earnestness of devotion and an amiable sympathy with the feelings of the poor, are of the very essence of the Clerical profession. Bishop Burnet often adverts to this defect in the character of the English clergy, with much bitter regret and with many a prophetic anticipation of evil.—

"Nor were the clergy," he says, in his History of His own Times, "more diligent in their labours among the people, in which respect, it must be confessed, the English clergy are the most remiss of any. The curates in Popery, besides their saying mass every day, their exactness to the Breviary, their attending on confession, and the multiplicity of offices to which they are obliged, do so labour in instructing the youth, and visiting the sick, that in all places in which I could observe them, it seemed to be the constant employment of their lives. And in the foreign (Protestant) Churches, though the labours of the ministers may seem mean, yet they are perpetually in them."

That Prelate's general opinions of the Clergy are thus expressed by Mr. Southey:—"It was not that their lives were scandalous; he entirely acquitted them of any such imputation; but they were not exemplary as it became them to be; and in the sincerity and grief of a pious and reflecting mind, he pronounced that they would never regain the influence which they had lost, till they lived better and laboured more."—Southey's *Life of Wesley*, vol. i. p. 325.

If fastidious lukewarmness, then, had relaxed the influence of the English clergy over the minds even of their own countrymen,—it might reasonably have been expected, that it would prove still more subversive of it, amongst a people of more ardent feeling and imagination. The tone of society in Wales has always been less reserved and aristocratic than in England; the peasantry are habituated to a more familiar intercourse with their superiors. Hence, the mere manner of the English clergymen who are from time to time introduced into the country, by the influence alluded to, inevitably becomes a source of offence,—and serves even in those districts in which the Welsh language is extinct, to repel the people from the Church. Thus, has the whole frame of the ecclesiastical institutions of Wales been debilitated, by the unpatriotic character of its system of polity. The object has been to "assimilate" the people to their fellow-subjects of England. But it is with nations as with individuals; their sympathies are not to be won by compulsion, or their feelings to be circumscribed within the scholastic narrowness of a metaphysical rule.

"Hamlet.—Will you play upon this pipe?

"Guildenstern.—I know no touch of it, my lord.

"Hamlet.—Why, look you, how unworthy a thing you would
"make of me? You would play upon me; you would seem to
"know my stops; you would pluck out the heart of my mystery;

"you would sound me from my lowest note to the top of my "compass; and there is much music, excellent voice in this little "organ; yet cannot you make it speak. Do you think I am "easier to be played upon than a pipe? Call me what instrument "you will, though you may fret me, you cannot play upon me."

Slavery is a thing of degrees, as the human race has its varieties of shade, from the swarthy tint of the Southern European, down to the midnight hue of the race who endure the last extreme of tyranny. To be bound with material fetters, to be made the mere cipher of another's will, to be constrained to build up the castles of a conqueror,—these are the dregs of the cup of bitterness, and it was of yore the lot of our forefathers to drink them; those times are past, but a more refined age may have its thraldom in the heart and spirit of a people! To bend down the elastic feelings of youth to the austere pursuits of manhood, is a violence against nature; nor is it a much more judicious or philosophical experiment, to attempt to recast the mental physiognomy of an imaginative and sensitive race, in the mould and model of a grave, sedate, and unimpassioned one—to arrest their religious education—to keep their intellectual instruction in abeyance, till—the butterfly has been fairly broken on the wheel! It may be glossed over with showy phrases; but it is neither a measure of justice, nor is it in the spirit of Christianity. The question lies in one word; are an imaginative taste and warm feelings a sin against the Christian code, and are the people of Wales more remote from its spirit because they happen to possess them? If they are, then were the first teachers of the religion of Christ—the nations to whom that religion was first taught, the most insensible of all others to the real nature of its doctrines. If I apprehend the Gospel Revelation aright, its main features are—hostility to all that is sinful, and sanction of all that is innocent; its object is not to change the tastes and intellectual dispositions of men, but to cleanse the moral depravity of the heart; like the living waters from the fountain, to which it is so often compared, which may at one moment hang in sublime cataracts from the mountain's side, and the next shed softness and verdure through the tranquil valleys,—without loosing, at either time, anything of its vivid light or its unsullied purity!

The moral and religious character of a people may be changed in a generation,—but their tastes and intellectual dispositions are almost unalterable : the Welsh of Queen Elizabeth's time were as peaceful and humane, as their ancestors, described by Sir John Wynn, of Gwydir, were warlike and ferocious ; in their love for poetry and music, both were alike : the Welsh of the last century were as irreligious and ignorant, as the Welsh of the present are pious and well instructed ; yet the love of sacred music and poetry, and of religious eloquence, evinces that their mental peculiarities have only migrated, as it were, into minds disciplined into a purer moral sentiment. And herein lies the fundamental error ; under the name of civilization, an attempt has been made to stifle those traits of national character, in which they are, perhaps, superior to their neighbours, and war has been waged against those nobler susceptibilities, which even under the guidance of an irregular zeal, have become the basis of a religious and intellectual civilization, perhaps unparalleled amongst a people similarly circumstanced.

Nothing can more energetically express the effect which the present administration of the Church in Wales has produced on her people, than the words of Shakespeare, "You may fret me, but you cannot play upon me." Instead of "assimilating" them to their English neighbours, it has divided them from each other, and split them into a variety of rival sects and parties. The consequence of a species of tuition unsuited to their temperament, has been (as it always must be with nations as with individuals) to pervert, not to foster, their better dispositions, and to draw from their very capacity for certain virtues, vices which bear a species of analogy to them ; hence their strong religious feelings are soured with uncharitableness, and their fervent and warm-hearted enthusiasm is alloyed with party spirit and fanaticism. A profound writer[*] has remarked,

[*] Dugald Stewart.

that the follies into which men are sometimes betrayed by the name of religion, is not a just ground of indifference,—but, on the contrary, affords a strong proof that a sentiment which thus at times dominates even over reason itself, must be founded on an intuitive principle of human nature ; and this opinion has been pursued by other writers with a closeness of reasoning that amounts to absolute demonstration.* But, still there are seasons when that divine light, which in its natural influences, is a source of nothing but tenderness and moral beauty,—is cast into dim eclipse by the clouds of human pride and passion. Such is human nature—religion, patriotism, every good principle, are at times associated with its weakness and its vices.

It is not unusual, in the present day, to look upon schism amongst Christians, as neither an evil nor a sin ; this question is best tried by the effects we see around us.† It is idle to say, that men may differ in opinion, and still continue united in heart ; such is what I may term the natural intolerance of human nature, that trifling divisions, on whatever subject, will alienate men from each other; and to these unhappy distractions Wales is peculiarly a prey.

There are also evils of a different kind, resulting from the dependence of the Dissenting clergy on the bounty of their flocks, —a system which leads to extremes, because by extremes, is popular favour to be won and sustained. Its evils prevail most amongst the Welsh Methodists, owing to their frequent change of preachers. The first Welsh Methodists were Calvinists, yet not intolerant or disposed to violate the unity of the Church ; probably, a venerable

---

* See Kant's *Reine Vernunft.*—Bishop Butler's *Miscellaneous Works.*—It is not a little remarkable, that Burns should have expressed this sentiment, with almost as much accuracy as his philosophical countryman. See Burns' *Letters.*—It is still more singular that a late noble Poet should have introduced a similar sentiment, in a passage which concludes with the opinion, that if the Church of England should ever fall, it would not be by the power of the enemies to religion generally, but by the zeal of "the Sectaries." Lord Byron's *Miscellaneous Works.*

† See the *Welsh Looking Glass.*

clergyman who had intimately known the body, has expressed their feelings. " Pious Calvinists and Arminians ought to co-operate, so long as both admit that salvation is of grace."* But no sooner did they separate from the Church, than they adopted an exclusively Calvinistic creed. The same is the case with the doctrine of the atonement. Perhaps the great difficulty of ethical instruction is not to make men understand their duty, but to create a sense of the obligation to amendment. In this respect, the doctrine of an atonement, wrought by the Divine Being himself, has been found a practical doctrine, as it gives a more affecting view of his benevolence, than is furnished by natural theology. The divines of the last century have been accused of making morality independent of Christian motives,† of never adverting to the atonement but as a subject of dry metaphysical reasoning. But the first Methodists appealed to the heart and the affections; they blended practical precepts with Christian doctrine; their manner was an imitation of the apostolic style of preaching. If we may judge of the tree by its fruits, of the preaching of the first Methodists by the lives of their disciples, there was nothing in it that was likely to bring dishonour on the Church of England. But their followers, for the reasons before mentioned, are too apt to carry to an extreme the principles of their predecessors. Their sermons are too frequently mere declamation on the grand leading doctrines of the gospel, often to the neglect of the practical application of theological truth. Thus, a doctrine of all others calculated to humble the pride of the human heart, becomes a source of intolerance and not meekness; indulgence of the imagination is mistaken for amendment of the heart; and humility to God and charity to man are exchanged for a religion which is little better than a strange and impassioned dream. It has frequently been remarked, that those who are most strongly affected by this visionary faith, are often deficient in feeling in the ordinary relations of life. This has been to hastily ascribed to hypocrisy; it is oftener in the nature of that morbid insensibility

* The *Welsh Looking Glass*.   † By Bishop Horseley.

to real suffering which is known to arise from indulging to excess in tales of fictitious sorrow. There is, in fact, a very striking analogy between the effect sometimes produced by the preaching of the Welsh Dissenters, and that resulting from the pomp and phantasmagoria of Popish worship; there is the same plausible but transient emotion, the same momentary enthusiasm, followed by a relapse of moral and religious energies.*

To these sad self-deceptions all mankind are, in some degree, liable; but there is much in the situation of the Welsh mountaineer that peculiarly exposes him to them. This is more especially the case in the Snowdonian districts, where Methodism has at times taken its extravagant shape. No one who has ever visited that wild and romantic district, can forget the fantastic, and if I may use the term, the visionary air of the whole scenery. All is splendid melancholy, yet all is shadowy and fitful; every cloud as it passes brings some new object into light, or envelopes some scenery in obscurity; every mountain shower gives, as it were, a new voice to the torrents that pour down in a hundred directions from the mountains. The whole district seems a link between the world in which we live and the fairy land in which Cambrian superstition has placed her patriot King Arthur!

It may now be asked how far Dissent has progressed in Wales? It may be answered, that it has gone as far as the means of her population will enable them to carry it. It may be replied that there are as many Dissenting Chapels in the remote parishes in Wales as there are in many flourishing English towns.†

---

* There are some able remarks on this subject in the *Natural History of Enthusiasm.*—I beg it may be understood, that I am far from intending this as a picture of the state of feeling amongst Dissenters generally. Both parties have their Extremes; the Church is too often lukewarm and inert; the Dissenters attach too much importance to incessant preaching and excitement, (as if the people had yet to be taught the elements of Christianity); and both parties think too lightly of that every-day pastoral intercourse, which is the most powerful means of identifying the whole life and softening every feeling with religious principle.

† In Chester there are eight chapels, (two of which are Welsh); in the parish of Llanfair, in Montgomeryshire, 12!

On this state of things, I may at least be permitted to say, that it is a melancholy one; but with a man of candour and of religious feeling, I would confidently appeal to it as a proof that there is something fundamentally wrong in the administration of the Church in Wales. There are men, I know—men, too, whom I can esteem and love, who find a justification for the present system in a supposed intellectual barrenness in our land: Wales, we are told, cannot furnish clergymen fit for her four episcopal dignities! Did not this sometimes come from those who have the good of our country really at heart, we might treat it as an insult, added to an injury, and be silent. But we may still remark that when those times are recollected which saw Archbishop Williams on one side and John Owen on the other, that when the origin of that great man is remembered, who first taught religious toleration as a principle,* of him who stood up alone in defence of it in a British House of Commons,† when it is remembered, how much England owes her constitution, the Church of England her Protestant freedom, to the firmness of a Welsh Judge,‡ and that one of the last Welsh Bishops who presided over a Welsh see was amongst her seven Bishops, it will perhaps still be thought that Welshmen may be found fit to guide the Christian principles of their own mountain land!

I will not, at present, stop to enquire whether the majority of our prelates, for the last century have been men of such lofty endowments—such active benevolence—such exalted piety,—as to reconcile us to a difference of language—to make us forget even a breach of the articles of our Church—to place them in the gratitude of our people above the best of the native clergy, such

---

* Dr. John Owen. See Orme's *Life*. Mr. Orme has proved this in the opinion of an Edinburgh Reviewer.

† Chief Justice Vaughan, in the case of the Nonconformists, after the Restoration.

‡ Judge Powel, at the trial of the seven bishops. It is an interesting circumstance, that Bishop Jeremy Taylor found an asylum in Wales during the civil wars, and composed his great Defence of Religious Liberty in the house of a gentleman in that country. Judge Powel was his pupil.—See Bishop Heber's *Life of Jeremy Taylor*, prefixed to his Works.

men as the Pastor of Llanddowror, who were the light of the age in which they lived, and whose goodness will leave its stamp on the whole Welsh nation for centuries yet to come :—upon this question I will, at present, say nothing; suffice it to remark, that to prognosticate the destruction of the Welsh Church from the sway of Welshmen, at a moment when the Dissenters, under Welsh rulers, have gained the whole country--and the Establishment, under English rulers, has most signally lost it, is rather an eccentric species both of logical inference and—nervous sensibility!

But who is there that does not discern that the cause, the very essence of the grievance, is mistaken for a justification of it? When all the wealth of the land is engrossed by strangers; and all the toil, drudgery, and odium, left to the native clergy, how can it be expected that great divines should be found amongst them? Wales has sent forth Missionaries to foreign lands, and ardent spirits to become the champions of Dissent: but her own Church repels her children from her bosom. Amongst the Dissenters in the last century, were Dr. Rees, the Cyclopœdist, Dr. Price, and Dr. Williams; than whom few men were more instrumental in organizing that combined opposition which a certain class of Dissenters now offer to the Church of England: and amongst the followers of Wesley, the most eminent was Dr. Coke, the founder of Wesleyanism in America and the West Indies, who was a native of Wales. The Church in Wales had also her ministers, whose genius and piety would have done honour to any station; but too many of them were driven to become wanderers over fell and mountain!

But the simple truth is, that Wales does not require Marshes or Blomfields for her Bishops; she has few Papists to refute, or sceptics to convince; her Dissenters require conciliation, and not argument. Her prelates had far better be men of respectable erudition; men like our own native Welsh Bishops, uniting the ordinary attainments of a gentleman with sincere piety, good sense, and above all things, a knowledge of the language and regard for the feelings of their countrymen. Such men have at all times amply sustained the dignity of their office. Such men are many of the most estimable of the present English Bishops; such men may be found amongst the parochial clergy of every district in the kingdom.

In favour of the present system, what one argument can be advanced, but theories refuted by a ride of half a mile, from almost any spot in the Principality? What is the object of episcopacy? To preserve Christian feelings and Christian unity? Are these objects attained in Wales? Never was any country so completely rent with bitter and complicated schisms!

In the last century the people were unenlightened, and the episcopal authority did nothing to improve their religious condition; and now that they are educated, it has turned even gospel light into a firebrand of division,—parcelled out the whole country into a multitude of sects and parties,—robbed the Church of all hold whatever on the humbler ranks,—nearly deprived her of all substantial—all vital influence on the principles of the higher classes. And yet no change must take place! To touch the system of abuse and corruption—(so we are told)—would be a dangerous innovation—calamities without end would result from restoring Wales to her just rights—the Church of England to a conformity with her own Articles! As if it were possible, even by the wildest exercise of the imagination, to conceive more forcible—more complete proofs, —indeed, I may say, any other proofs—of the utter inefficiency of the system on which the Church of England is now administered in Wales, than those evils to which I have just adverted—evils which are not a matter of imagination, but of experience—and endurance; I say it is impossible to conceive a more complete demonstration of an unsound system of administration, than Dissent thus nearly universal, from a Church, to the purity of whose doctrines even Dissenters themselves are, for the most part, ready to bear testimony!

And what is the defence of the present system? An argument which is in effect a mere taunt against the people whom it professes to evangelize! I have yet to learn that Christianity is less a religion of affection than of reason. I have yet to learn that it is a slight grievance when Christian institutions are turned against one of the best feelings of our nature—a feeling sanctioned by the Divine Author of our faith, when he wept over the sins and sorrows of Jerusalem. Christianity is not a religion of Stoical abstractions; it should live in the hearts and feelings of men; it delights to draw to itself even the generous weaknesses of mankind! The present system of the Church in Wales is cold, is repulsive, it is not in the true spirit of Christianity. The Scottish Church is generally spoken of as highly popular and efficient; but how long would it continue so, were Dr. Chalmers all at once plucked from his professor's chair, to make room for a stranger, and all the more estimable part of the Scottish clergy degraded into mere drudges to some fine "Southron" gentlemen, who would appear in the country but once in a year, and then abuse Scotch air, Scotch morals, and everything Scotch, with all the extravagant virulence of a Johnson!

The following illustrious Catalogue will amply prove, that in arguing for the restoration of a better system, "we have the dead with us, and only the living against us!"

LIST OF WELSHMEN WHO ATTAINED THE EPISCOPAL DIGNITY,*

FROM THE YEAR 1558 TO 1714; (BEING A PERIOD OF 156 YEARS;)

That is, from the commencement of Queen Elizabeth's Reign, to the end of that of Queen Anne.

	NATIVE OF.	DIED.	REFERENCES.
1 Thomas Young, Bish. of St. David's, and A'bishop of York	Pembrokeshire	1568	Wood, vol. i. 595. Camb. Reg. ii. 210.
2 Richard Davies, Bishop of St. Asaph and St. David's	Denbighshire	1581	Wood, vol. i. 605. Camb. Reg. ii. 210. Gwed. Hist. 105.
3 Rowland Meyrick, Bishop of Bangor	Anglesey	1565	Wood, vol. i. 595.
4 Nicholas Robinson, Bishop of Bangor	Caernarvonshire	1584	Pet. Williams. Gwed. Hist. 105.
5 Thomas Devies, Bishop of St. Asaph	Caernarvonshire	1573	B. Willis. Gwedir History, 107.
6 Marmaduke Middleton, Bishop of Lismore & St. David's.	Cardiganshire	1592	Wood, vol. i. 608.
7 William Hughes, Bishop of St. Asaph	Caernarvonshire	1600	B. Willis. Wood, vol. i. 615. York, page
8 William Morgan, Bishop of Llandaff and St. Asaph	Caernarvonshire	1604	B. Willis. Gwed. Hist. 109.
9 Richard Parry, Bishop of St. Asaph	Denbighshire	1623	B. Willis. Wood, vol. i. 622.
10 Richard Vaughan, Bishop of Bangor, Chester, & London.	Caernarvonshire		Pet. Will. York. B. Willis, Chester, 332. Gwedir Hist. 102. Ath. Oxon. i. 756.
11 Henry Rowland, Bishop of Bangor	Anglesey	1616	Wood, vol. i. 620. P. Williams. Gwed. H. 102.
12 Lewis Bayley, Bishop of Bangor	Caermarthenshire	1631	
13 David Dolben, Bishop of Bangor	Denbighshire	1633	
14 Edmund Griffith, Bishop of Bangor	Caernarvonshire	1637	Gwedir Hist, 111.
15 Hugh Jones, Bishop of Llandaff	A Welshman	1574	Wood.
16 William Blethin, Bishop of Llandaff	A Welshman	1590	Wood.
17 Morgan Owen, Bishop	Caermarthenshire	1644	
18 Hugh Lloyd, Bishop of Llandaff	Cardiganshire	1667	
19 Francis Davies, Bishop of Llandaff	Glamorganshire	1674	
20 Godfrey Goodman, Bishop of Gloucester	Denbighshire	1655	
21 John Williams, Bishop of Lincoln and Archbishop of York	Caernarvonshire	1650	
22 Thomas Howells, Bishop of Bristol	Caermarthenshire	1649	

23	George Griffiths, Bishop of St. Asaph	Caernarvonshire	1666	Gent. Mag. Supplement, 2nd part, 1826.
24	Robert Morgan, Bishop of Bangor	Montgomeryshire	1673	York, page 21.
25	Humphrey Lloyd, Bishop of Bangor	Merionethshire	1688	Gent. Mag. Supplement, 2nd part, 1826.
26	Humphrey Humphreys, Bishop of Bangor and Hereford	Caernarvonshire	1712	
27	John Evans, Bishop of Bangor and Meath	Caernarvonshire	1687	
28	John Lloyd, Bishop of St. David's	Caernarthenshire	1703	
29	Edward Jones, Bishop of St. Asaph	Montgomeryshire	1743	
30	John Wynne, Bishop of St. Asaph, 1712	Flintshire	1650	
31	Lancelot Bulkeley, Archbishop of Dublin	Anglesey	1671	
32	Griffith Williams, Bishop of Ossory	Caernarvonshire	1646	
33	Lewis Jones, Bishop of Killaloe	Merionethshire	1597	Wood.
34	Richard Meredith, Bishop of Ferns and Leighlin	A Welshman	1665	
35	Robert Price, Bishop of Ferns and Leighlin	Merionethshire	1573	B. Willis, Man, 367. Gent. Mag. May, 1825.
36	John Salesbury, Dean of Norwich and Bishop of Man	Denbighshire	1599	B. Willis, Man, 368.
37	John Meyrick, Bishop of Man	Anglesey	1615	B. Willis, Chester, 337. Do. Man, 368.
38	George Lloyd, Bishop of Man and Chester	Caernarvonshire	1633	Wood, vol. i. 692, B. Willis, Man, 363.
39	John Phillips, B. of Man, Translator of the Bible into Manx	A Welshman		Newcome, p. 37.
40	Hugh Bellot, Bishop of Bangor and Chester	Denbighshire†		B. Willis, Peterb. p. 509. Magna Britannia, vol. iii. page 396.
41	William Lloyd, Bishop of Llandaff, Peterboro' & Norwich	Merioneth‡	1709	Gwedir History, page 108.
42	William Glyn, Bishop of Bangor	Caernarvonshire		B.N.W. 443.
43	Maurice Griffith, Bishop of Rochester	Caernarvonshire		

* I am indebted for this interesting document, to the kindness of the Widow of my late excellent and revered friend, the Rev. J. Jenkins, Vicar of Kerry, in Montgomeryshire. It bears abundant marks of that laborious and enthusiastic spirit of enquiry, which so honourably distinguished him, on all questions that affected the interests or history of his native country. The occasion on which it was drawn up will appear from the following letter:—

Extract from a Letter of the Rev. John Jenkins, to Archdeacon Beynon.

"I have now drawn from the few books in my possession, a list of our countrymen who arrived at the Episcopal Dignity, from the commencement of the reign of Queen Elizabeth, to the end of the reign of Queen Anne. And though the number is considerably beyond what might be expected,* I have no doubt but several names are omitted, for want of proper books to refer to. To carry on the list from the year 1714 to the present time, will require but little research, for the number is very limited indeed."

† He was of a Cheshire family.—B. Willis, Chester, 332.   ‡ A Non-juror.

* The period being one of 156 years—the number of Prelates 50—the List affords us one Prelate to every three years,—a very generous allowance!

BISHOPS CONNECTED WITH WALES BY RELATIONSHIP, EDUCATION, OR LONG RESIDENCE.

		DIED.	REFERENCES.
44	John Dolben, Bishop of Rochester, and Archbishop of York: Nephew of Archbishop Williams; of the Family of the Dolbens, of Denbighshire, but born at Stanwich, Northamptonshire, where his Father was Rector.	1686	A. Wood, vol. ii. 684. Walk. Suff. 107.
45	William Thomas, Bishop of St. David's and Worcester; born at Bristol, but of a Caermarthen Family, and educated at Caermarthen. He kept a School at Llangharn, during the great Rebellion, & was the Rector of Pembryn, Cardigan.	1689	
46	John Hanmer, Bishop of St. Asaph: born at Pentre-pant, in the parish of Selatyn, Salop, a border parish, being descended from a branch of the Flintshire Hanmers	1629	
47	John Owens, Bishop of St. Asaph; born at Burton Latimer, Northamptonshire, where his Father was Rector, but descended from the Family of the Owens, of Bodsilin, Caernarvonshire. He probably was partly educated in Wales, as he was well skilled in the Welsh language.	1651	
48	William Roberts, Bishop of Bangor; He was previously Archdeacon of Anglesey. He was a Benefactor to the Cathedral, and founded a Scholarship at Queen's College, Cambridge, for the Diocese of Bangor. I know nothing of his parentage or connections	1665	Pet. Will. Wood, vol. i. 632. Walk. Suff. 2. Lloyd's Mem. 599.
49	William Lloyd, Bishop of St. Asaph, Lichfield and Coventry, and Worcester, born at Tilehurst, Berkshire, where his Father was Vicar. He was descended from the Lloyds of Henblas, Anglesey. He was a very learned man	1717	B. Willis. Bio. Dict. Gent. Mag. Supplement, 3rd part, 1827.
50	William Lloyd, Bishop of Llandaff, Peterborough, and Norwich, was contemporary with the last: I know nothing of him. The two namesakes are at times confounded. William Lloyd of St. Asaph, was one of the seven bishops sent to the Tower by James the Second		

Thus, we have fifty Bishops natives of Wales, or connected with it by origin, in the course of one hundred and fifty-six years; forty-three of the former, and seven of the latter, giving us the average of about a Bishop every three years, an allowance which we should have no objection to see restored to us. But there is another circumstance much more gratifying than numbers, the eminence of many of these Prelates; it appears that Dr. John Philipps, the Bishop of Man, was the translator of the Scriptures into Manx, and taking him, together with our countryman Tindal, and Bishop Morgan, we may form a triad of the three translators of the Scriptures into three out of four of the languages of the British Isles.*

Amongst Englishmen, and those who value the principles of the Church of England, I can hardly believe there will be much difference of opinion on the subject. It cannot be that a nation which has sent missionaries to teach the remotest nations in their own tongues, will long submit to see the principles of the reformation trampled upon in the land of their fellow-subjects and friends. Never, till of late, did this system exist, in its full extent, even in Wales, though no country has endured more oppression: she was comparatively free from it even during the midnight darkness of Popery: it did not form a part even of the first insolence of conquest.† Alas! that an event which gave religious freedom to all besides, an event to which her children had so much contributed, should have made Christianity itself a source of degradation to her.‡

But, no! there is one period which affords a parallel; it is furnished—not by the conduct of those who had conquered our country, but of those who were aiming at conquest. At a time when all the weapons of priestly craft and secular violence were combined to enslave her, then was a petition framed, which describes the Welsh Church—as it is in the nineteenth century! In

* English, Welsh, and Manx.

† After the conquest by Edward the First, though some Englishmen were mitred, there was no systematic exclusion of Welshmen.

‡ The revolution, from which period Welshmen have been almost systematically excluded from Welsh bishoprics.

the time of Henry III. Giraldus Cambrensis presented a petition to the Pope from the Princes of Wales. Leaving the present good Archbishop of Canterbury out of the question, this petition may furnish an appropriate conclusion to this chapter.

"Petition of the Welsh Princes to the Pope.*—To the Right Reverend Father and Lord, Innocent, by the grace of God, Pope,—Llywelyn, Prince of Gwynedd; Gwenwynwyn and Madoc, Princes of Powys; Gruffydd, Maelgwn, Rhys, and Meredith, sons of Rhys, Prince of South Wales, send health and true obedience in all things. Be it known to your fatherly goodness the great sufferings and the danger of loosing souls that have fallen upon the Church of Wales, since, by kingly oppression, and not by the authority of the Bishop of Rome, she became subjected to the authority of England and the Archbishop of Canterbury.

"At first, the Archbishop of Canterbury, as a matter of course, sends us English Bishops, ignorant of the manners and language of our land, who cannot preach the word of God to the people, nor receive their confessions but through interpreters.

"And besides, these Bishops that they send us from England, as they neither love us nor our land, but rather persecute and oppress us with an innate and deep-rooted hatred, seek not the welfare of souls; their ambition is to rule over us, and not to benefit us; and on this account, they do not but very rarely fulfil the duties of their pastoral office among us. And whatever they can lay their hands upon, or get from us, whether by right or wrong, they carry into England, and waste and consume the whole of the profits obtained from us in abbeys and lands given to them by the King of England. And like the Parthians, who shoot backwards from afar as they retreat, so do they from England excommunicate us as often as they are ordered so to do.

"The lands which were bestowed by the devout bounty of our forefathers of old, upon the cathedrals of Wales, (as they do not love our country,) they sell, give away, and alienate to the clergy and others who may happen to covet them. And because the lands

* See Mr. Theophilus Jones's valuable *History of Brecknockshire*.

belonging to the churches are liable to be taken from them, we ourselves have taken part of them into our own hands, and they are in our possession at the present time. From these causes, the Cathedral Churches of Wales have been reduced to the greatest poverty; but if they were blessed with good and godly Bishops, they would soon again be rich and flourishing.

"Besides these things, when the Saxons (English) rush into Wales, the Archbishop of Canterbury puts the whole land under an interdict; and because we and our people defend our country against the Saxons and other enemies, he places us and our people under judgment of excommunication, and causes those Bishops whom he sent amongst us, to proclaim this judgment, which they are ready to do on all occasions. The consequence is, that every one of our people who falls on the field of blood, in defence of the liberty of his country, dies under the curse of excommunication. We, therefore, with sighs and tears, beseech your Holiness, to whom belongs the government of the Universal Church, to give us effectual relief from these grievances, and others which will be communicated to you by the mouth of the Canons of St. David's, and Giraldus, their Bishop elect, who is a discreet and reverend man. And with one voice, we implore you to liberate your children from the oppression they have endured from the three last Bishops that have been placed at St. David's, in consequence of the subjection of that see to the Archbishop of Canterbury. For, before the time of the three last Bishops, St. David's was the seat of an Archbishop of all Wales, who, as Archbishop, was subject to none except to the Mother Church of Rome.

"If thou wilt deign to look upon us with eyes of pity, whatever service is in our power, we will willingly do to the holy apostle Peter: therefore, our dear father, farewell in the Lord."

Thus far the Princes of our land and the heroic Giraldus, in language as eloquent and pathetic as it is applicable to our own time. But even in this case the parallel is incomplete; the Romish Church was bound to an unintelligible ritual; the Church of England is built on a protestation against it. Hitherto, I have spoken only of the effects of English episcopacy; I must now advert to its principle; to those who consider this question apart from the unchristian apology of expediency, it will certainly suggest many melancholy reflections! Whilst it is granted that many of the English Bishops of Wales, were in many respects an honour to their Church, it is impossible to reconcile their *bare acceptance* of their dignities with those thirty-nine Articles to which they were pledged as the very passport to their profession, and which form a confession of faith, which it is the very object of the episcopal office to preserve inviolate. The 24th Article is fearfully explicit.

" The 24th Art. Of speaking in the congregation in such a tongue as the people understandeth.—It is a thing plainly repugnant *to the word of God* and to the custom of the Primitive Church, *to have public prayer* in the Church, or to minister the sacraments, in a tongue not understanded of the people!" *

* "It is extraordinary, that such a dignity should be either granted or accepted!"—*Five Letters on the state of Religion in Wales.*—Chester, 1826.

As the only apology that has ever been offered for the practice of thrusting Englishmen into every valuable piece of Church Preferment in Wales, is the supposed advantages of abolishing the Welsh language, I trust I shall be excused for the length of the following extracts, which serve to elucidate two propositions:—First, That such measures tend to counteract the very object they seek to attain. Secondly, That if they were calculated to ensure it, they are most unjustifiable.

ENGLISH SCHOOLS FOR WELSH CHILDREN.

Griffith Jones, whose experience and discrimination make his opinions on this subject of peculiar value, has left us some admirable remarks upon it.

"To be able to read one Language does not increase the difficulty of learning another, but always renders it easier : It is common for all nations to learn their own Language first; and it is the most natural method to begin with the easiest, and then proceed to the hardest things.

"The English Charity Schools, which have been tried, produced no better effect in country places; all that the children could do in three, or four, or five years (though but few of the poor could stay so long in them) amounted commonly to no more than to learn very imperfectly to read some easy parts of the Bible, without knowing the Welsh of it, nor the meaning of what they said when they repeated their catechism; nor should this be thought strange, considering they were learning to read an unknown language, and had none to speak it to them but the Master, and he too obliged to talk to them often in Welsh: Insomuch that those who have been so long in the English Schools could not edify themselves by Reading, till many of them lately learned to read their own language in the Welsh Charity Schools. Should these be turned into English Charity Schools, to propagate the language?

"Sure I am the Welsh Charity Schools do no way hinder to learn English but do very much contribute towards it : and perhaps you will allow, Sir, that learning our own language first is the most expeditious way to come at the knowledge of another; else why are not your youths in England, designed for scholars, set to learn Latin and Greek, before they are taught English?"

He argues that the Welsh language has its advantages, and those very great ones, to all who make moral sentiment the first consideration.—

"But with respect to a more important concern, our spiritual and highest interest of all, there are some advantages peculiar to the Welsh tongue favourable to religion, as being perhaps the chastest in all Europe. Its books and writings are free from the infection and deadly venom of Atheism, Deism, Infidelity, Arianism, Popery, Lewd Plays, Immodest Romances, and Love Intrigues; which poison the mind, captivate all the senses, and prejudice so many (conversant with them) against their duty to God, and due care of their own souls; and which, by too many books in English and some other languages, are this day grievously propagated."

He shows the impossibility of a rapid abolition without the sacrifice of what is far more valuable. He then decides that the question ought to be left to the free choice of the people themselves,—a conclusion at once consonant with sound policy, and with sound feeling.—

"She has not lost her charms nor chasteness, remains unalterably the same, is now perhaps the same she was four thousand years ago; still retains the beauties of her youth, grown old in years, but not decayed. I pray that due regard may be had to her great age, her intrinsic usefulness; and that her long standing repute may not be stained by wrong imputations. Let it suffice, that so great a part of her dominions have been usurped from her; but let no violence be offered to her life."

Of the scandalous practice before alluded to, of imposing English clergymen on Welsh parishes, he expresses himself in a spirit of manly indignation, and uncompromising independence, worthy of Giraldus Cambrensis himself.—

"It is not my present business to enquire, *who this is owing to;* but *be they who they will*, and how little soever they lay it to heart for the present, they will hereafter find themselves *answerable to a grievous charge*. This has, in too many places, reduced the country into heathenish darkness and irreligion, and (what some are apt to declaim against as more damnable,) into different communities and separations from the Established Church. By means of these clergymen officiating in English to Welsh congregations, we may say, a trial has been made, in some sort, whether the people would learn their language, and forget their own, till they have almost forgot the name of Christ. The sheep could not know their shepherd's voice from first to last; and must therefore perish, or go astray, for want of pasture. If pastors will continue to have no more compassion for the people in this world, what sort of greeting will pass between them about it when they meet in the next, is not hard to guess. We cannot help thinking, that English sermons to Welsh congregations are neither less absurd, nor more edifying, than Welsh preaching would be in the centre of England, or Latin service in the Church of Rome. In some respect, a greater severity this than is imposed by the Romish Antichrist; who, notwithstanding his robes are red with the blood of the saints, yet ordains that preaching be in the known tongue through all his provinces. This grievance of some people here is too insufferable not to be loudly complained of. Wherein have our forefathers been more barbarously used by their adversaries in the worst of servitudes?"—See *Welsh Piety*, vol. i. pages 33, 36, 37, 38, 51.

LLYWELYN'S HISTORICAL SKETCH OF THE VERSIONS OF THE WELSH BIBLE.— HIS VIEWS AS TO THE MEANS WHICH HAVE BEEN ADOPTED TO ABOLISH THE WELSH LANGUAGE.

"Here again, I own it seems to me of very little moment; I mean to those who are residents, or stay at home; who in every country must be by far the majority. The general, the common business and concerns of civil, of religious, and social life, may be transacted, I suppose, as well in Welsh as in English. A Cambro-Briton may mind his farm and his merchandise, if he has any; he may sow his corn and bring home his harvest; he may live as long, and do as much good, with only his own mother tongue, as if he had twenty tongues besides. But as to those who are non-residents, who leave their native country and come over to England; as to those who cross the Severn, the Wye, or the Dee; those who come up to London and have a mind to distinguish themselves in the metropolis; to them the Welsh, or another language is not indifferent. The English is of advantage, is necessary, and it is their personal concern to learn and attain it.

"This matter in this way of considering it, cannot appear of any great consequence. It is a mere *affair of convenience*, of convenience comparatively to few, to one in a hundred, to three thousand, may be out of three hundred thousand inhabitants; to whom in general it is of little importance. It might be convenient, if all the world was now, as it was in the days of Noah, of one speech and of one language. This might facilitate travelling: it might promote trade and correspondence among the different countries and nations of the earth; but for all that, I never heard of any law made, nor of any bill brought into any Senate, for extirpating tongues in general, and establishing some one common and universal language. If a formal decree may have been proper for the purpose of extirpating the Welsh tongue, why not another equally formal and weighty to abolish all dialects of the English but one? To put an end to Irish inaccuracies and blunders? And to give a pure pronunciation, and a sweet accent to the inhabitants of Edinburgh, of Northumberland, or Devonshire? Again,

"If we grant *the end* here to be worthy and of greater importance than it seems to be; *the methods* made use of to accomplish this end will yet remain very improper and disproportioned. To bring about an *uniformity of language* between two neighbouring nations, subjects of the same sovereign, in a state of perfect harmony and peace: what must be done? Why, *the Holy Bible* must be withheld from one of them; *the word of God* must be withdrawn from a people, till they can all understand it, in another tongue: that is, it must be for ever withheld from thousands who never can, nor will learn any other. To describe here, is to expose. The very naming of these means must surely be sufficient to show them to be, to the last degree, improper and preposterous. They affect the religion of a people; they infringe the rights of conscience; they interfere with their duty to God, the care of their souls, and their eternal salvation: with which no schemes of human policy should interfere, *on any account*, much less on account of a mere trifling convenience.

"Here lies the great, the unanswerable objection to these measures for a change of language. They affect, they deprive a man of, what he considers as essential to his most important interests for a trifle, for nothing to him! He is born in a certain country, he learns the language of his parents, and of his country, as naturally and as innocently, as he sucks his mother's breasts, or breathes the common air. He has neither opportunity nor ability to learn any other tongue. And what is the consequence? He must never hear of a Saviour or salvation: not because the gospel was never heard in the land: nor because he is under an Antichristian government! No. His superiors are Christians, are Protestants: the gospel is in his neighbourhood; and may be preached in his language as well as in any other! But it must not be read nor preached in it; *because*, should it be, it will obstruct *the spread and progress of another language*. Thus disproportioned are the means to the end. They appear highly absurd and preposterous, when considered only in their aspect or relation one to another. They appear still worse, if considered as coming from a Christian magistracy or government. They are diametrically opposite to the genius and spirit of Christianity.

"After all, these disproportioned and preposterous, these *unprotestant* and *unchristian* methods, though pursued with rigour and severity, will not *insure the end proposed*. Suppose neither the name nor the religion of Christ to be known or heard of, in the Principality of Wales; yet the language of it might subsist, in spite of every effort of this nature to destroy it. Violent measures hardly ever answer the expectation. In general they soon spend themselves and end in nothing. They may do mischief; they may distress a person or a party; they may show the disposition and temper of the times; or they may gratify the rage of a persecuting tyrant: and but very little more."

In accounting for the Cornish dialect having become obsolete, he ascribes it to the superior justice with which the people have been treated.

"No Offa's dyke in that part of Britain. They have never been cooped in by hedges and ditches, or other barriers, less rustic indeed, but more disagreeable and hostile. They were never slaughtered by multitudes for a song. They were never punished for being Cornish: never excluded the protection of government: never denied legal redress on complaints of injustice or oppression: nor even disqualified as a people, by Acts of

Parliament, from holding places of honour or of profit in any part of the kingdom."

The sum of his reasoning is, that the abolition of the Welsh language ought to be the result of education, and not the basis of it. There can be no doubt that if the people are well instructed in their own language, they will be ready enough to discern the advantage of acquiring another, so well calculated to advance their wordly interests.—

"Upon the whole, in whatever view I consider this design of discontinuing the language of Wales, and of establishing the English in its stead: I cannot think it any way so important as is pretended. It seems to me to be very immaterial, especially to England; and I should therefore be a good deal unconcerned about it. But when I consider the measures proposed to accomplish this end, I can no longer be indifferent. I feel, I avow, a warmth and emotion; and I think it becomes me. Were I an Englishman or a Scotchman, my feelings here, I apprehend, would be the same. And I should look upon it as a duty, to the utmost of my power, to bear a public testimony against measures so preposterous and ineffectual; against measures of such pernicious and destructive consequences; against measures tending, not to answer the end proposed, or to make the people of Wales cease to be Welsh, and become English—but tending to make them cease to be Protestants—to make them cease to be Christians—cease to be loyal subjects and good men."—See *Dr. Llywelyn's Historical Account of the Welsh Versions and Editions of the Bible*, pages 73, 74, 75, 76, 77, 79, 80, 82, 83, 89, 90.

In January last, a Memorial* was addressed by a Welsh Antiquarian Society in London, to the present Bishops of Wales, on the subject of the orthography of the Welsh Bible. It concludes with the following intimation:—

"At the same time, however, your Committee must not close this address without throwing out a hint, that in future it will be more consistent to address the Bible Societies on this subject, than again to acknowledge the authority of men in whom we cannot confide, on account of their being unacquainted with the Welsh language. And they would respectfully submit the suggestion to the attention of their brethren in Wales, who have proposed to act in reference to the orthography in question."

To this Address an Answer has recently issued from the pen of the Rev. John Jones, Archdeacon of Merioneth. It is written in a mild and gentlemanlike spirit; but leaves untouched the main subject of the Memorial—the competence of the present Bishops of Wales for the ordinary duties of their office.

* Memorial of the Cymreigyddion to the Welsh Bishops.

CHAPTER III.
THE TWO ERAS.

THE INFLUENCE OF THE NATIVE WELSH BISHOPS COMPARED WITH THAT OF THEIR ENGLISH SUCCESSORS:—1. ON CHURCH PATRONAGE.—2. ON RELIGIOUS AND GENERAL EDUCATION.

> "Look here upon this picture, and on this!"—*Hamlet.*
>
> "Quanto præstantius esset
> Numen aquæ, viridi si margine clauderet undas
> Herba nec ingenuum violarent marmora tophum."—*Juvenal.*
>
> "How had the sacred stream more sweetly rolled,
> Still edg'd with rural verdure as of old,
> If still in nature's modest charms it shone,
> And marble ne'er defiled its genuine stone."—*Owen's Translation.*

EXPEDIENCY, as opposed to simplicity of purpose and integrity, is sufficiently revolting, when made a rule of conduct in matters of mere civil policy; but, when the doctrine, that evil may be done for the sake of the good it may produce, is admitted into religious institutions,—we cannot expect for them the blessing of Providence; a temporizing and crooked policy will always appear a most unnatural vehicle for the Christian injunctions to guilelessness and purity! The doctrine, that the Welsh Church may be best governed by natives of England, has many zealous friends, and for very obvious reasons; and yet I never have heard one of them reconcile this practice with the Article of our Church, or those Gospel principles which it so forcibly expresses. The only vindication is, that it has been found salutary in practice!

Now, though this defence of English Episcopacy savours as strongly of one peculiarity of Popery, as the system itself of another, I am perfectly willing, for the sake of argument, to descend from the vantage-ground of principle,—and to try, by the fair test of historical experience, how far Wales and the cause of religion generally, have been benefitted by the policy that has long been pursued towards her. I am willing, in the outset, to admit, that during the times when Wales was governed by Welsh Bishops, instances may be found of great favouritism and corruption,— and it will not be denied, on the other hand, that similar examples may be found amongst the English Bishops of Wales—examples, it is to be feared, of a far more corrupt feeling, when we consider the additional check that is imposed in our days, by the vigilance of public opinion. But, in comparing the merits of conflicting theories, it will always be the aim of candid men to avoid extreme cases on both sides, and to search out for some test by which they may judge of the even tenor of the ordinary workings of their respective systems. Happily, we possess a criterion on this subject, which is, in every respect, free from objection. From the year 1601 to 1640, the diocese of St. Asaph was governed exclusively by Welsh Bishops; from 1761 to 1800 is a space of time of exactly equal length, during which its prelates were exclusively Englishmen. During both these periods, there was a tolerably rapid change of Bishops; and it is singular, that in both cases, they were exactly four in number.

It is difficult to conceive a state of circumstances more favourable to a fair comparison. I have selected the diocese of St. Asaph, because it is, in many respects, the most important in Wales, and because a publication relating to it has furnished us with the means of following up the investigation with peculiar minuteness (Brown Willis's St. Asaph). To inquire into the appropriation of all the benefices in the diocese would, of course, be alike tedious and unprofitable; I propose, therefore, to confine the inquiry to the higher branches of Church Patronage, which will be sufficient for all useful purposes.

DIOCESE OF ST. ASAPH.

The state of Patronage under the ancient native Bishops of the Principality, as compared with the mode in which it has been since exercised under English Prelates; exemplified by a Statement of the preferments enjoyed by the higher Dignitaries of the Diocese, during two periods of forty years each; in the former of which the Bishops of St. Asaph were exclusively Welshmen, and in the latter they were exclusively Englishmen; and each period including four Prelates.

WELSH PERIOD.—From 1601 to 1640.

Distinctions and Connexions.	Preferments held with Bishoprie.
1. BISHOP MORGAN, 1601. He translated the whole Bible into Welsh, almost single-handed, from the original languages.—Llywelyn, page 60.—Preferred by Queen Elizabeth, *expressly on this ground.*—Cambrian Plutarch.—"Pertinaciously conscientious in the exercise of his episcopal functions."—Idem. —"In his original conception of this great design, it is likely that Morgan had little hopes of emolument or honour: he was satisfied, we may presume, with the reward of his conscience, in a case so pregnant with that peculiar species of consolation."—Idem.	

ENGLISH PERIOD.—From 1761 to 1800.

Distinctions and Connexions.	Preferments held with Bishoprie.
1. BISHOP NEWCOME, 1761. "He had at the same time under his care and private tuition, Willm. Lord Marquis of Brackley, son of the Duke of Bridgewater, and Lord Hartington. To these lords he was indebted for his future advancement in life, and the preferments which he enjoyed. He was translated to St. Asaph, holding his living of Whitchurch in commendam. He rebuilt the Rectory House there entirely, and was therefore fond of the place, and made it his principal residence, being very conveniently situated for the business of his diocese, and going only occasionally for a month or two in the summer to his palace at St. Asaph, where he performed all episcopal duties with the utmost regularity. He published a few occasional Sermons."—B. Willis.	FIVE: viz.—1 Whitchurch, Salop.—2 Llandrillo-yn-Rhos.—3 Llandrinio.—4 Llansannan.—5 Northop.

2. BISHOP PARRY, 1604. He published a corrected, or new, version of the whole Welsh Bible, being the edition now in use in our Churches.—Llywelyn's Historical Account of the Editions of the Welsh Bible, p. 28. "When King James, who had an especial regard to his learning, came to the English throne, he promoted him to the see of St. Asaph."—B. Willis.	Two : viz.	1 Llangwm. 2 Llanrwst.*	2. BISHOP SHIPLEY, 1769. Clerk of the Closet to George II. Chaplain to the Army, 1744. He published occasional Sermons, and a Speech intended to have been spoken on the Bill for altering the Charter of Massachusetts Bay. Eloquence and political consistency cannot be regarded as the only desiderata in the character of a Christian Bishop. Of his application of his patronage we shall presently have the means of judging.	FIVE : viz.— 1 Llandrillo-yn-Rhos. 2 Llandrinio. 3 Northop. 4 Deanery of Christ Church. 5 Rect. of Chilbolton.
3. BISHOP HANMER, 1623. Chaplain to James I. Descended of an illustrious Flintshire family distinguished by its patriotism and the number of great men it has produced.—Pennant's Whitford and Holywell.	ONE : viz.— Prebendary of Worcester.		3. BISHOP HALIFAX, 1787. Professor of Arabic, and then of Civil Law, at Cambridge. Chaplain to his Majesty. A very learned and able man, and author of many valuable works on Divinity and other subjects.	THREE : viz.— 1 Llandrillo-yn-Rhos. 2 Llandrinio. 3 Northop.
4. BISHOP OWEN, 1629. He was the son of Owen Owens, of the House of Bodsilin, Caernarvonshire, though born in England. "He was preferred to this see by King Charles I, to whom he had been Chaplain, while he was Prince of Wales, on supposition, as saith Fuller in his Worthies, that he was a Welshman, which indeed he distinguished himself to be in all respects (except that the place of his nativity was English) by his incomparable skill in the Welsh language, and zeal in promoting the good of his Bishopric. Upon his repair to St. Asaph, June 16, 1630, he immediately began to set about several great works. He began first by his order and decrees, to establish preaching in Welsh in St. Asaph Parish Church, and, as it is supposed, in other Parish Churches in his diocese. He repaired his Cathedral at his own cost, and set up a new organ in it. His benefactions, were a few years after put an end to by the great rebellion breaking out in 1641."—B. Willis.	Two : viz.— Llanvyllin and Rhuddlan Vic.		4. BISHOP BAGOT, 1790. Son of Lord Bagot.	FOUR: viz.— 1 Llandrillo-yn-Rhos. 2 Llandrinio. 3 Northop. 4 Llangwm.

* Bishop Parry at one time held Cwm Rectory and Kilken; but he gave up the former, and (as it would appear,) the latter, on receiving Llangwm and Llanrwst.

The result of this comparison is very strongly indeed in favour of the native dynasty.

FIRST.—As regards fitness for the duties of their office.—Three out of the four Welsh Bishops (viz., Morgan, Parry, and Owen), were, as we have seen, men distinguished by piety and a high degree of talent, applied entirely to professional objects; and the fourth (Bishop Hanmer) seems to have been a man of worth and competent endowments. On the other hand, three out of the four English Bishops (Newcome, Shipley, and Bagot), were certainly not remarkable for great professional attainments, though one of them (Shipley) was distinguished as a parliamentary debater. The fourth (Bishop Halifax) had great professional claims; but was Bishop of St. Asaph only during a short period.

All the Welsh Bishops understood the language* of Wales; three of them were distinguished by the peculiar depth of their knowledge on this subject, and were preferred on that very ground. The English prelates were all utterly ignorant of the Cambro-British tongue.

SECONDLY.—As regards the comparative disinterestedness with which the episcopal influence† was employed in each era, the contrast between the number of "additional preferments," in the two periods, speaks volumes. The total number of "additional preferments" enjoyed by the Welsh Bishops is FIVE, whilst those possessed by their English successors is SEVENTEEN!

But, upon this subject, we possess much more decisive evidence in the minute account preserved by Brown Willis and his editor, of the mode in which sinecure rectories and other high preferments were appropriated during the two periods. The reader will find, at the end of the Chapter, details which sufficiently establish the following conclusions:—

"We are apt to think," says a French writer, "that yesterday

* Bishop Hanmer was born at Selatyn, Shropshire. In his time, the Welsh language was spoken in this parish, and we may presume he understood it.

† Commendams are, it is true, the gift of the Crown; but the royal bounty is abused when they are enjoyed to excess.

never existed because we were born, but to-day;" and thus it is with Wales, the pure flame of patriotism has been so long smothered by the strong arm of an unrighteous policy, that we are apt to regard the sickly and unnatural light which has supplanted it, as the only security against total darkness. The more, however, we investigate the subject, the more clearly shall we perceive, that the intellectual backwardness of the Welsh Church is the effect of a system of intellectual proscription, and therefore no vindication of it.

During the Welsh period, we shall find, that though the higher preferments were almost exclusively confined to men whose names imply their Welsh origin,—there were amongst them, perhaps, as many persons of eminence as amongst those who were promoted under the English regimen.*

During the English period, the best benefices were generally bestowed on gentlemen conspicuous only for their connection with the prelates or their patrons—even when given to men celebrated for their theological acquirements, it will appear, that those individuals were possessed elsewhere of professional emoluments, which surpassed, even their high professional attainments, —that they were constant absentees from Wales, and that neither reason nor justice required that the Principality should be drained to reward them. On the other hand, though pluralties existed in the Welsh era, it was to a much less extent, and on principles much less injuries to the rights and interests of Wales,—as those who were benefitted by them were almost uniformly natives of the country—generally residents in some part or other of the diocese, and—not like most of the present modern English sinecure pluralists of St. Asaph, stationed on another cluster of pluralities in the remotest counties of England.

I shall now proceed to a brief review of the progress of religious and general education in Wales, beginning with

A HISTORY OF THE WELSH BIBLE AND ITS EDITIONS.

From the Reformation to the time of Elizabeth was a period of English Bishops. The consequences of the system were similar

* See Table at the end of this Chapter.

to what they now are; the people were, during the whole of that period, without a translation of the Scriptures.

"For upwards of *seventy years*, from the Reformatian to the reign of Queen Elizabeth; for nearly *one hundred years*, from the separation from the Church of Rome — there were *no Bibles* in Wales, but only *in the cathedrals or in the parish churches and chapels*. There was no provision made for the country, or for the people in general; as if they had nothing to do with the word of God, at least no farther than they might hear it in their attendance upon public worship, once in the week. This is astonishing!"— *Llywelyn*, p. 36.

No sooner did that wise and patriotic Princess ascend the throne than she filled the Welsh bishoprics with native Welshmen—men to whom Wales, in fact, owes all the religious light she at present enjoys,—and but for whom it is more than probable she would have been, at this moment, a Popish Country, exposed to the superstitions and miseries of a neighbouring and a kindred people.*

* Bishop Richard Davies's Preface to his Edition of the New Testament.

WELSH BIBLE.

Editions of	When Published.	By whose Instrumentality.
1st, folio....	1588	Bishop Morgan of St. Asaph. He undertook and accomplished the translation of the Scriptures solely from patriotic and religious principle.—*Llywelyn's History of the Welsh Bible* p. 17.
2nd, folio...	1620	Bishop Parry, of St. Asaph, aided by Dr. John Davies, of Mallwyd. "Parry was entirely a volunteer in this affair, induced to undertake it merely from a consideration of the absolute wants and necessities of his country. Many, if not most of the churches were without Bibles, and we may rest assured there were none elsewhere; yet no provisions was made, or likely to be made, but for the voluntary, but for the spontaneous undertaking of this truly Protestant, and very venerable Bishop."—*Llywelyn.*
3rd, 8vo.....	1630	Rowland Heylin and Sir Thomas Middleton, two patriotic Welshmen.
4th, 8vo.....	1654	In the times of the Commonwealth. Supposed by Dr. Llywelyn to have originated with Cromwell, who was of Welsh origin. 6000 copies.
5th, 8vo.....	1678	Thomas Gouge, a pious and charitable Non-conformist, of London. 8000 copies.
6th, 8vo.....	1690	Stephen Hughes, a Dissenting Minister, patronized by Lord Wharton.
7th, folio....	1690	Bishop Lloyd, of St Asaph (one of the 7 Bishops).
8th, 8vo.....	1718	Society for promoting Christian Knowledge.
9th, 8vo.....	1727	Ditto. ⎫ At the instigation of Griffith Jones, and in
10th, 8vo ...	1746	Ditto. ⎬ consequence of the demand created by his
11th, 8vo ...	1752	Ditto. ⎭ Schools.—See *Welsh Piety*, vol. i. p. 20, 25. In all 30,000 copies.
12th, 8vo ...	1770	Ditto. — At the instigation of Dr. Llywelyn, a Dissenting Minister.
13th, 8vo ...	1789	Ditto.—By the Rev. H. Parry and Mr. John Thomas.
14th ⎫ 15th ⎬ folio 16th ⎭ 17th 18th	At the end of this century.	The Rev. Peter Williams, a Methodist Clergyman, with Notes. In the whole, about 20,000 copies. Charles, a Methodist Clergyman. The Society for promoting Christian Knowledge.— At the instigation of a Welsh Clergyman, the Rev. T. Jones, Curate of Creaton, Northamptonshire.
19th		The Bible Society, which was formed in consequence of Mr. Jones failing to procure an additional supply from the Society for promoting Christian Knowledge.

Since the commencement of the Bible Society, the number of Welsh Bibles sent by it into Wales, are as four to one, compared to those issued by any other institution.

From the foregoing sketch, the reader may draw the following inferences :—

1st.—That when Wales was blessed with native prelates, they led the van in the progress of religious knowledge.

2ndly.—That since she has been ruled by English Bishops, all her great religious benefits have been traceable either to the influence of Dissenters, or of a class of Clergymen such as Griffith Jones, who experienced few marks of episcopal favour.

OTHER RELIGIOUS WRITINGS.

An immense number of tracts, pamphlets, periodicals, &c., good, bad, and indifferent, have been published in the Welsh language by Dissenters. They issue about 4,000 copies of magazines every month. The clergy have written very few religious books of any description. Those who have written, have belonged to a class by no means in favour with their rulers; and the monthly magazine, called the GWYLIEDYDD, the only publication of the kind connected with the Church, is supported almost exclusively by Curates, and the poorer part of the beneficed clergy, and a smaller number of it are sold than of any other Welsh periodical.

SCHOOLS.

Many were endowed in the times of the Tudors and Stewarts, the funds of which are now most grossly abused.

About the time of the Revolution, Gouge, a clergyman, but a Non-conformist, established three or four hundred Schools in Wales, by aid of Subscriptions.—(See Archbishop Tillotson's Sermon on his death).

Of Griffith Jones's and Mrs. Bevan's Schools, which spread over the whole country, an account has already been given. £30,000, the accumulation of the legacy left by that lady's will, are still employed in a similar way. But the chief instructors of the people are the Dissenters.

Statement of the number of Schools Established by Griffith Jones and Mrs. Bevan, and the number of Scholars instructed in them from the commencement in 1737 till the death of that lady in 1777, a period of Forty Years.

	Schools.	Scholars.		Schools.	Scholars.
In the year 1737	37	2400	In the year 1759	206	8539
1738	71	3981	1760	215	8687
1739	71	3989	1761	210	8023
1740	150	8767	1762	225	9616
1741	128	7995	1763	279	11770
1742	89	5123	1764	195	9453
1743	75	4881	1765	189	9029
1744	74	4253	1766	219	10986
1745	120	5843	1767	190	8422
1746	116	5635	1768	148	7149
1747	110	5633	1769	173	8637
1748	136	6223	1770	159	9042
1749	142	6543	1771	181	9844
1750	130	6244	1772	219	12044
1751	129	5669	1773	242	13205
1752	130	5724	1774	211	11685
1753	134	5118	1775	148	9002
1754	149	6018	1776	118	7354
1755	163	7015	1777	144	9576
1756	172	7064			
1757	220	9037	Total	6465	314051
1758	218	9834			

In one word, both religious education and general education has sprung from the efforts of Dissenters and the most discouraged part of the clergy. What can be expected from such a state of things but Dissent—deep-rooted Dissent? The influence of the English Bishops on all these good works, has been like that of the stream which flows through Bala lake—but, as it is thought, without mingling with the waters!

SUMMARY OF THE COMPARISON.

WELSH PRELATES, 1601.	ENGLISH PRELATES, 1701.
They found a people immersed in Popery; they left a nation of Protestants.—*Dr. Davies's Address to his Countrymen, Prefixed to his translation of the New Testament.*	They found a nation of Churchmen; they left a nation of Dissenters.
In the last century, there was not one Welshman acquainted only with the Welsh language, who professed the Roman Catholic religion. — *Welsh Piety, by Griffith Jones.*	In the present century, in most districts of Wales, there is hardly one Welshman acquainted only with the Welsh language, who does not frequent the Dissenting Chapel oftener than the Church.
The period of Welsh Bishops terminates with the civil wars, (1641,) during which North Wales was more faithful than any other part of the kingdom to the Crown and the Church.—*Walter Davies's Life of Hugh Morris, the Bard.*	The period of English Bishops ends in 1700, with the general predominance of Dissent, which has continued to progress ever since, and is still progressing.

Comparative View of the Appropriation of the higher Preferments of the Diocese of St. Asaph, during two periods of 40 years each; during the first of which, its Bishops were exclusively Welshmen, and the latter exclusively Englishmen.

WELSH PERIOD.—From 1601 to 1640.			ENGLISH PERIOD.—From 1761 to 1800.		
Names.	Other Preferments.	Distinctions & Connections.	Names.	Other Preferments.	Distinctions & Connections.
DEANERY.			DEANERY.		
T. Bank, E.*	Llandrillo-yn-Edeyrnion		W. Herring, E.	Rector of Bolton Ferry, Yorkshire Precentor of Salisbury Prebendary of Apesthorp	Son of Archbp. Herring, and appointed by him Dean of St. Asaph.
A. Maurice, W.†	Llanycil Corwen, Vicar Llansaunan, R.	Chaplain of All Souls' College, Oxford.	W. D. Shipley, E.	Ysceiviog—Wrexham Llanarmon Chancellorship	Son of Bp. Shipley, of St. Asaph.—Published a Sermon for the benefit of the Chester Infirmy.
SINECURE RECTORIES AND PREBENDS.			SINECURE RECTORIES AND PREBENDS.		
Cum.			*Cum.*		
J. Pickering, W.			O. Batley, E.		
J. Griffith, W.	Caerwys, one year		W. Adams, E.	Cundover and St. Chad's, Shropshire	Master of Pembroke Col. Cambridge.—Author of two vols. of Sermons and Tracts.
Bishop Parry, W.					
J. Price, W.			Hon. D. Finch, E.	Prebend. of Gloucester Harpsden Rectory	Brother of the Earl of Aylesford.
H. Griffith, W.					
Corwen.			*Corwen.*		
Edmund Meyric, W.			John Morgan, W.		
Henry Rainsford, E.	Prebendary of Licfield		W. D. Shipley, E.	Prebendary of Meivod Ysceiviog—Wrexham Llangwm—Chancellor	Son of Bishop Shipley, of St. Asaph.

* E. denotes Englishmen.   † W. denotes Welshmen.

Incumbents' Names.	Other Preferments.	Distinctions & Connections	Incumbents' Names.	Other Preferments.	Distinctions & Connections.
Corwen.			*Corwen.* George Prettyman, E	Dean of Westminster Bishop of Lincoln	The Prettymans, both distinguished by the number of their preferments. Brother of the Bishop
			J. Prettyman, E. R. Sneyd, E.		
Darowain. William Griffith, W... John Davies, W......	Cemaes, and Canon 4th Mallwyd Llan-yn-Mowddwy	A distinguished divine and a most erudite Welsh scholar & bard. Author of an elaborate Welsh & Latin Dicty. Assisted Bp. Parry in his translation of the Scriptures	*Darowain.* Burleigh, E. Peter Newcome, E... John Randolph, E...	Rector of Shorley, Herts Canon of Christ Church	Nephew of Bp. Newcome and author of the History of St. Albans. Professor of Divinity.— Bp. of Oxford, Bangor and London
Clitoph Brayn, E......	Preb. of Llan Nevydd		*East Hope.* W. Worthington, W Bishop Shipley, in commendam......	Llandrillo-yn-Rhos Llandrinio—Northop Llandysilio	A learned and excellent Welsh clergyman
East Hope. Richard Pydleston, E. Edward Puleston, E.			Thurlow, E.		Nephew of Ld. Thurlow, the Chancellor
Kilcain. Thomas Yale, W. Bishop Parry, in commendam............	Bishop of St. Asaph Llangwm—Llanrwst	A distinguished Welsh scholar	*Kilcain.* John Allen, E. Benj. Newcome, E...	Preb. of Worcester, and Rector of St. Mildred London.	Dean of Rochester Brother of Bp. Newcome

Name	Position	Notes	Name	Position	Notes
Kilcain.			*Kilcain.*		
Morgan, Wynn, W....	Rector of Llanrwst, and Archdeacon of Lincoln		Charles Poyntz, E..	Lewes, Sussex	Relative of the Hon. S. Poyntz
Llanarmon-yn-Ial.			*Llanarmon-yn-Ial.*		Author of Hecuba, and Royal Suppliants
J. Williams, W	Rector of Llandrinio	Professor of Divinity & Principal of Jesus Col	J. Delap, E.......... H. Lushington, E... J. Eyton, E............	Not resident in diocese Comportion of Westbury, Lichfield	
Godfrey, Goodman, W		A distinguished foreign Protestant, preferred by the King		Deanery Ysceiviog—Wrexham Llangwm—Chancellor	
P. Du Moulin, French					
Llanbryn Mair.			*Llanbryn Mair.*		Dean of St. Asaph, and son of Bishop Shipley
Peter Williams, W	Marchwiail Llansannan, 2d portion Rhiwabon		Walter Ward, E.... Robert Gibson, E... William Gibson, E...		
Humphrey Morgan, W					
Arthur Hodslow, E...					
Llandrillo-yn-Edeyrnion.			*Llandrillo-yn-Edeyrnion.*		Neph. of the Chancellor, Enjoys a sinecure in the Court of Chancery
Thomas Banks, E......	Dean of St. Asaph		John Upton, E ..... Charles Bertie, E ... — Thurlow, E.......	East Hope Rectory	
J. Griffith, W.					
Llansannan.			*Llansannan.*		A learned geometrician
W. Vaughan, W.			Brakenbridge, E.....		
G. Goodman, W.		Bishop of Gloucester	Bishop Newcome, E	See of St. Asaph Llandrinio—Llandysilio Northop	
J. Griffith, W.					
R. Pritchard, W					
E. Powell, W			C. Sampson, E.......	Rect. of Ripley, Yorksh.	

Incumbents' Names	Other Preferments	Distinctions & Connections	Incumbents' Names	Other Preferments	Distinctions & Connections
Llanvavor.			*Llanvavor.*		
E. Griffith, W	Llandwrog	Bishop of Bangor	Gibson, E	Other preferments in Eng Llandysilio—Llandrinio. Northop.	Relation of Bp. Gibson
A. Williams, W	Mallwyd and Llan-yn-Mowddwy	A very learned man	Bishop Shipley, E	Llanrhaiadr	
J. Davies, W			W. Worthington, W	Prebendary of Durham	A very learned W. clerg. Son of the Hon. Stephen Poyntz
			C. Poyntz, E	Rector of North Creek, Norfolk	
Llan Newydd.			*Llan Newydd.*		
Richard Gwynne, W	Archdeacon of Bangor Rector of Llantrisant		Venn Eyre, E	Archdeacon of Carlisle Rector of Stambridge, in Essex	
John Davies, W	Rector of Mallwyd and Llan-yn-Mowddwy and Llanvawr sinecure	See distinctions given under Darowain	George Watts, E	Vicar of Dunford, Wilts, and of Uffington	
Llanvair Tal Haiarn First Portion.			*Llanvair Tal Haiarn. First Portion.*		
A. Williams, W.			H. Jones, W	Vicar of Gresford	
J. Berkley, E.			Peter Newcome, E	Rector of Pitsea, Essex Prebendary of Llandaff	Nephew of Bp. Newcome Author of Ht. St. Albans
T. Mostyn, W.			H. Newcome, E	Rector of Gresford and Castle Caereinion	Nephew of Bp. Newcome
R. Kynaston, W.					
J. Salodyne, E.					
Second Portion.			*Second Portion.*		
F. Price, W	Rector of Llandrinio		J. Swynton, E		Well versed in oriental languages
E. Price, W	Vicar of Rhuddlan		T. Baker, E	Prebendary of Exeter	
Meivod.			*Meivod.*		
P. Williams, W	Rector of Marchwiail		J. Morgan, W	Rector of Cwrm, and one of the priests of the Chapel Royal	
T. Kyffin, W	Vicar of Pool				
E. Morgan, W	Rector of Denbigh		W. Worthington, W	Preb. of York, V. of Llan-rhaiadr, R. of Llanvawr, V. of Guilsfield & Meifod	A learned and worthy Welsh clergyman
R. Evans, W	Vicar of Llanasaph		W. Brown, E		

Llangwm.		*Llangwm.*		
Owen Vaughan, W.		J. Price, W.		
Hugh Griffith, W.	Cwm	W. D. Shipley, E.	Ysceiviog—Wrexham	Son of Bishop Shipley Professor of Chemistry & Divinity at Cambridge; afterwards bishop of Llandaff. A very eminent man.
	Chancellor of Bangor	Richard Watson, E.		
Llan St. Ffraid-yn-Mechain.		*Llan St. Ffraid-yn-Mechain.*		
Herbert Thelwall, W.		Watson, E.		
G. Powell, W.	"He was esteemed a prodigy of learning."—*B. Willis.*	C. Everard, E. Bishop Bagot, E.	Llandrinio—Llandysilio Northop	
Meliden.		*Meliden.*		
Roger Thomas, W. by Hughes		Gilbert Bouchry, E.	Rector of Swaffam, Norfolk, and of Llan St. Ffraid	He had been Curate to Bp. Lisle, at Norehoil, in Middlesex
David Gwynne, W.	Vicar of Wrexham			
Robert Lloyd, W.	Vicar of Oswestry	H. Stephen Milner, E	Rect. of Dumton, Bucks	Son of Sir Stephen Milner, Nun Appleton, Yorkshire
John Kyffin, W.	R. of Castle Caereinion			
Edward Pulceston, E.				
Pennant.		*Pennant.*		
Peter Sharp, E.		Murray, E.	Erbistock	Chaplain to the King
H. Burchcs, E.	First share of Llandinam	Wm. Sturges, E.	Chancellor and Prebendary of Winchester	Author of several works in Divinity
Evan Morgan, W.				
Whitford.		*Whitford.*		
George Smith, E	Rector of Northop	Roger Mostyn, W.	Rector of Castle Caereinion	
J. King, E.	Canon of Windsor			
Robert King, E.		J. Jeffreys, W.	Rector of St. Nicholas, London	Brother of Chancellor Jeffreys
Bp. Owen, in comdm W				
George Griffith, W.			Rector of Berkhampstcd, Herts, &c	
William Thelwall, W.	Canon of Westminster			

Incumbents' Names.	Other Preferments.	Distinctions & Connections.	Incumbents' Names.	Other Preferments.	Distinctions & Connections.
Vaenol.			*Vaenol.*		
David Dolben, W.	Prebend of Vaenol Vicar of Hackney, and Llangerniw	Bishop of Bangor	J. Marsden	Rector of Bolton Percy in Yorkshire Prebendary of Southwell in Nottinghamshire Rector of Llandysil	
David Yale, W. by Bishop T. Davies	Prebendary and Chancellor of Chester.	Chancellor of Chester			
Hugh Williams, W. by Bishop J. Owen	Rector of Llantrisant, and Llanrhuddlad in Anglesey. — Comportionist of Llaudinam		W. Bagot, E.	Rector of Bithfield and Leigh, in the patronage of the family in Staffordshire	Brother of Bishop Bagot

CHAPTER IV.

PRIMARY AND DERIVATIVE CAUSES OF DISSENT IN WALES DISTINGUISHED. ECCLESIASTICAL MISGOVERNMENT THE SOLE CAUSE OF ITS PREDOMINANCE.

"It was merely the crisis to which things had been tending for some centuries; and if the fire did at last run over the country with wonderful rapidity, it was because the trees were all dry."—*Blunt's History of the Reformation.*

NOTHING is more common than to hear the wide-spread sectarianism of Wales referred to a variety of causes;—causes (as it is generally assumed) of a totally distinct and independent origin. Now, that the moral impulses to Dissent are various, is a proposition which—taken in a certain narrow sense—it is impossible to deny; but the question is, whether these various impulses were not at first communicated from one single source, whether they are not themselves mere effects of one simple solitary cause. Nothing, for instance, can be more unsatisfactory than to rank ignorance and individual eccentricity, as in themselves, causes of Dissent in Wales; these are mere common infirmities and foibles of the human race, and not more predominant in the heart of her mountains, than in many lands in which separation from the established religion is almost unknown; besides, Dissent has advanced with knowledge, and not with ignorance,—and individual eccentricity will not explain the sectarianism of a whole nation. Nor is it more philosophical to ascribe the strength of Dissent to the influence which views of worldly advantage may sometimes possess, in swelling its numbers; mercenary views may, indeed, make converts to a cause already prosperous, but can rarely contribute to raise it into prosperity.

A good deal of weight is sometimes attached (and with more reason,) to the continual change of preachers, and other attractions employed by Dissenters, more particularly the Welsh Methodists; but here, again, we must remember that a numerous clergy implies a sect already numerous, and cannot therefore be reckoned amongst the original causes of its establishment, though it may afterwards serve still further to secure its predominance. "There is nothing new under the sun," says the proverb;—there is very little in the expedients of modern Dissenters, which would not readily occur to men having similar views. Many of my readers will feel no difficulty in pointing out the antitype of the following picture:—

"They" (the Mendicant Friars) "practised all the stratagems of itinerancy, preaching in public streets, and administering the communion on a portable altar. Thirty years after their institution, an historian complains that the parish churches were deserted, that none confessed except to these friars; in short that the regular discipline was subverted.* He" (the Mendicant Friar) "could preach where he would; if he could not lawfully take possession of the church of the minister, he could erect his ambulatory pulpit at any cross in any parish, and rail (as he generally did) at the supineness and ignorance of the resident pastor. * * * He would confess whosoever might come to him. It was to *no purpose that the parish priest refused absolution* to any black sheep of his flock; away he went to a Franciscan, and absolution was given him at once."—*Blunt's History of the Reformation.* p. 37.

"Indeed, the frailty of human nature soon found out the weak places of the Mendicant system. Soon had the primitive zeal of its founders burnt itself out,—and then its censer was no longer lighted with fire from the altar: a living was to be made; the populace were to be alarmed, or caressed, or cajoled out of a subsistence. However humiliating may be the truth, experience has sanctioned it as a truth, that an indigent church makes a corrupt clergy."—Idem, p. 42.

* Hallam's *Middle Ages*, vol. ii. p. 291.

The reader of Chaucer will also be struck by observing, that his Mendicant Friar is distinguished from the secular priest, by his gloomy views of religion; whilst in his beautiful character of the latter he says, "but chiefly on the joys of heaven he loved to dwell;" and this disposition to dwell on judgments, rather than on mercies, is the peculiarity which, more than any positive difference of doctrine, distinguishes the Methodist minister of the present day from the clergy of the Church of England. It is, in fact, the natural tone of thought with those who secede on the ground, that the Establishment is in a state of great moral corruption.

Again, the result is sometimes referred to causes of a very different character,—the zeal and industry of Dissenters on the one hand, and the apathy both of the clergy and lay members of the Establishment on the other.

1.—Of the zeal of Dissenters, it is enough to remark, that it can be attractive only in proportion as it stands contrasted with the inactivity of the clergy.

2.—As to the apathy of the Welsh clergy,—it may reasonably be asked, whence is it that they are open to this imputation?

Is religious indifference a feature of the community from which they are taken? Undoubtedly not;—the virtues and vices of the Principality are both of a very different complexion. It is enough, then, to remark, that the dissimilarity in character between the Welsh clergy and the Welsh people cannot be explained in any other way than by the system of Church patronage, which attracts indolence into the Church, and repels excellence from it,—which holds out a kind of bounty to mere negative characters, and looks coldly on patriotism and piety, and those attainments on which the usefulness of a parish priest in Wales will mainly depend.

3.—The lay members of the Church, it is said, are extremely indifferent to her interests. Whilst Dissenters are in the habit of subscribing thousands to establish schools, and build chapels, the laity of the Establishment are by no means anxious for the extension of her influence. Hence, instead of chapels of ease connected with the Church being erected to accommodate our increasing population,—the ground is left vacant for Dissenters who never fail to occupy it. Upon this subject also, it may be asked, is indifference to the interests of religion characteristic of the Welsh as a nation? To this question, their liberality to the Dissenting clergy of the present day,—the generous endowments granted by our forefathers in Roman Catholic times—are a sufficient answer. Whence then the present indifference of the lay members of the Church in Wales to the extension of her communion? Without approving of that indifference, I cannot help observing, that its causes are perfectly obvious. They will do nothing for the Church because she will do nothing for herself; it is sufficiently plain that if one half of that preferment which is engrossed by absentees and strangers, had been employed in extending the religious privileges of the people, there would have been but little need of voluntary contributions. It is no answer to tell us, that the prelates of Wales have no power so to apply those revenues; if such had been their disposition they might have obtained power from the legislature.

Upon this subject, I may advert to the case of the new College of St. David's, at Lampeter, an institution, which, with all its abuses of administration, has been of no small benefit to the Church in Wales. Before its establishment, the young clergy of the Principality were of necessity educated either in academies in Wales, where the education was of an inferior stamp, or at an English University, where they generally lost the free use their native dialect, and were apt to contract habits of expense and ambitious views,* which unfitted them for the pastoral duties

* It has been before observed, that the clergy of Wales are, for the most part men of a humbler rank than those of England. Hence it is, that their brief residence in an English University tends so often to dazzle and unsettle their minds, and produces in too many instances, a most unfavourable change on the character and disposition. Placed in the vicinity, as it were, of young men more blessed by fortune than themselves, yet jealously excluded from familiar intercourse, they may witness and imbibe the follies and affectation of those above them, but they have no means of profiting by their superior intelligence. The inferior rank of the Welsh clergy arises in South Wales from the poverty of the Church; but in North Wales, (where this difference does not, however, exist to the same extent,) solely from the way in which all the higher emoluments are engrossed by strangers, which induces a kind of artificial poverty.

in the seclusion of their native country. The object of St. David's College was to avoid the evils of both these courses of education, and combine all that was good in both; its site being in the Principality, it was free from the evils attendant on an English University; on the other hand, it might reasonably be presumed, that it would be the means of affording, in a much more economical way, that limited degree of erudition to which its students would have been restricted by their scanty resources, even at an University which flung wide the portals of learning to those who were in possession of the golden key. In support of this excellent institution, many of the Welsh gentry and clergy, and, indeed, some distinguished Englishmen, contributed most generously.* If, then, there ever was a time when disinterestedness was called for on the part of the rulers of the Welsh Church, it was then. But, how did they emulate the good example that had been thus set them? Did they sacrifice a sinecure rectory, a prebend, or any of those superfluous revenues which are professedly intended to provide learning, though, in reality, they are generally far otherwise employed? Alas, no! The College was endowed with a cluster of poor livings in the county of Cardigan, which were in some instances so completely stripped of their scanty revenues, that the parishoners were left without funds to support a resident minister!

Poor as the parochial clergy are in Cardiganshire, that county abounds in sinecures. The only apology that is found in the present day for the continuance of this species of Church patronage is its alleged tendency to promote learning; and it is still more worthy of remark, that the support of institutions similar to that of St.

* Amongst the benefactions of this institution, the generous donation of Archdeacon Beynon is particularly worthy of remembrance. In addition to his subscription, this patriotic Welsh clergyman bestowed on the new institution a fine of £742, accruing from his prebend of Penboyr.—The Principality will also remember, with gratitude, a donation of £100, from Mr. Justice Burton, who, though an Englishman, evinced in this instance the affectionate munificence of a son.

David's College, was the very object for which they were preserved at the Reformation.

"Although bishops, priests, and deacons, are the only sacred orders known to the Church of England, there are certain ecclesiastical offices and distinctions peculiar to her system, which require to be noticed. Such are deaneries, prebends, canonries, and similar situations connected with our cathedrals. Burnet, in his History of the Reformation, observes, that the design of these institutions was to form nurseries for the sees in which they were respectively situated; and that it was an object with the venerable Cranmer, (whose interest at court was unfortunately too low to effect it,) to restore them to their proper use, by 'setting up readers of the learned tongues and of divinity in them, that so a considerable number of young clerks might be trained up, under the bishop's eye, both in their studies and in a course of devotion, to be by him put afterwards in livings, according to their merit and improvements.' If the revenues belonging to the cathedrals were appropriated to such uses, they might be highly conducive to the general advantage and credit of the Establishment. The purposes to which they are applied are, however, purely political; and the general consequence is precisely what might be anticipated; not to raise modest merit out of obscurity—not to mitigate the infirmities of the superannuated labourer—not to train up a fresh generation of able theologians; but, proh pudor! to aggrandize the pride, and pamper the luxury of the richest and best provided members of the profession."—*Solemn Appeal on behalf of the Church of England*, by the Rev. Daniel Nihil, perpetual Curate of Forden, in Montgomeryshire.

The question, in what way the patronage of the Welsh Church has of late been applied, is, however, one of too grave a character to be considered, except through the medium of an enlarged view of facts; to facts, therefore, I shall appeal. The following pages present a sketch of the state of Church property in two counties, which being in the centre of Wales, and at the junction of several dioceses, may be assumed to furnish a fair specimen of the state of patronage throughout the Principality.

SOUTH WALES.—RADNORSHIRE

Contains 42 parishes (exclusive of chapels of ease). Of these, 21 (one half) are in the hands of non-residents; 16 of whom are absentees even from the county!

Of the 16 livings enjoyed by absentees from the county, six are in the hands of clergymen residing severally in London, at Portsmouth, at Harrow, in Lancashire, and other parts of England; the remaining ten are shared between individuals living respectively in Brecknockshire, Pembrokeshire, and Glamorganshire. The incumbent of St. Harmon's, not very long since, received both that benefice and Llanwrthwl, in Brecknockshire, in both of which the Welsh language prevails; in St. Harmon's it is more generally spoken than in any other parish in Radnorshire. Yet, he is unacquainted with it!

Since the publication of the first edition of this Essay, a letter has appeared in the St. James's Chronicle, defending the union of parishes in Radnorshire, on the ground of their extreme poverty and the scantiness of their population. Now, I may take this opportunity of observing, that I am fully sensible that *some* of the livings in Radnorshire are too poor to afford a decent maintenance to their ministers,—much less an adequate recompense for a long life of piety and usefulness. But, still, I may be permitted to enquire, what defence is this of the sixteen instances of incumbents who are absentees from the county altogether? If the resources of the Church in this district are naturally scanty—too scanty to do justice to the people—too scanty to do justice to the deserving clergy,—does not this place in a tenfold more odious light, those abuses which impoverish it still further, by handing over the revenues of its secluded Churches to gentlemen living in Hampshire, Lancashire, and the Metropolis!!

But unhappily, if we look closely into the real facts of the case, we shall find, that the poverty of *some* of the benefices in this county will afford anything but an exculpatory comment on existing

9

abuses; for, how stands the fact? Are unions *confined to the poorer parishes?** So far is this from being the case, that of all the benefices in the district, which are too rich to receive augmentation from Queen Anne's bounty—two-thirds are enjoyed by absentees from their parishes,—one-half by absentees from the county!†

NORTH WALES.—MONTGOMERYSHIRE.

In North Wales, the Church is peculiarly opulent,—but as little of the spirit of justice is discernible in the distribution of its Church patronage as in South Wales. In discussing this subject, I shall, in the first place, adopt two plain criteria, which will at once serve to place the truth of this proposition in an unequivocal light, and relieve me from entering into an invidious comparison of the individual merits of the clergy. I shall consider the parishes in this county in reference, first, to their value; secondly, their population.

And first, with reference to their value. One-half‡ of the livings above the annual value of £300 are appropriated as follows:

Three to absentees from the county { Llanvechain, Newtown, and Llan St. Ffraid.

Two to connections of the Bishops of Wales, but resident on their beneficos . . . . . . } Kerry and Llanllwchaearn.

Two to gentlemen connected with the Bishops of Wales, absentees from the county, and possessed of other benefices of equal value . } Castell Caereinion and Berriew.

Two to gentlemen ignorant of the Welsh language. . . . . } Llanrhaiadr and Machynlleth.

* I might venture, with much humility, to suggest, that the only satisfactory restraint on pluralities, would be a specific rule for each individual parish, according to its circumstances. At present, two evils arise,—the incumbent of two poor benefices is exposed to unjust odium, and the incumbent of wealthy "unions," is sheltered from his due share of censure.

† See table of Radnorshire in the appendix. On this subject see also Carlisle's Topographical Dictionary of Wales,—a useful and elaborate work.

‡ More than one-half, if we exclude from this computation two livings bestowed by the Crown, viz.—Montgomery and Llandysil.

Secondly, I shall take the test of population. It is almost needless to remark, that it will always be an object with a conscientious distributor of patronage, to render the Church most efficient in those places where her energies are most extensively demanded. Keeping this principle in view, we may now take a survey of the state of the Church in the four largest towns in Montgomeryshire.

NEWTOWN, £400.—The largest is held by a clergyman residing in Gloucestershire. A great part of the population of this place are but very imperfectly acquainted with English; yet, the officiating minister has for many years, uniformly been *a person ignorant of the Welsh language.*

MACHYNLLAETH, £400—is held by a clergyman ignorant of the language of the inhabitants. There is no town in the county in which English is less understood.

WELSH POOL — Christ Church, Oxford, £900, Vicar £300—is held by a clergyman who devotes himself to the duties of his parish with exemplary assiduity; and, much to his credit, maintains a curate out of its revenues, which are by no means ample when we consider the expenses incident to a populous parish. The merits of the individual are, however, a stigma, and not an eulogium on the system of patronage, which, instead of employing the sinecure rectories in this county in augmenting the religious funds of its more populous parishes, has conferred them on individuals living in remote counties of England, possessing no peculiar claim on the Church in Wales, or the Church generally. These observations are, however, much more forcibly applicable to the next instance, where merit is not combined with youth and fortune.

LLANIDLOES—Dean and Chapter of Bangor, £180, Vicar £180.— The incumbent is upwards of seventy years of age; forty-four years of his life has he spent as its officiating minister, (fourteen as its curate and thirty as its incumbent.) His clear income as vicar has rarely exceeded £100 per annum; and, till about a year ago, he had no prospect of such an increase of his resources as might enable him to obtain the assistance of a curate, in the performance of those duties for which his growing infirmities must shortly have incapacitated him. At length, however, in the 70th year of his age, his income was augmented; but, by what means? By a prebend or a sinecure?—By preferring him to a parish at once more opulent and less laborious? No! but, by adding another small benefice to that of which he was already in possession—thus depriving another parish of a resident incumbent—throwing upon him the odium of a pluralist, without conferring upon him, even for the few brief years, which he might yet expect to live, an income equal to that of any one of those benefices in this county, which are accumulated into pluralities—for men in the extreme of youth —unconnected with Wales—connected only with the dispensers of its Church patronage! I have dwelt at length upon this case, because it is a specimen of the system. The best livings are squandered in pluralities, from mere nepotism; and thus it comes to pass, that plurality in the small livings is the only expedient left for securing any thing like a decent maintenance for the meritorious part of the clergy!

ABSENTEEISM.—Putting sinecure rectors out of the question, ten of the parishes in Montgomeryshire are held by gentlemen who are absentees from the county altogether. Besides the benefices already enumerated as belonging to this class, are the following:—

GARTHBEIBIO, held by a gentleman resident in Caermarthenshire.

LLAN ST. FFRAID.—The rector and vicar are both absentees, resident in remote districts in England! Of this more by and by.

LLANWYDDELAN, held by a gentleman residing on the borders of Denbighshire and Caernarvonshire.

CARNO, LLANWYNOG, AND TREVEGLWYS.—These three, together with Llanidloes and Llandinam, constitute what is termed the comportion of Llandinam. In the reign of James the Second, more than two-thirds of the ecclesiastical tithes of this district were vested in the Dean and Chapter of Bangor, as trustees, for the following purposes:—one-third for the support of the vicars of these parishes, and the remaining two-thirds, first, for the repair of the cathedral—secondly, for the maintenance of the choir.

In the year 1812, the tithes thus vested in the Dean and Chapter had so much improved in value, that they came to a resolution of applying for an Act of Parliament, to enable them to borrow a sum of £5,000, on the security of the tithes, to be employed first, in erecting a Welsh church in Bangor; secondly, enlarging the cathedral; thirdly, augmenting the salaries of the vicars of that town, and in building dwelling-houses for the accommodation of those gentlemen. This project was thwarted by Dr. Pring, the organist of the cathedral, and other members of the choir, who presented a petition to the Court of Chancery, praying that the tithes might be applied in strict conformity to the Act of James, viz., first, to the support of the Montgomeryshire vicars; secondly, the repair of the cathedral; and thirdly, the maintenance of the choir; insisting that the whole of the surplus remaining after the accomplishment of the first two objects, ought, according to the Act, to be divided amongst the members of the choir. The Court decided in favour of this application; one of the results of its decision was to give—

To the organist, £138, double his original salary.

To the vicars of Bangor,* £249.

To each singing man, £40, four times his original salary!

To each singing boy, £20, being about eight times his original salary!

Though the Dean and Chapter of Bangor thus failed in changing the law as it stands under the Act of James, their attempt to do

* Before the decision in this case, it was never supposed that the vicars of Bangor (as members of the choir) had any claim to a portion of the fund; nor is it easy to reconcile such a claim (by whatever authority it may be supported) with the letter or spirit of the Act of James. That statute is framed for the relief of the choir, expressly on the ground, that it had at that time "no income or allowance;" now, the vicars of Bangor had then, and have now, *the tithes of the parish of Bangor:* it is impossible, then, to suppose that they were intended to be included in the Act, under the term "Choir."—See *Dr. Pring's Account of the Suit in Chancery,* page 249.

so relieves me from any difficulty which I might otherwise have felt, in contending, that, that act ought to be repealed; for, that, it ought to be repealed, is a principle which they themselves—the trustees under it—have thus irrevocably sanctioned. The only question is, to what purpose the tithes should be appropriated which are now fettered by its provisions? Which possesses the better claim—the town of Bangor, or the parishes on which they are levied, and from which they were taken by that act? On this subject, as a more matter of justice, there can hardly be much difference of opinion; but, when we recur to the present state of patronage in this part of Montgomeryshire, we shall find other grounds for arriving at a decided conclusion.

Of the five parishes in the comportion of Llandinam, the vicars of four are non-residents—three absentees from the county; in short, in the five parishes, there is only one resident incumbent—the vicar of Llanidloes! Two of the benefices, Llanwynog and Carno, have only one officiating minister between them,—a man whose kindness of disposition and exemplary life might, one would think, have exempted him from the fate of being, at an advanced age, the curate to two absentees—in the charge of two extensive parishes—with a salary from both, not amounting to £100 a-year!

These five benefices, together with that of Llangurig, constitute the hundred of Llanidloes, the population of which hundred, in the returns of the present year, amounts to 12,159

The population of the whole hundred of Is Gwyrfai, in which Bangor is situated, is scarcely more numerous . . 12,844

Yet, the tithes enjoyed by the resident clergy of the hundred of Is Gwyrfai are at least treble the amount of those in the hands of the clergy of the hundred of Llanidloes. Nay, what will be thought when it is added, that the two vicars of Bangor alone are possessed of emoluments which far exceed in amount the whole tithes set apart for the vicars of all these parishes put together! Still more singular is it, that in addition to the immense funds drawn from this district by the Cathedral, the scanty residue left for its religious wants should be squandered on absentees!!*

I shall now proceed to comment a little more at length on the state of some of the parishes just enumerated.

LLANVECHAIN, £750—is the richest living in the county; and, perhaps, of all its parishes, practically enjoys the smallest portion of it own endowments.

KERRY—Bishop £660, Vicar £330.—It is certainly a little hard upon this parish, the remotest in the whole diocese of St. David's from the episcopal residence, that, whilst one part of its tithes belongs to the Bishop, his connections should enjoy the remainder! The Bishop's tithes are on lease to his predecessor, Dr. Burgess, now Bishop of Salisbury, who when Bishop of this diocese, granted to a person connected with him, a lease, to commence after the expiration of an existing lease to a family in the neighbourhood; on his translation to another diocese, this new lease was assigned to him, and thus, his lordship (the Bishop of Salisbury) is now lessee of the tithes of Kerry! It is but justice to Dr. Burgess to add, that the revenues of the see of St. David's were, on the whole, augmented considerably by his disinterested refusal to renew leases of this kind.† Nor do I think that his conduct, in this instance, is deserving of any great censure; as he merely left the rights of the see, in this parish, in the same condition in which he had found them. It is, however, worthy of consideration, how far the power of granting concurrent leases at present possessed by our Bishops, is consistent with justice to their successors and the community. This grievance, of anticipating the income of the Church, by granting beneficial leases, is of great antiquity as far as this parish is concerned. "Upon July the 9th, anno 1637, the King (Charles I.) commanded him (the then Bishop of St. David's) that neither he nor his successors should renew the leases of the

---

* Before the Act of James, the Cathedral was repaired at the expense of the Bishop and Chapter (B. Willis's Bangor, p. 44); and, as stated in the Act, the annual income of the bishopric was not then more than £200. Since that time, an immense number of sinecure rectories have been annexed to the see.

† Dr. Burgess's general conduct, when Bishop of St. David's, entitled him to the gratitude of the Principality.

rectories of Kerry and Glascwm, then ready to expire, but hold them in demesne."—*Manby's St. David's*, p. 160.—The present vicar was intruded on the parishioners against their expressed wishes and feelings; and it may safely be affirmed, without any disparagement of his general merits, that his previous habits neither qualify him, in any peculiar degree, for the duties of a sequestered parish in Wales, nor to exhibit, in a very favourable light, the motives of those to whom he is thus indebted. The curate of the late vicar, in whose favour the parishioners petitioned, has remained since the death of the late vicar, not only without preferment, but—without employment in the Church!

CASTELL CAEREINION, £600—has been held for two-thirds of a century without intermission, by the relatives of the prelates of Wales; and during the whole of this time, the rich living of Gresford, in Denbighshire, at the other extremity of the diocese, has been enjoyed with it! (See *Brown Willis's Castell Caereinion and Gresford.*) The present incumbent, the Rev. Heneage Horsley, is resident in Edinburgh! His curate, who is upwards of seventy years of age, and at least twenty years older than his rector, is a man, whose pious attention to the duties of his profession is deserving of a far better fate. I have heard it alledged, indeed, that some apology is to be found for the mode in which he has been treated, in the circumstance, that he derives about £20 a year from a living in a neighbouring county, in which he has never resided. And, undoubtedly, this is a very good reason to those who choose to make it a reason; beyond question, there are laws in our day like those of classical fame, which, like cobwebs, may serve to strangle small flies, though large ones may easily break through them. This will be exemplified by the next instance.

BERRIEW, £450.—If non-residence be so peculiarly odious to the dispensers of patronage in Wales, it is rather singular, that they should have embarrassed the incumbent of this living, on his first entry into his profession, with two parishes at once, to one of which he must of necessity be a non-resident. Yet, this was literally the case; he received from his uncle, Bishop Luxmoore, two benefices, each worth £450 a-year—at the same time, and i the 24th year of his age, the earliest period at which any preferment could be either bestowed or accepted! The curate of Berriew is 73, more than double the age of his vicar. No one who considers the rights of the inhabitants of this extensive parish to such an appropriation of their religious funds as may ensure them the services of a youthful officiating minister,—as may relieve them from the repulsive spectacle of age burdened with labours fit only for youth, and youth enjoying emoluments that could not, with any degree of justice to the parishioners, have been awarded even to age,—will envy the feelings of those who are content to profit by such an arrangement.*

LLANRHAIADR.—The rectorial tithes, £1,000, were appropriated by an Act passed in 1680, to the repair of the Cathedral of St. Asaph, and the maintenance of the choir. The vicar's share, £450. He is unacquainted with the Welsh language. It is stated by Brown Willis, that before the passing of the Act of 1680, "the four singing men, choristers, and organists, and the reparation of the fabric, were maintained chiefly by subscriptions of the Church members, who, if they had not been gentlemen of generosity and zeal for the place, which may be attributed to their having been most of them natives of the diocese, the Church must have lain in ruins, and the inferior members could not have subsisted." Hence,

* Population of Berriew in 1815, 2,334. Under a recent statute, passed for the purpose of ensuring to stipendiary curates a salary proportioned to the population of parishes, the curate in this case was entitled to a salary of £150 from the present vicar; and yet, till Dr. Carey became Bishop of St. Asaph, he never received more than £100. This is a strong practical instance of the impossibility of regulating the income of curates by legislative compulsion. However clearly his liabilities may be defined, an avaricious incumbent will always have it in his power to find an individual, willing, either from local attachments or other motives, to accept a curacy on the terms of a compromise of his just legal claims. The Romish Church wisely provided for the working clergy, by giving them a share of the tithes,—and by transferring the right of appointment from the rector to the bishop. The curates were thus really safe from the encroachments of the rectors.

it appears, that there was a time when the Welsh people were as liberal to the Church as they now are to the Dissenting Chapel.

This Act, which originated with Bishop Lloyd, was, no doubt, well meant, as is proved by a provision it contains, by which seven other sinecure rectories were merged in the vicarages,—a measure, the disinterestedness of which will be duly appreciated by all who are familiar with the selfishness which is generally so conspicuous in the distribution of sinecure rectories. In the present day, however, it is well worth consideration, whether it is altogether just, that the immense sum of £1,000 should be annually drawn from this single parish, to be plunged into a sort of quicksand, in the shape of the Cathedral of St. Asaph! Were the edifice one of the noblest monuments of ancient architecture, we might well question the propriety of devoting to its support a fund sufficient to establish parochial schools through the whole county from which it is exacted;[*] and, we believe that those who can best appreciate the sublimity of art, would be the first to deem its very choicest relique an insignificant object compared to the general intelligence of a people. Nothing, then, ought to reconcile us to such a sacrifice, for the sake of a Cathedral, in a very common style of architecture. Rich as she is in the unfading magnificence of Nature, Wales would do well to leave to more favoured realms the inferior ornaments of art. The beauties of nature, an educated and religious people,—these are the true glories, and should be the only pride of the humble land of rock and mountain.

But, to return: if there ever was a case in which the feelings of a people ought to have been peculiarly consulted, it was in the application of the tithes still left to the vicar of this benefice. What, then, are we to think, when we find, that even the vicarial tithes belong to a gentleman unacquainted with their language![†] The Act of 1680 begins by reciting, that "The Cathedral Church

[*] This is not literally correct, as some part of this parish is in Denbighshire; this, however, does not affect the principle of my remarks.

[†] My remark is directed against the appointment, not against the individual.

of St. Asaph, by reason of the high and bleak situation thereof, near the sea, is much exposed to storms, and requireth great and frequent repairs." Those who look abroad, through the diocese of St. Asaph, will suspect that cathedrals may flourish at the self-same time that the living members of the church are fast fading away, and that it is high time for the friends of the Church of England to fortify her by nobler bulwarks than those which are proof only against—"seas and storms!"

GUILSFIELD.—Christ Church, Oxford, £900, Vicar £300.—Is in the possession of a gentleman of the name of Luxmore; neither of the clergymen of that name before alluded to. At least one-half of this parish is inhabited by people who do not understand the English language, and he is ignorant of Welsh, nor is Welsh service ever celebrated in the Church. At the same time, I feel it a duty to bear testimony to the pastoral assiduity of the reverend gentleman. When we consider the extent of his parish, and that he has been in the habit of maintaining a curate, it must be apparent, that his real emoluments are but trivial. He is worthy of a better system than that with which he has chosen to identify himself,—and under a better system, would have been deserving of a higher reward.

POOL, GUILSFIELD, MEIVOD, BUTTINGTON, £2,500—the greatest portion of the tithes of these four parishes were conferred on Christ Church, Oxford, in the time of Henry the Eighth; they originally belonged to the monastery of Strata Marcella, in this county. Without disputing, that the advantage of individual districts must, sometimes, and in some slight degree, be sacrificed to wide national improvements,—it is impossible not to feel, that the Principality has a stricter claim upon this fund, than is realized by its present application; particularly, when we remember, that in no part of the kingdom has the cause of education* been so much neglected by the government. That a direction of these revenues to some purpose more exclusively connected with her intellectual

* I may remark (and, I trust, without any feeling of intolerance), that Wales possessed at least as strong claims on the British Government, as the Catholic College of Maynooth.

privileges would not be injurious, but conducive to the general interests of learning—is a proposition supported by a writer, whose experience, piety, eloquence, and philosophical acumen, have given to his opinions on the subject of endowments an almost despotic authority. "There can be no doubt, that it would serve to multiply and diffuse the higher scholarship through England, were the Colleges of Oxford and Cambridge more dispersed than they now are over the face of the country. The distance of these great seminaries, or rather of these mighty aggregates of seminaries, is a barrier in the way of many families. Let these aggregates be, in some degree at least, broken up—by detaching so many of the separate institutions, and transferring them, with all their endowments, to other parts of the land; and we feel confident, that the whole amount of the nation's literature would be greatly increased. Each vicinity so blessed would brighten into a more highly lettered region than before, and we should there behold a more refined and accomplished society. The juxtaposition of a college would tell on the general habit of education in every town and neighbourhood wherein it should happen to be situated."—*Dr. Chalmers on Endowments*, p. 167.

PREBEND—MOCHDRE.—Jackson, Cambridge, £200, Vicar £100. —The tithes belonging to the Prebend are let on a lease for lives, and the Prebendary receives but a small sum from the lessee. This, however, does not improve the case, as far as the community are concerned; the only effect of leases of this description is to benefit one ecclesiastic at the expense of his successor;* the tithes are equally lost to the parishioners and the diocese, whether they

* The following is a description of the effects of the system of leases in question,—which is as gross an injustice to the Church and the community, as if those who granted the first lease had attempted to sell nine-tenths of the tithes.—The tithes of Mochdre belong to the prebendal stall at Brecon; but they are held on a lease for lives by a family in Brecknockshire. This sort of tenure is very common in regard to lands and tithes belonging to stalls in Cathedral and Collegiate Churches, and forms, in fact, a considerable part of the income of great and even noble families in England. A small reserved rent is annually paid to the Prebendary, and a fine of about two years' net

are enjoyed by a Prebendary at Cambridge, or (as is the case in this instance) by a lessee in Brecknockshire. Prebends were originally stipends for certain duties connected with the Cathedrals; at present, they are mere sinecures. In taking leave of this branch of Church preferment, I cannot help remarking that if it ever is applied in the promotion of learning, this certainly is not the case in this county. The only one of its resident clergy who has contributed to English theological literature is, at the age of forty, a curate, with a salary of £100 a-year, and he owes even this curacy to a lay corporation.* But, as this is an instance which belongs rather to England than to Wales, I will choose one which does indeed belong to the Principality. The name of Walter Davies is well known to all who are informed upon any one subject in which his country is peculiarly interested; independently of his merits as a pious and exemplary pastor, he has contributed to almost every work calculated to promote the honour and welfare of Wales: in addition to his researches into her past history, his works on those arts which most conduce to her advancement in wealth and civilization, are acknowledged to be the very best that have been written on those subjects. Is it possible to conceive higher claims—at least as far as this county is concerned? And what is his reward at that age when the strength of ordinary men is but labour and weakness? Neither prebend nor sinecure—but a mere third-rate benefice!

SINECURE RECTORIES.—Originally, every rector was bound to income is paid for the insertion of every new life in the lease. This, in common cases, occurs seldom, because the lessee always nominates a young and good life; and few incumbents, at the age when they usually are promoted to stalls, will have the temerity to *run* their lives against two others. Therefore, the lessee has always an advantage in negociating for the insertion of a *third* life; and, in fact, this sort of property is far more valuable to him than to his ecclesiastical principal. Mr. Jenkins, the late Prebend, received from his stall nothing but the reserved rent. One, indeed, of the lives "*dropped,*" but the fine offered for a renewal was so trifling, that he declined taking it!

* The Rev. Daniel Nihil, Curate of Forden.

reside; gradually, however, they contrived to devolve the whole duty on their vicars, who, like our modern curates, were paid by an arbitrary stipend. In the time of Henry the Third, an Act was passed, conferring on the vicars a portion of the tithes; generally, it is supposed, about one-half. *(Burn's Ecclesiastical Law.)* This Act was not meant to sanction the non-residence of rectors, but merely to improve the condition of vicars; and according to Dr. Burn, the non-residence of what are called sinecure rectors, is even yet nothing better than a venerable abuse ratified by no express statute or decision.

LLAN ST. FFRAID.—Sinecure Rector £500, Vicar £250.—Both absentees in remote districts of England! Curate's salary £90. This is a singular case indeed! The rector is an absentee, and takes with him two-thirds of the tithes; thus far we have merely an imitation, though certainly a very zealous one, of the worst abuses of Popery; but this is not all; with us, even the vicar also is allowed to play the non-resident,—the vicar, whose very duty, even in Popish times, it was to atone for the absence of another;—the vicar (himself a curate in the middle ages) is permitted in these days of light, to revive, in his own favour, the system of stipendiary curates,*—that very grievance, the removal of which was the only object of his endowments!†

LLANBRYN MAIR.—Sinecure Rector, W. Gibson, £300.—Absent in a remote part of England. Vicar £300. This sinecure has been held by gentlemen of the name of Gibson since the year 1775.

DAROWAIN.—Sinecure Rector, C. S. Luxmoore, Dean of St. Asaph, £120. Resident in Herefordshire. Vicar £120. The Vicar is in his 77th year—double the age of the rector. Without adverting to the claims of the Vicar, it is impossible not to feel

* The curate is an amiable and worthy man, which may, in some measure, enable the parishioners to endure the injustice that is accumulated upon them.

† "When a vicar is instituted, he (besides the usual forms) takes, if required by the Bishop, an oath of perpetual residence; for the maxim of law is—vicarius non habet vicarium."—*Blackstone's Commentaries*, vol. i. page 389.

the strongest indignation at an arrangement thus unjust to the parishioners—which leaves the duty of their parish to the oldest clergyman in the county, and confers half its scanty revenues upon an individual, who, though an absentee from the county and the diocese, enjoys a larger share of the income of the Church in Wales than any other clergyman whatever!

BISHOPS' LIVINGS.

Llandrinio	Bishop of St. Asaph in commendam.	£550	......	Curate	£120
Llandysilio		450	......	Curate	120
Pennant		300	......	Vicar	120*

£1300

The two first of these parishes were added to the bishopric since the restoration,—the third within the last twenty years! Thus, in the course of a century and a half, has the immense sum of £1,300 been added to the see of St. Asaph from this single county. Most of my readers are probably aware, that the term "commendam" signifies, in this case, a power vested in the Crown, of enabling a Bishop to hold other preferments in addition to his regular revenues.

The alleged object of this power is the augmentation of poor bishoprics; and if the possessors of power were free from human infirmities, this would be a good defence of the system of commendams. Unhappily, however, the three parishes in question afford us abundant proof, that "the augmentation of poor bishoprics," is not the purpose to which it has generally been applied; as we have seen—the two first of these livings were annexed to the see at the restoration, a period when, according to Burnett, the Church was profusely rich, owing to the funds which had accumulated during the civil wars; *(History of his own Times)*—and the third benefice was added at a time of growing agricultural prosperity! Next to the practice of translations, nothing tends so much to infuse into the Church a spirit

---

* £120 is the proper income of the vicar. The present Bishop, Dr. Carey, has augmented the vicarage by the addition of £80 of the rectorial tithes; he has evinced similar liberality in other instances. In treating of the principle of this case, I have adhered to the usual division.

of political subserviency as that of commendams; and I cannot help expressing my regret, that the present estimable head of the Church of England should have defended the latter, at the same time that he admitted the impropriety of the former. The argument advanced by his lordship in favour of commendams, viz. that they are a part of the prerogative of the Crown, is equally applicable to translations, which are also a prerogative of the Crown. The prerogatives of the Crown may be limited by Parliament, when clearly at variance with religion and liberty; nay, our Protestant Church is secured by such restrictions—restrictions of a far more extensive character than that now contended for—and wrung from Monarchs who set a far higher value upon corrupt influence than our present excellent sovereign.*

A considerable portion of the tithes of this county are in lay hands: of individual lay tithe owners, no peculiar remarks suggest themselves; one parish, however, which is in the hands of a Lay Corporation, cannot be passed by without some observations.

CHURCHSTOKE, £900.—Its tithes belong to "the Warden and poor men of Clun Hospital," an Institution which strongly demands Parliamentary enquiry. In addition to Churchstoke, and other property, the tithes of Knighton, in Radnorshire, belong to it. When we consider the amount of these funds, and when it is added that the sums paid by the Hospital, to the late curate of Churchstoke, at the age of seventy, did not exceed £60, we may conjecture, that a smaller portion of the tithes of this parish were

* The sees of St. Asaph and Bangor were both, in the time of Elizabeth, rather poor; but now, owing to the continual additions that have been made to them out of the Church property of the dioceses, they are two of the wealthiest in the kingdom. St. Asaph is double the value of Oxford, Bristol, and several other bishoprics, the duties of which are of a far more arduous character than those of the Welsh dioceses. It is, perhaps, needless to remark, that the efficiency of our Bishops has not increased with increased wealth, which has only served as a new temptation to the Ministers of the day, to employ our sees for political purposes, in contempt of the religious wants of the country.

expended on him, than on any one of the paupers, maintained in idleness by the Hospital! I am fully aware, that his income was, in some degree, augmented by Queen Anne's bounty; but this circumstance can only make us regret, that the pious benevolence of that Princess, which was intended for the benefit of the poorer clergy, should, in so many instances, only serve to swell the mass of existing abuses, by exonerating the lay tithe owners and the more opulent clergy, from those burdens, which in all reason, they ought exclusively to bear.* Curate's income, £200, of this, £60 comes from Queen Anne's bounty.

From the foregoing detail, it will appear, that at least one-half of the parishes of this county, are scenes of abuses, which, it is equally impossible to justify and to deny—abuses which, he that runs may read! I shall now compare the amount of Church property, in the hands of absentees from the county, clergymen ignorant of the Welsh language, &c., &c., with the aggregate revenues of the clergy generally.

TITHES HELD BY

ABSENTEES FROM THE COUNTY.—Berriew, £450.—Castell Caereinion, £600.—Garthbeibio, £100.—Carno, £100.— Llan St. Ffraid, £250.—Llanwyddelan, £300.—Newtown, £400.—Llanwynog, £205.—Treveglwys, £110.— Llanvechain, £750...................................... 3265

BISHOPS.†—Llandrinio, §£550.—Llandysilio, §£450.—Pennant, §£300.—Kerry, £660.......................... 1960

PREBEND.—Mochdre 200

SINECURES.—Darowain, £120.—Llanbryn Mair, £300.— Llan St. Ffraid, £500................................. 920

CATHEDRALS.—Llandinam, §£560.—Llanwynog, §£410.— Carno, §£90.—Llanidloes, £180.—Treveglwys, §£65.— Llanrhaiadr, §£1000 2305

* I have good authority for stating that so far back as 1809, there was an accumulation of money belonging to the Hospital, of upwards of £12,000; since which period, the tithes in this parish have nearly tripled in annual amount.

† The rectoral tithes of all those parishes marked thus § have been added to the Cathedrals and the bishoprics within the last two centuries. The collective value of these tithes is £3,605!

CHRIST CHURCH, OXFORD.—Guilsfield, £900.—W. Pool, £900.—Meivod, £500.—Buttington, £200............ 2500
CLUN HOSPITAL 906
INCUMBENTS IGNORANT OF THE WELSH LANGUAGE.—Llanrhaiadr, £450.—Machynllaeth, £300*.................... 850
RELATIVES OF THE BISHOPS.—Guilsfield, £300.—Kerry, £330.—Llan-llwchhaearn, £400†...................... 1030

Sum Total, held as above......£13,930

FROM THE ABOVE, IS TO BE DEDUCTED, THE SALARIES OF THE CURATES, OF BISHOPS AND ABSENTEES, VIZ :—

Llandrinio, £120.—Llandysilio, £120.—Berriew, £150.—Castell Caereinion, £70.—Treveglwys, £70.—Carno, £40. Llanwynog, £55.—Llan St. Ffraid, £90.—Llanwyddelan, £70.—Llanvechain, £70.—Garthbeibio, £60.—Newtown, £100.—Churchstoke,‡from Clun Hospital, £100 1115

Sum Total, enjoyed as above......£12,815

GENERAL BODY OF RESIDENT INCUMBENTS.

Aberhafesp, £250.—Buttington, £100.—Bettws, £250.—Cemaes, £350.—Churchstoke,‡ £100.—Darowain, £120.—Forden, £100.—Hirnant, £180.—Hissington, £160.—Llanbryn Mair, £300.—Llandinam, £290.—Llangurig, £200.—Llanidloes, £180.—Deuddwr, £100.—Llanerfyl, £300.—Llanvair, £400.—Llan Vihangel, £350.—Llanvyllin, £500.—Llangadvan, £300.—Llangynyw, £350.—Llangynog, £120.—Llanllugan, £50.—Llanmerewig, £100.—Llanwyddyn, £100.—Llanwrin, 400.—Llandysil, £450. Manavon, £300.—Mochdre, £100.—Meivod, £500.—Montgomery, £400.—Welsh Pool, £300.—Pennant, Vic. £102 (and £80 added by Bishop Carey).—Penegoes, £300. —Penystrowed, £140.—Snead, £90.—Tregynon, £81.

Total, enjoyed as above......£8511

* Besides these, the Prebendary, the three Sinecurists, and four of the absentees, are ignorant of the Welsh language.

† Berriew and Castell Caereinion, are held by Bishops' relatives, who are classed amongst the "Absentees."

‡ Queen Anne's Bounty—house and garden, £100.

Great as are the abuses, which form the subject of the foregoing remarks, they are, after all, a mere index to the general spirit in which the patronage of the whole Church is administered. I do not mean, of course, to affirm that worth and piety are uniformly in poverty, or that the emoluments of the Church always fall to the share of the profligate priest; but I leave it to the experience of a certain class of my readers, whether the estimable clergy are not depressed *quite as often* as the undeserving. But it is not so much by neglect of the broad distinctions between the extremes of vice and virtue, that an unjust spirit is manifested, as by a disregard to degrees of merit—by the manner in which the best preferments are generally conferred on mere negative characters, whilst men of first-rate professional claims are past over altogether, or receive only mere second-rate rewards. In short, the best that can be said of the system of patronage is, that it apportions its boons like the lottery wheel, if not in hostility to merit without any respect to it.

And here I may take the opportunity of declaring, that nothing is farther from my intention than to cast an indiscriminating stigma upon the resident clergy of the county of Montgomery; and I may appeal to those who possess opportunities of forming a judgment on such a subject, whether I have not, throughout the whole of the preceding remarks, evinced the utmost anxiety to do justice to individuals, without reference to the passions or the parties of the day. This humble claim will, I feel confident, be admitted; and I cannot help believing, that should any trivial error of judgment or of fact have occurred in the previous observations, candid men of all parties will feel inclined to ascribe it to the infirmity of human judgment and the intricacy and delicacy of some topics, ratner than to a spirit of factious and wilful misrepresentation.

Of a very large portion of the clergy of this county, I might truly say, that they are amiable, pious and charitable; of a large majority, that their lives are in strong contrast with those of their predecessors of the last century, who spent six days out of the seven in tippling in ale houses, or in the rude sports of the demoralized squirarchy of their day. My remarks, I repeat it, are not directed against the clergy as a body, but against that base system of ecclesiastical mal-administration, which is no less unjust to them than to their country. Yet, notwithstanding the reform that has to a great extent taken place in the lives of the clergy, it is a fact too well known to be questioned, that Dissent has of late years progressed with an increased momentum; and this is perfectly consistent with an opinion previously expressed,* that the virtues of individual ministers always operate against a Church, which, as a whole, is in a corrupt state of administration. Nothing, then, but a fundamental reform of her system can save the Church in Wales.

In that part of Montgomeryshire which lies in the Welsh dioceses, the Dissenting Chapels are in more than a treble proportion to the Churches of the Establishment.†

Churches and Chapels of Ease belonging to the Established Church 49
Dissenting Chapels 154

More than one-half of these Dissenting Chapels have arisen within the last twenty-two years; the number ascribed to this county for the year 1810, in Peter's *Hanes Crevydd*, is 74.

Strong as are the expressions contained in this chapter, the reader will find terms still more unqualified employed, in an able article, published since the first edition of this Essay, in the *British Critic and Theological Quarterly*, a publication which cannot be suspected of any other feelings but those of attachment to the true interests of the Church.

"With the House of Hanover and Sir R. Walpole came parliamentary management and corruption; and that abominable exercise of a most important function of the Crown, which has prevailed, with little intermission, to the present day. Without having

---

* See account of Griffith Jones's Schools in the first Chapter.

† To those parishes in Montgomeryshire which are situated in the diocese of Hereford, the principles evolved in this Essay do not apply, the people have but little of the Welsh character, and their language is English. There is but one Chapel in the whole district.

recourse to exaggeration, we may safely say, that not *one* Bishop in *five* was appointed from proper motives, during the long period which elapsed between the administration of Walpole and of Liverpool." p. 224. "Such as are the Bishops which the Crown is pleased to place over it, such, in point of efficiency, order, and strength, must be the Established Church; and what probability is there, in the nature of things, or from the results of experience, that the Crown will generally and wisely consult the interests of religion. Looking to the almost universal practice of mankind, we see that patronage of every description is used more as an instrument of the gratification of power, than under any sense of duty. And looking to the manner in which the Church patronage has been exercised, from the Revolution to the present day, what hope can we entertain of seeing it made effectual for the promotion of religion?" * * * "And we implore the reader to reflect, for a moment, upon the consequences of such a system. In the first place, most men raised to the bench by the abuse of patronage are found to show respect to their patrons, by faithfully imitating their example. When a Bishop owes his consecration to a job, he will, in nine cases out of ten, be a jobber himself. Ministers make a Bishop from private and unworthy motives, and then wonder that he should be guilty of nepotism!" * * * "If all clergymen holding public preferment were meritorious persons, not only would they stimulate the rest of their brethren to become so likewise, but lay patrons would feel that their sons and brothers must be disgraced, if they did not acquit themselves respectably in the performance of their sacred duties. Whereas, while the Minister of the Crown creates inefficient prelates, and such prelates prefer their inefficient sons, nephews, and cousins, to the fourth and fifth generation, what can be expected of a private gentleman possessing an advowson? Why should he be required to have a greater regard for the Church than the head of the Church!" * * "In the matter of patronage, therefore, that poison which is thrown into the spring at its source, may be detected in every drop which is drawn from the stream as it flows, in every ripple which creeps along the bank, and in every billow which rolls in darkness to the sea." * * * "Such are a few of the evils arising from a bad appointment of Bishops; it leads to other and more numerous abuses—it gives a sanction to every species of ecclesiastical irregularity—it checks and stints the education of youth—it fills the Church and country with inefficient ministers of the Word of God." p. 227.

As is stated by the reviewer, the decay of the Church of England, as an institution, may be dated from the administration of Walpole. But the unhallowed policy of that minister brought a double blight upon the religious institutions of the Principality. The Welsh were attached to the cause of the unfortunate House of Stewart; and hence, in his conduct towards that people, it was natural for the minister of the House of Hanover, to be guided no less by political resentment, than by his habitual disregard to things sacred. The practice of introducing Englishmen into the Welsh bishoprics had been frequently adopted since the Restoration; and, we know that the seeds of Dissent had already been widely sown, even by this occasional deviation from principle. But from the days of Walpole, the Welsh sees have uniformly been filled with Englishmen; and it is highly important to observe, that the establishment of the system of perfect exclusion was accompanied by a coincidence too strong to have been merely accidental—for, it was coeval with the commencement of Methodism in the Principality!

The extent to which Welshmen have, since that time, been excluded from the higher dignities of their Church, may be judged of, by comparing, in this respect, two periods of eighty-five years each; the first beginning at the Restoration in 1660, and ending in 1745, (the date of the great rebellion,)—the second era beginning in 1745, and ending in 1830.

ST. ASAPH DIOCESE.

Number of Englishmen and Welshmen, in possession of higher Preferments, compared.

I.—FROM 1660 TO 1745.

ENGLISHMEN.	WELSHMEN.
9 BISHOPRIC. — Glemham,* Barrow, Hooper, Beveridge, Fleetwood, Hare, Tanner, Maddox, Lisle.	4 Griffith, Lloyd, (born in England, of Welsh origin,) Jones, Wynne.
3 DEANERY.—Stratford, Bright, Stanley.	4 D. Lloyd, H. Lloyd, Price, Powell.
SINECURE RECTORIES.	5 Foulkes, Davies, Williams, Jones, Morris.
2 *Cwm.*—Rogers, Babington.	
1 *Corwen.*—Wells.	2 Eyton, Wynne.
1 *Darowain.*—Mardaveil.	7 Hughes, Lloyd, Jones, Owen, Rowland, Jones, Parry.
0 *East Hope.*	6 J. Parry, B. Parry (doubtful), Edwards, Lloyd, Wynne, Jones, Powel.
1 *Kilcain.*—Clopton.	2 Lloyd, Davies.
4 *Llanarmon-yn-Ial.* — Backhouse, Hare, Tanner, Maddox, Lisle.	5 Lloyd, Eyton, Maurice, Davies, Wynne.
2 *Llanbryn Mair.*—Lloyd, Ward.	2 Foulkes, Vaughan.
3 *Llandrillo-yn-Edeyrnion.* — Clutterbuck, Carter, Tanner.	0
1 *Llangwm.*—Weston.	2 Davies, Powel.
2 *Llan St. Ffraid.* — Nicholson, Stratford.	4 Lloyd, Price, Edwards, Wynne.
5 *Llansannan,* 1st portion.—Herault, Ford, Montford, Holborn, Hare.	6 J. Lloyd, D. Lloyd, E. Lloyd, Richards, Wynne, Owen.
4 2nd portion.—Barker, Todd, Fleetwood, Horsley.	1 Ellis.
3 *Pennant.* — Hitchcock, Ashton, Dubois.	1 Richards.
1 *Whitford.*—Swan.	3. Lloyd, J. Mostyn, R. Mostyn.
0 CHANCELLORSHIP.	6 Jones, Powel, Edwards, H. Wynn, R. Wynn, Salisbury.
43 Total Englishmen.	60 Total Welshmen.

* My evidence of national origin, in most of the following cases, are NAMES, which, although not a perfectly accurate criterion, are sufficiently so for the purpose of this comparison; an Englishman may sometimes have a Welsh name, and vice versa; but the errors will balance each other.

II.—From 1745 to 1830.

ENGLISHMEN.		WELSHMEN.
7 BISHOPRIC. — Drummond, Newcome, Shipley, Bagot, Horsley, Cleaver, Luxmoore.		0
3 DEANERY.—Herring, Shipley, Luxmoore		0
SINECURE RECTORIES.		0
5 *Cwm.*—Hay, Batley, Adams, Halifax, Finch.		1 Morgan.
7 *Corwen.*—Lisle, Palmer, Shipley, Geo. Prettyman, J. Prettyman, Sneyd, Cleaver.		
7 *Darowain.*—Murray, Burleigh, Newcome, Randolph, Huddersford, Barnard, C. S. Luxmoore.		1 Worthington.
3 *East Hope.*—Hay, Shipley, Thurlow.		1 Worthington.
6 *Kilcain.* — Wells, Allen, Newcome, Poyntz, Delap, Corrie.		0
3 *Llanarmon-yn-Ial.*—Lushington, Shipley, J. M. Luxmoore.		0
2 *Llanbryn Mair.*—R. Gibson, W. Gibson.		0
3 *Llandrillo-yn-Edeyrnion.*—Upton, Bertie, Thurlow.		2 Holland, Price.
4. *Llangwm.*—Shipley, Watson, Everard, Bagot.		1 Holland.
3 *Llan St. Ffraid.*—Bouchery, Beauclerk, Thorton.		0
7 *Llansannan*, 1st portion.—J. Johnson, Palmer, Drummond, Brakenbridge, Newcome, Smith, Sampson.		1 Strong.
3 2nd portion.—Shipley, Poynts, W. Cleaver.		2 Worthington, Clough.
6 *Pennant.* — Shipley, Poyntz, Murray, Sturges, Bp. Cleaver, Bp. Luxmoore.		0
2 *Whitford.*—Gouch, J. M. Luxmoore.		1 Jeffreys.
2 CHANCELLORSHIP. — Shipley, C. S. Luxmoore.		0

73 Total Englishmen.   10 Total Welshmen!!

CHAPTER V.—Conclusion.

PROGRESSIVE SPOLIATION, BY THE ENGLISH GOVERNMENT, OF THE RELIGIOUS AND LITERARY ENDOWMENTS OF WALES.—THE SYSTEM ON WHICH THE CHURCH IS AT PRESENT ADMINISTERED NO LESS INJURIOUS TO HER INTELLECTUAL ADVANCEMENT AND TEMPORAL PROSPERITY, THAN TO HER RELIGIOUS INTERESTS.

"The funds that were absorbed during the period of that unprincipled scramble, would not only have sustained a sufficient number of functionaries, for the purposes both of literary and Christian education; but there would have been enough, and to spare, for the decent and respectable maintenance of them all. . . . . This also has gone to wreck along with the other noble interests which perished in the wildness of that revolutionary storm; and in this little age of calculators and economists, there are patriots who can rejoice in such a consummation. The age of moral chivalry is gone!"
Dr. Chalmers on Endowments.

"The like or greater difficulties have the poor Welsh people often and of old laboured under, to rekindle the Lamp of God in their Sanctuary."
Griffith Jones, of Llanddowror.

THE history of the Cambro-British Church is the record of one unremitting wrong. Planted in primitive, if not in apostolic times,* she was the last among the western nations to bend to the usurpations of the Romish hierarchy; and it is the opinion of the eloquent Monsieur Thierry, that her attachment to the cause of ancient religious liberty, made her over afterwards an object of persecution to that fearful despotism. From the day that the Cambrian ecclesiastics renounced the claims of her emissary, the Monk Augustine,† every enemy of the Britons became the ally of Rome!

* Bishop Burgess's Works. Hughes's *Horæ Britannicæ.*

† The conference with Augustine (A. D. 607) was attended by seven British Bishops and a great number of religious men, chiefly from the great monastery of Bangor on the Dee. "We will never acknowledge," said those among them who were appointed to speak, "we will never acknowledge the pretended rights of Roman ambition, any more than those of Saxon tyranny."

She blessed the ferocities of the Saxon Pagans; she hallowed the aggressions of the Norman with her consecrated banner.* In later times she sanctioned the power assumed by the Norman Kings of England, of filling all the dignities of the Welsh Church with their creatures,—that dreadful oppression so beautifully described in the petition of the Welsh Princes, which set the brand of sacrilege on the most exalted chivalry, and turned even the rites of religion against the expiring liberties of their land.

These were dark days of open hostility; and we may pass on to the reign of Henry the Seventh, in whose person the Welsh once more vanquished their oppressors in a fair-fought field,—recovered that freedom which they had lost, and realized the proudest aspirations of their nation, by restoring the throne of Britain to the descendants of their ancient Kings.† The accession of the House of Tudor might have been expected to open a new era in the history of the religious institutions of Wales; and, undoubtedly the general dispositions of Henry the Seventh and of several of his successors, toward that country, were eminently kind and paternal. But, unhappily, notwithstanding the patriotic views of individual Sovereigns,—the most important measures adopted by the English Government towards her, since his time, were marked with such striking features of injustice, that the eloquent foreign writer alluded to—an impartial authority,—has declared, that even since the reign of that Monarch, almost equally as before, Wales has been treated in the contemptuous style used towards a conquered country, rather than in that spirit which is due to a faithful and free ally. The following is an extract from the French historian, whose profound research is surpassed only by his eloquence, and whose minute knowledge of Welsh history may put many of our country-

We owe to the Pope of Rome, as to all Christians, the submission of fraternal charity; but as for the submission of obedience, we owe it only to God, and after God, to our venerable superior the Bishop of Ker-leon on the Usk.' *M. Thierry's History of the Norman Conquest*, vol. i. page 68.

* Thierry.

† Two thirds of Henry the Seventh's army at Bosworth were Welshmen.

men to shame. It is impossible to read the following passage without feelings of the deepest humiliation, when we recollect, that it is a narrative of the first fruits experienced by Wales, of the reformation and the revival of learning in England!

"When the religious supremacy of the Pope had been abolished in England, the Welsh, to whom the Roman Church had never chosen to lend any aid for the maintenance of their independence, adopted, without reluctance, the changes decreed by the Government of England. But the Government, whilst it gave every encouragement to the translation of the Bible into English, did not cause it to be translated into Welsh. On the contrary, some persons of that country, zealous for the new reforms, having undertaken at their own cost, the translation and publication of the Scriptures, so far from being praised for it, as had been the case in England, orders were given for the seizure and destruction af all copies, which were carried off from the Churches and publicly burnt. The English authorities attacked about the same time the manuscript and historical documents, more numerous at that time in Wales than in any other European country. Many families which had private archives were obliged to bury them in the earth, in order to secure them from the requisitions of the royal agents!!"—*Thierry's History of the Norman Conquest*, vol. i. p. 376.

Amongst the complaints urged by the Welsh Princes against the English Bishops of those days are the following. "And whatever they can take from us, either by right or wrong, is carried away by them into England, and squandered in the abbeys that are given to them by the King of England."

"Because they do not love our country, the lands which were given by our forefathers of old to the bishoprics, they transfer to priests and others who may happen to covet them."

To understand the full import of these expressions, requires a brief digression:

Long before the conquest of North Wales by Edward the First, the most fertile and beautiful districts in South Wales had fallen successively a prey to the incursions of the Norman knights and barons. In conformity to the religious views of their day, these adventurers generally devoted a portion of the spoil to the foundation of some religious house, which they filled with monks of their own nation; at other times, they conferred a large share of the tithes of their new territory on English or even Norman monasteries. In addition to these extortions, Wales was at last exposed to the grievances which form the subject of the petition of the Welsh Princes; a considerable time before the accession of Edward I., the Kings of England contrived, by the connivance of the Roman Pontiff, to render the Welsh Church subject to the Archbishopric of Canterbury, and thus to intrude their dependents on her sees in both divisions of the Principality. Thus, before the final subjugation of Wales, a considerable portion of her Church revenues had passed into the hands of foreigners. It is a singular fact, that during the three first reigns after that event, the North Welsh had very few English prelates imposed upon them;* it would seem, that in those days this measure was regarded as so far partaking of the character of sacrilege, that even her conquerors did not care to resort to it, after they had once completely achieved their favourite object of conquest. But in the time of Henry the Fourth, the insurrection of Glyndwr awakened a stern spirit of resentment in her English rulers, which made North Wales the scene of the most horrible calamities. Her ancient aristocracy were degraded by oppression into so many captains of banditti, who preserved their territories only by waging an incessant and ferocious warfare against the English authorities and each other. Welshmen were excluded from all offices of authority and trust in their own country,—from that of "a judge, a viscount, or a chancellor," down to the humble rustic dignity of "a forester."† And, to return to my subject, the Welsh bishoprics were again transferred to English ecclesiastics, and the revenues of the Church in North Wales (as had previously been the case in the South), became the booty of monks of the English nation.

* B. Willis's Bangor and St. Asaph. † Thierry.

Such, then, was the condition to which the Welsh Church had been reduced shortly before the Reformation; and at that bright era in the history of England—of Christianity, and of mankind; remembering that that great revolution was consummated under a dynasty indebted to the Welsh people for their throne,—who is there that does not expect to learn that some important boon was conceded to the Principality? Who is there that is not prepared, at least, to find that she was then relieved from those complicated burdens which ages of Popery and of bondage had accumulated? To rescue her scanty Church revenues from the monks and sinecurists of England,—this was nothing more than the rudest sense of justice might have dictated; and had this been done, not only would a fund have been provided—ample enough to maintain her ministers in decency,—but colleges might have been endowed for the education of her higher classes, and parochial schools for the benefit of her peasantry. But, alas! the measures of those days were any thing but those of justice or of conciliation! Not only were no steps taken to restore to the Principality those revenues of which she had most unrighteously been deprived,—but the robbery in times of peace proved worse than the spoliation of the times of war, and the rapacity of the Reformation was added to the rapacity of Popery! In North Wales, the poor county of Merioneth was stripped—for the erection of the new bishopric of Lichfield—of tithes equal in amount to nearly one-half of the whole income of all her resident clergy put together! Caernarvonshire was, in the like manner taxed for that of Chester;* and the new Bishops in other parts

* This bishopric is by no means wealthy; and, perhaps, there never was a time when it was less for the public interest that it should be poor. But, why should Wales be forced to contribute to the support of the religious Establishment of England, as well as her own? The revenues of the Bishops of St. Asaph and Bangor arise solely from their dioceses; why should not this be the case in the more fertile provinces of England? Every principle of justice demands that those funds which are exacted from the Principality, and which were, beyond a question, conferred on the Church solely with a view to her religious interests should be restored to her. Neither would national justice work injustice to individuals, as the life interests of individuals might be

of England were pensioned upon South Wales! Whatever, in the present day, may be urged in defence of these abuses, they are still —what they were at first—mere remnants of servitude—an unjust tribute wrung from a poor country, to swell the wealth of one already immensely opulent, a tribute, not like that of "wolves' heads," which King Edgar is said to have exacted from our forefathers,—but levied on the virtue, intelligence, and civilization of our land! In other parts of North Wales, the richest parishes were made the perquisites of English Colleges, from which the Principality derives very little benefit indeed—compared to the amount of her contributions.

In South Wales, the pillage was more fearfully complete; the great tithes of almost every parish were conferred upon laymen— the descendants of its Norman invaders, or on families which have now become estranged from it for many generations. Even what was preserved to the Church, was, to a great extent, lost to the Principality. As before stated, a perpetual tax was imposed on South Wales, for the support of several of the English bishoprics; and the patronage of most of the puny endowments still spared for the religious emergencies of the country, was parcelled out amongst lay tithe-owners—the Crown—the Bishops of English dioceses— sinecurists in England,* and the sinecurists of the Welsh Cathedrals. From such a system of patronage nothing could be expected but a corrupt, an unpopular Church; lay patrons are rarely actuated by strong religious motives; the patronage of the Crown has almost uniformly been employed in converting the ministers of religion into the leaders of a petty local faction; and ecclesiastics resident in England must, of course, feel an inclination to favour their

preserved; nor would any injury be done to the Church, as an institution, by applying her revenues in stricter conformity to the purposes for which they were bestowed.

* In the county of Glamorgan alone, no fewer than ten parishes, (including many populous towns,) are in the gift of the Dean and Chapter of Gloucester! Nothing can be more unfair to Wales, than this privilege of introducing Englishmen into her benefices; (for such it is practically)—nothing more injurious to the Church.

English friends, in preference to men conversant with the language and feelings of the country; and when it is remembered that the Bishops of Wales themselves have not set any very high example of self-denial, it was hardly to be expected that these distant ecclesiastical bodies would evince any peculiar sense of their responsibility to the parishes at their disposal. The effects of the measures adopted by Henry the Eighth in South Wales have been already pretty fully described, in the extracts which I have from time to time made from the writings of Griffith Jones, of Llanddowror. From the Reformation to the end of the last century the clergy of that country, for the most part, consisted of men sunk in poverty, and little raised in intelligence above the populace. I may quote the words of a worthy friend, a native of that division of Wales. "The livings in South Wales are so poor, that very few gentlemen's sons are brought up to the Church; and in my recollection, the clergy in South Wales, (I mean many of them,) were so ignorant, that they could not write a common English letter correctly, and were also addicted to low company, and fond of tippling in taverns."

It was this general ignorance and immorality of its ministers which prepared the minds of the people in South Wales for that sudden revolt from the Church which has already been narrated. The Dissent of North Wales is of later date. In the present day, many of the clergy of South Wales are very pious and excellent men; and I believe, that the character drawn by my informant is not very applicable to any of them; but, nevertheless, the Church, as an institution, is in a most melancholy condition! It is impossible for the mind of man to conceive a more appalling picture of devastation, than is presented by a mere muster-roll of the names of the present possessors of Church property in many of the South Wales counties. Opposite to the most valuable part of the endowments of the most valuable benefices, we shall generally find the name of some English nobleman or gentleman, resident in London, in Devonshire, in the most distant parts of the kingdom; and again, in juxtaposition with the paltry pittances left to the clergy, we shall continually meet with the name of some reverend pluralist, living equally remote—the incumbent, it may be, of a rich benefice in Northamptonshire—or residing, free from all parochial duties, in London! Would that this were an imaginary picture; but, alas! it is but a too literal description of the Church, as it exists in Radnorshire and Cardiganshire, the two poorest counties in South Wales.* Thus, in our days, the miserable stipends which even the tender mercies of Henry the Eighth reserved for her pastors, have, in many instances, followed her nobler endowments—and, like them, been scattered to the four winds of heaven! To the Church Establishment of South Wales, we may almost apply the sentence inscribed by a traveller, on the remains of Strata Florida—(that venerable abbey, which was the depository of her history—the asylum of her poets—the sepulchre of her ancient kings,)—"ipsæ periere ruinæ,"—even its ruins have perished!

Of late years, invidious comparisons have occasionally been drawn between the mental claims of Wales and those of other parts of the kingdom, more particularly Scotland; as if the Welsh were themselves to blame for that Tartar spirit which has crushed the very elements of learning and of genius in their land! Would it not be more just to award them their meed of praise, for sustaining the character of an eminently moral, religious, and loyal people, even under an abused Church, and a Government anything but paternal?

Adverting to the scantiness of her population, it can hardly be affirmed, after all, that Wales has been more barren of illustrious men, than her more highly favoured neighbours—even in modern times; and down to the time of Chaucer, she was more fertile in works of imagination, the only literature of those days, than any part of the island.† The enthusiasm with which her peasantry

* See table of Radnorshire. In Cardiganshire the most considerable tithe-owner is a gentleman of the name of Chichester, resident in Devonshire.

† See Sharon Turner's Defence of the Bards, and various parts of the periodical called "The Cambrian Quarterly."

availed themselves of Griffith Jones's schools—the advances which they have made since his time—and without any intrinsic aid, amply demonstrate, that they are naturally fond of knowledge, and industrious in the pursuit of it.

In his valuable work on Endowments, Dr. Chalmers ascribes the mental forwardness of Scotland to two causes; the appropriation of her Church endowments to a clergy exclusively national,—parochial schools extended through the whole country—her three national colleges, which communicate a competent and diversified share of attainment to the many, and at the same time afford opportunities of distinguished excellence to the few: by these means, every latent seed of genius has been, as it were, detected, economized, and matured; and the result has been a high degree of national greatness. Wales, unhappily, has had no such schools or colleges; and whenever a seminary has been founded by individuals, it has generally fallen into an abuse in less than a century. But to complete the parallel, or rather the contrast, would be to retrace the thorny path which I have already trodden.*

One measure only was still needed to consummate the intellectual nakedness of the land—and to lay the whole Principality open to the inroads of sectarianism or irreligion. Protected by their poverty, the benefices of North Wales had in a great measure escaped the rapacity of Henry the Eighth; neverthe-

* I may take this opportunity of stating a fact, probably little known to most of my readers, that a Society has recently been established, for the publication of Essays in the Welsh Language, in connection with the Society for the Promotion of Useful Knowledge. The Principality is chiefly indebted for this excellent project to the present Lord Chancellor and Mr. Bellenden Kerr. The former has presented the Rev. J. Blackwell, to whose able management it has been confided, and at whose suggestion it originated, with the living of Maenor Deifi, in Pembrokeshire. No doubt, this Society will itself be hailed with gratitude by all well-wishers to Wales,—and by some it may perhaps be regarded as an augury of better times—of a disposition to consult the feelings and existing circumstances of that country, in the policy that may hereafter be pursued towards her.

less, after the lapse of centuries, the locusts gleaned what the palmer-worm had left! By a policy already detailed—commenced at the Restoration—continued at the Revolution—and consummated under the House of Hanover, even these also became another tribute from Wales for the benefit of Englishmen! Those revenues which had afforded literary leisure to the founders of the Protestant faith in the Principality,*—were turned into pensions, for a class of men, from whom she experiences little other return than she did of yore from the Roman tax gatherer—

"The ivy which has hid her princely trunk,
And suck'd her verdure out on't!"

Well would it have been for Wales, if her people could have dealt with their endowments as with their ancient manuscripts—buried them in the earth!†

* It cannot be too often repeated, that the injustice thus done to Wales, does not depend on the difference of language; for, surely, it is most unjust, that strangers should be thrust into all the best benefices of any country, to the exclusion of men, equally, or, indeed, more meritorious, connected with that country! No part of Wales has suffered so much, in this way, as those districts where English is understood, as this renders them more convenient for the English connections of our Bishops. It is almost literally true, that all the border parishes of North Wales (with the exception of a few, in the gift of laymen,) are in the hands either of the Bishop of St. Asaph and the Cathedral dignitaries—or of the relatives of the former, and of individuals introduced by them into the country, from well-known motives of self-interest. Starting from Kerry, on the borders of South Wales, which is divided between the Bishop of St. David's and his connections,—and resting at Flint, in the northern extremity,—we have an almost unbroken chain of parishes, circumstanced as above mentioned—viz., Newtown, Llanllwchhaearn, Berriew, Castell Caereinion, Guilsfield, Llandrinio, Llandysilio, Melverley, Llanymynach, Llan St. Ffraid, Llanyblodwel, Llansilin, Llanrhaiadr, Chirk, Erbistock, Rhiwabon, Marchwiail, Gresford, Hope, Northop, Flint! This line is only once broken, viz., by Bettws, in Montgomeryshire, a benefice of small value!!

† It has been before stated, that at the Reformation, many Welsh families were obliged to bury their manuscripts in the earth, to preserve them from the English agents.

Considered merely in a temporal point of view, a well-regulated national Church is one of the greatest blessings a country can enjoy; if it were merely because, amongst all the fluctuations of property, it secures to each district one resident of competent fortune, and bound by peculiar ties, to works of benevolence. But it needs hardly be remarked that the effect of the Church in Wales is to draw wealth from its remoter districts; and the immense sums that are enjoyed by the absentee clergy may be considered as a fertile source of pauperism. Pauperism is still further increased .by Dissent (which is the result of Church abuses); this can hardly admit of a doubt, when the immense expense of erecting chapels and of maintaining ministers is remembered—a burden which falls mainly on the more indigent classes of society.

A national Church, conducted on pure principles, would be an invaluable bulwark to the liberties of the people; and I feel convinced, that in Wales, where large districts are often in the hands of one great proprietor, the Church is even now a check on local oppression. The mere presence of an educated body of men, independent of the rich members of their flock, is a kind of channel, through which the force of public opinion is extended to the darkest corners of the land. But, at present, the spirit of the Church is not in unison with the affections of the people. How can it be, when the clergy owe their advancement, almost in every instance, either to their connection with strangers, or to the influence of their own absentee aristocracy? One would think that there is no insult which an English Bishop would repel with so much indignation as political dictation in the exercise of his most sacred functions; yet nothing is more common than to hear clergymen avow their obligations to a political patron for benefits which none but their Bishop could have bestowed! An eminent prelate is reported to have advised his clergy "to keep aloof from scenes of popular excitement, if they wished to preserve their spiritual authority unimpaired." If the rulers of the Church had spurned the least attempt to make the clergy, through their means, the instruments of faction, we never should have seen their spiritual authority so far impaired.

Nor are our present religious divisions favourable to the real end of Christianity; schism is no imaginary evil; it is perfectly appalling to see the whole face of a Christian land studded with hostile sectarian churches, each a kind of lowering conspiracy against the rest. One of the great principles of the Christian worship is thus abandoned; the lessons of humility and of Christian equality can hardly be expressively taught when the peasant and his superior no longer meet together in the same temple. I cannot help thinking that the most intelligent Dissenters are more opposed to the abuses of the Church than to its principles; that it requires but a little kindness and a little wisdom to make Wales once more a united country. The people have been scattered, not by the logic of controversy, but by the foreign accents of the hireling.

Every one who feels strongly towards Wales, has a right to complain, not merely of the effect, but of the principle of the present absentee system. Tithes, we are told, are the property of the Church; but why is it forgotten, that upon the same principle, and to the same extent, the tithes of each parish are the property of that parish; and, *a fortiori*, the tithes of a country belong to that country! The object of these donations was the spiritual good of the districts to which they were given; their donors had no view to the religious instruction of remote parts of England, nor to the *personal* advantage of the clergy, any further than as *instruments of edification*.

But perhaps in no respect are the evils of the system more apparent than in their ill effect on the higher ranks in Wales; the clergy ought to be, and generally are, the link of intelligence between the aristocracy and the lower and middle ranks; but in Wales, the clergy being all either strangers or men of very humble rank, this link is broken, and what is the consequence? Why, that the higher classes, though in other respects often highly gifted and well disposed, will frequently be found ignorant of all that is going on in their own country, of the very rudiments of her literature, and even of her language!

It is deeply to be regretted, that the aristocracy of Wales should have allowed their Church thus to grow up into a prescriptive abuse; it has been the means of weakening that attachment which the people once felt to them and their fathers. To see the peasantry of a country and their rulers ranged under conflicting religious teachers, is surely a sad, if not a fearful sight! The traditions of Wales record a tale of a sluggard, who, by allowing a sea rampart to fall into decay, let the ocean in upon the loveliest valleys of our land. To our times this incident has but too obvious an application; yet, I trust it is not even yet too late to restore the best bulwark of the social edifice, a Church built not merely in name, but in reality, on the principles of the Reformation—a Church uniting within itself all classes of men.

Of one thing I feel assured, that Wales is fast verging to a condition which none who love her as the land of their nativity, can regard without feelings of anxiety, if not of alarm. Who is there that does not behold in her present divisions the germ of those evils which afflict a neighbouring country? Religious differences generally end sooner or later in civil commotions. The Welsh are still a loyal people, but it cannot be disguised, that their loyalty is on the wane,—and all who are experienced in the character and history of Celtic nations will agree, that when once the tide of their affections is turned, the ebb is as rapid as the flow. When ruled with kindness, the gentlest—the most affectionate of people; under misrule, they become impatient of the very elementary bonds of society. As an instance, we may contrast Ireland as she is now —Wales as she was before the time of Henry the Seventh—with that same Wales as described by an English poet, under the patriotic, the chivalrous sway of Queen Elizabeth.

"Whiles quarrels rage did nourish ruynest wracke,
And Owen Glendore set bloodie broyles abroach,
Full many a towne was spoyld and put to sacke,
And cleane consum'd, to countries foule reproach :

> Great castles raste, fayre buildings burnt to dust,
> Such revell raingde, that men did live by lust:
> But since they came, and yeelded unto lawe,
> Most meeke as lambe, within one yoke they drawe.
>
> Like brethren now doe Welshmen still agree,
> In as much love as any men alive;
> The friendship there, and concord that I see,
> I doe compare to bees in honey hive,
> Which keep in swarme, and hold together still,
> Yet gladly showe to stranger great good will;
> A courteous kynd of love in every place,
> A man may finde, in simple people's face.
>
> Passe where you please, on plaine or mountain wilde,
> And beare yourself in sweete and civill sort,
> And you shall sure be haulst with man and childe,
> Who will salute, with gentle comely port,
> The passers by; on braves they stand not so,
> Without good speech, to let a trav'ler go;
> They think it dett and duetie franke and free,
> In towne or fielde, to yeeld you cap and knee.
>
> They will not strive to royst and take the way
> Of any man, that travailes through their land;
> A greater thing of Wales now will I say,
> You may come there, beare purse of gold in hand,
> Or mightie bagges of silver stuffed throwe,
> And no one man dare touch your treasure now;
> Which shewes some grace doth rule and guyde them there,
> That doth to God and man such conscience beare."
>
> Thomas's *Churchyard's Worthies of Wales*, p. 2, 3.

The same natural sensibility may be traced in the character of the people for ages—though it has at all times been but little cherished by their rulers.

"These feeble remains of a great people" (says M. Thierry),* "had the glory of keeping possession of their last corner of territory, against the efforts of an enemy immensely superior in numbers and resources; often vanquished, but never subjugated, and bearing through the course of ages the unshaken conviction of a mysterious eternity reserved for their name and their lan-

---

* *History of the Norman Conquest*, vol. i. English Translation.

gungo. This eternity was foretold by the bards of the Welsh, from the first day of their defeat :* and whenever, in after times, a new invader crossed the mountains of Cambria, after the most complete victories his captives would repeat to him: ' 'Tis all in vain; thou canst destroy neither our name nor our language.'* Fortune, bravery, and above all, the nature of the country, formed of rocks, lakes, and sands, justified these predictions, which, though rash ones, are a remarkable evidence of vigorous imagination in the little people who dared to make them their national creed."

"It is hardly too much to say, that the ancient British *fed* on poetry; for in their political axioms which have been handed down to us, the bard, at once poet and musician, is placed beside the labourer and the artisan, as one of the three pillars of social life.‡ Their poets had one great and almost only theme—their country's destinies, her misfortunes, and her hopes. The nation, poetical in its turn, extended the bounds of fiction by ascribing fantastic meanings to their simplest words. The wishes of their bards were received as promises, their expectations as prophecies; even their silence was made expressive. If they sang not of Arthur's death, it was proof that Arthur yet lived; if the harper undesignedly sounded some melancholy air, the minds of his hearers spontaneously linked with this vague melody the name of some spot rendered mournfully famous by the loss of a battle with the foreign conquerors § This life of hopes and recollections gave charms, in the eyes of the latter Cambrians, to their country of rocks and morasses: though poor, they were gay and social,‖ bearing the burden of distress lightly as some passing inconvenience, looking forward with unabated confidence to a great political revolution, by

* Taliesin.—*Archæology of Wales*, vol. i. p. 95.
† See Book XI. of Thierry's *History of the Conquest of England*.
‡ Trioedd Ynys Prydain, Sect. 21, No. 1.
§ Morva Rhuddlan, Rhuddlan Marsh. See Book VI. of Thierrry's *History of the Conquest of England*.
‖ Giraldi Cambrensis Itineraarium Walliæ, passim.

which they should regain all that they had lost, and (as one of their bards expresses it) recover the crown of Britain."*

If we remember the wrongs, by which the fertile plains of England were wrested from our forefathers, it is only as a theme for the moralist or the bard; may every feeling of affection link their present possessors with the natives of "the country of rocks and morasses!" But, we should be less than Christians—less than men—unworthy of an alliance with the great nations with whom we are united—were we to contemplate with similar feelings, that crafty and encroaching policy, which, under the mask of free institutions, has deprived us of the free enjoyment even of the humble territory that is left to us,—consigned every noble, every civilizing institution to the mole and to the bat—and doomed us to a worse evil than the splendid solitudes of rocks and mountains,—an insufferable—an ignominious intellectual wilderness! The Reformation—the Revolution—the accession of the House of Hanover—every event, which has been as an era of light to the liberties and religion of England, has been the signal of some new injustice to Wales, as if the destinies of that country were like the lake described by the poet of Ireland, which is ever dark, even at noon-day:—

> "The lake, whose gloomy shore
> Skylark never warbled o'er."

Most of those who have visited our land have spoken of the Welsh as a people deserving a better fate. No people of these islands have endured more for liberty, perhaps none more for conscience' sake; to their fathers was the Gospel first preached in Britain, and a hatred to Popish despotism was a great source of all their national misfortunes.† Nor have they been wanting to themselves, or the great nation with whom they are united, in any of those great struggles which secured their constitutional liberties. In our own times, the soldier of the Principality has

---

* Taliesin.—*Archæology of Wales*, vol. i. p. 95. Armes Prydain, Ibid. p. 156—159. Myrddin's Avallenau.—Ibid.

† Thierry.

fought side by side with the bravest of his English fellow-subjects. The philosophical English historian* has fairly and generously admitted, that Wales has contributed her full share to the intellectual wealth of the kingdom. Not even the contemptuous treatment that she has experienced for centuries, has extinguished those graceful feelings of chivalry, that love of poetry and song, which belonged in the very earliest ages to her children.† Notwithstanding her unhappy religious divisions, there is no part of the kingdom more united in a feeling of fervent and enthusiastic loyalty; no country where the gentry are more courteous and hospitable to strangers; and of her peasantry, I need only use the words of an eloquent bard of our time. "With them, though justice has sometimes to adjust her balance, she has rarely to use her sword."

Were the people of Wales ambitious of temporal privileges, they might not sue in vain; but when they only seek the ordinary means of religion and of virtue, of preserving those good dispositions which they have hitherto evinced, so beneficially to themselves and their fellow subjects, it is to be hoped that they pursue no other boon than a patriot King will delight to bestow. "The darkest hour is nearest the dawn;" the time may not be far distant when the peasantry of the Principality shall be gathered once more to the Church of their forefathers, and the children of her gentry shall cease to be the mere Ecclesiastical Helots of their own land.

About 15 years ago, an eminent London divine was preaching at Bala; amongst his audience appeared a venerable old man, the patriarch of the Welsh Methodists in that metropolis of Methodism. The next day the clergyman of Bala, with some friends, went to pay the old man a visit. The latter addressing Mr.————, the

* Sir J. Mackintosh.

† The Welsh, or rather British origin of the Stories of Chivalry have been proved by Mr. Ellis, in his Specimens of Ancient Romance.—See also an eloquent article on Brittany in the *Cambrian Quarterly Magazine*, for January, 1831.

clergyman of Bala, in Welsh, and in that singular style of metaphor which these sectaries have always affected, began to enquire about the stranger. "Have you," said he, "many such men as I heard yesterday, to beat the pan?" Mr.——— replied, that "The Church of England could certainly boast of an increasing body of zealous and eloquent ministers." "Then," replied his interrogator, with animation, "the bees will all return to the old hive again!"*

  * "Bydd y gwenyn yn dychwelyd i'r hen gwch eto."

 Page 147.

"*Societies for the Promotion of Useful Knowledge, by the Publication of Essays in the Welsh Language.*"—The first idea of associations, on this plan, is ascribable to the late Mr. Richard Evans, of Llanbryn Mair, in the county of Montgomery,—of whose sound and patriotic conceptions, the measures about to be pursued, under the superintendence of Mr. Blackwell, are merely the realization. The reader will find evidence of this in an article entitled "The Peasantry of Wales," published in the *Cambrian Quarterly Magazine* for July, 1830. This statement, I consider due to the memory of a respected friend and one of the most excellent of men ;—a nobler tribute to his merits will be found in the adoption of his views, by the illustrious nobleman to whom I have alluded, and in the steps he has taken towards the general education of the Principality.

 It is a highly interesting circumstance, that a prospectus was issued about the same time, of a monthly periodical, for the diffusion of general knowledge, to be entitled *Y Dynolydd*, or *The Philanthropist:* the author has since learned that its projectors were a few poor labouring men employed in the iron-works in South Wales.

APPENDIX I.

Number of Churches.—Progressive increase of the number of Dissenting Chapels.—Peculiarities of the different Sects in Wales.

	Number of	
A.D.	Dissenting Chapels.	
1715	35.	Presbyterians and Independents, 26.—Baptists, 9.
1801	954.	*("Peter's Hanes," i.e. Hist. of Dissenters in Wales, p. 616.)*

NORTH WALES.—*From Peter's Hanes, p. 700.*

COUNTIES.	Independents and Presbyterians.	Baptists.	Calvinistic or Welsh Methodists.	Wesleyan Methodists.	Total of Dissenting Places of Worship and Methodist Societies.	Churches and Chapels of Ease.
Anglesey	10	11	33	15	69	73
Caernarvonshire	20	13	41	17	91	69
Denbighshire	13	12	34 }	24	66	56
Flintshire	8	1		18	44	27
Merionethshire	16	13	33	24	86	38
Montgomeryshire	15	9	31	19	74	46
	82	59	172	117	430	309

SOUTH WALES.

Brecknockshire	15	14	23	7	59	63
Cardiganshire	26	11	42	16	95	62
Caermarthenshire	56	35	43	14	148	82
Glamorganshire	45	28	32	22	127	128
Pembrokeshire	30	19	20	15	84	136
Radnorshire	4	5	...	2	11	53
	176	112	160	76	524	524
Total in North and South Wales.	258	171	332	193	954	829*

1832, 1428.
Welsh Methodists 500
Independents, (260 in S. Wales and 180 in N. Wales)... 440
Wesleyans 250
Baptists 200
Unitarians or Presbyterians.. 23
Quakers 9
Roman Catholics 6

Total number of Dissenting Chapels in 1832 1428
Places of Worship belonging to the Church*.......... 829

* The latter have been for a century past rather on the decrease; some new Chapels have been built, but more have fallen into ruins; the feelings of the people have grown cold towards the Church.

I am indebted for the last list to the courtesy of a gentleman who has peculiar means of accurate information on the subject. In nine of the counties in Wales, the Dissenting chapels are in about a treble proportion to the churches and chapels of the Establishment. Caermarthenshire, Pembrokeshire, and Glamorganshire, are exceptions, because the churches are there unusually numerous; and in Radnorshire, where little Welsh is spoken, and where it is said the people are of English race—*(Malkin's South Wales)*—there is very little Dissent, in spite of all the Church abuses in that county.

DISSENTERS GENERALLY

Punish flagrant offences, and frequent absence from divine service, with expulsion from their societies; inferior transgressions, by exclusion from the sacrament. These rules serve to check open vice; but their abuse, like auricular confession in the Romish Church, generates habits of slyness and deceit.

WELSH METHODISTS.—Their doctrine is that of the thirty-nine Articles, "taken in a Calvinistic sense," their discipline like that of the Scottish Church, i. e., they have a monthly synod for each county, and a "general assembly," which meets quarterly, and alternately in North and South Wales, to which the general business of the body is referred. Their preachers hardly ever preach in the same chapel two Sundays together. Hence, hearers are secured by novelty; but excitement and partial views of Christianity are also the consequence,—and thus the means are sacrificed to the end. Their preachers, who are rarely educated men, generally depend on some trade for support. Besides their chapels in Wales, they have three in London, three in Liverpool, and one respectively in Chester, Shrewsbury, and Manchester. The Welsh Methodists still profess attachment to the Church; and though a practice, which is too common amongst them, of building their chapels close to the churches, seems rather irreconcilable with this profession, still it would be more charitable to ascribe the blame to the spiritual factiousness of a few, than to duplicity in the whole body.*

---

* This is the case, to my own knowledge, in the following parishes in Montgomeryshire:—Montgomery, Llangadvan, and Llanfyllin. It is also now a common practice with the Welsh Methodists to assemble in their chapels during the hours of service in the Church; formerly, they acted more consistently with their professions.

INDEPENDENTS—Descendants of the old Nonconformists. In 1740, they had only six places of worship in North Wales. They began to revive at the first breaking out of Methodism, and we may gather from Griffith Jones's writings, that if the Methodists had not occupied the country, the Independents would have done so. "It was not" (says that writer) "any scruple of conscience that gave occasion to scarce one in ten of the Dissenters (Independents) in this country, to separate from us at first, whatever objections they may afterwards imbibe against conforming. No, Sir, they generally dissent at first for no other reason than want of plain, practical, pressing, and zealous preaching, in a language and dialect they can understand, and freedom of friendly access to advice about their spiritual state."* They are a liberal body in their views of secular learning. In the last century, their ministers were all men of education; this is not generally the case now, though some of them are men of respectable erudition.

WESLEYANS.—Though Dr. Coke, the most celebrated of Wesley's missionaries, was a native of Wales, the Wesleyans had not one preacher in the Welsh language till the year 1800.—*(Peter's Hanes,* p. 674.) Their great success since that time, appears from the tables above; it arose, in some measure, from the attractive style of singing introduced by them,—but where various classes of Dissenters succeed, there must be some general predisposing cause of Dissent.

BAPTISTS.—It has already been stated, that a schism on the rite of baptism divided the Welsh Independents in very early times. In the time of Howel Harris, the Baptists were very few in number; since then, they have rapidly increased.

PRESBYTERIANS OR UNITARIANS.—Many of the descendants of the old Nonconformists adopted Unitarian opinions in the beginning of the eighteenth century. The preaching of Griffith Jones, Harris, and Rowland, contributed to revive an orthodox style of preaching, both in the Church and out of it.

* *Welsh-Piety* for 1740-1.

QUAKERS.—They seem to have been numerous in the time of the civil wars.

ROMAN CATHOLICS.—Notwithstanding their long struggle against the power of the Romish see, its influence was at last firmly established over the people of Wales;* but, owing to the piety and zeal of the early Welsh Reformers, this influence was most completely destroyed; and in the present day, there is no part of the kingdom, or indeed of Europe, in which Popery has been so signally annihilated. Griffith Jones says, that in his day, there was not a single Welshman *acquainted with no other language than his mother tongue* professing the Roman Catholic religion.

The mere number of Dissenting chapels (enormous as it is), furnishes but an inadequate idea of the popular feeling towards the Establishment; in many districts the churches have hardly any congregations whatever. Many of those who frequent the church go quite as constantly to chapel; and it is a very common remark, that when the clergyman is beloved, it is generally rather as a benevolent layman than as a clergyman; and that even then the people chiefly confide in Dissenting ministers for religious guidance and consolation.

* Several of the Welsh Bards levelled the shafts of their ridicule against the Romish priesthood; and it is not improbable, that the minds of the people were, in this way, prepared for the Reformation, as those of the English nation were thus disposed by the writings of Chaucer. Davydd ap Gwylym, a Welsh Bard, who lived a short time before the great English Poet, attacks the monks and priesthood of his day with irresistible humour, and with great powers of imagination; at one time, he calls a Grey Friar " Y dyn llygliw," the " Mouse-coloured man ;" at another, having stumbled over a heap of snow—he compares it to a bear's head, and to a Friar of the same order.

APPENDIX II.

THE STATE OF THE CHURCH AND CHURCH REVENUES OF SOUTH WALES.

My information respecting this division of the Principality is taken chiefly from *Carlisle's Topographical Dictionary*, which gives the value of the smaller livings from the diocesan returns of 1809.* Incomplete as that information is, it will enable the reader to form a tolerably clear view of the state of the Church in that district. The tithes of South Wales were almost completely taken from the Church by Henry VIII. and the clergy are consequently very meanly provided for indeed. Nevertheless, were due economy practised in what is left, and were the numerous sinecures abolished, an income of from about £150 to £200 a-year might still be furnished to each of the working clergy; except where the churches are unusually numerous, in proportion to the population and the extent of country.† This will appear more clearly from the following computations:—

In BRECKNOCKSHIRE, the united value of the smaller
benefices is................................. £3133 12 1¾

We may assume the largest benefices to average
£250 each, which is perhaps a tolerably fair
average. In this county, there are about 22
of those, which (at £260 each) would amount to 5500 0 0

Supposed value of Church property in Brecknockshire....................................... 8633 12 1¾

This calculation, which, though, of course, very far from being perfectly accurate, is, perhaps, sufficiently so for the purpose of

* The value of benefices has much improved since that time.

† The recklessness of the patrons of the South Wales benefices, has already been exhibited in the case of Radnorshire. Cardiganshire is still worse off; for more than half of its parishes are held by absentees, many of whom reside in the remotest parts of England.

this comparison, would give a provision of £200 a-year to 43 incumbents. It will be remembered that the whole income at present enjoyed by the resident clergy of Montgomeryshire, where the Church is rich, does not much exceed this amount; and the population of that county is about a third more than that of Brecknockshire.

Making the same computation for the remaining counties of South Wales, the result will be as follows:—

	£	s.	d.
CAERMARTHENSHIRE. — United value of smaller benefices	£4561	9	5
14 larger benefices, at an average value of £250 each	3500	0	0
Total	8061	9	5
CARDIGANSHIRE.—Smaller benefices	5973	17	3
11 larger ditto, at £250 each	2750	0	0
Total	8723	17	3
GLAMORGANSHIRE.—Smaller benefices	7382	15	2½
29 larger ditto, at £250 each	7250	0	0
Total	14632	15	2½
PEMBROKESHIRE.—Smaller benefices	6678	7	11
28 larger ditto, at £250 each	7000	0	0
Total	13678	7	11
RADNORSHIRE.—Smaller benefices	3085	10	4¼
15 larger ditto, at £250 each	6250	0	0
Total	9335	10	4¼

The above remarks are thrown out rather as suggestions for further inquiry, than as affording any thing like an authentic statement of the revenues of the Church in the counties alluded to; at the same time, I cannot help inferring, from the details furnished in *Carlisle's Topographical Dictionary* as to the extent and fertility of many of those parishes where all the tithes still belong to the Church, that I have rather underrated the value of the higher livings,—and, consequently, that the collective amount of the Church property will be found to be much greater than it is assumed to be in the above calculation. At any rate, I am fully persuaded, that the deficiencies of the South Welsh Church are ascribable much more to the mal-administration of its revenues, than to its intrinsic poverty.

As before intimated, most of the Church patronage in South Wales is shared between Laymen—the Crown—and Sinecurists in England and in Wales; hence, under the influence of personal friendship or political connection, the parishes are filled with ministers unsuited to them. The Bishops usually take but very little pains to encourage deserving pastors, and often prefer Englishmen to Welsh benefices. Pluralities and absenteeism exist to a great extent. Thus a very small fund is left for the generality of the clergy, who are reduced to abject poverty. Many of them are obliged to keep farms, situated often in distinct parishes from those which they serve. A great many of them serve two or three places of worship every Sunday; in many churches, service is performed only once a-day, and that at an inconvenient hour. These abuses exist to a less extent in the southern parts of South Wales; but in Cardiganshire, Radnorshire, and Caermarthenshire, this is the general course of things.

Of seventy-one parishes in Cardiganshire (including chapels of ease), not more than thirty are held by residents. At the same time, the revenues of the Church are squandered in sinecures, which, whatever may be their benefits (real or imaginary) in richer districts—are very unjustifiable under the local circumstances just described. The following is a list of the Prebends which are attached to the Collegiate Church of Brecon only, taken from Mr. Theophilus Jones's *History of Brecknockshire.*

PREBENDS IN THE COLLEGIATE CHURCH OF CHRIST, IN BRECKNOCK,

THEIR RESERVED RENTS, ETC.

From *Mr. Theo. Jones's Hist. p. 834.*

PREBENDS.	Reserved Rents.			Lease.	Provisions to the Lecturer.			Provisions to the Schoolmaster.			REMARKS.
	£	s.	d.		£	s.	d.	£	s.	d.	
Llangatwg	20	0	0	Years.				16	0	0	
Llanddeusant				Ditto.							Annexed to the Deanery.
Llangammarch	60	0	0	Ditto.	2	6	8				Annexed to the Treasurership in lieu of Mortuaries. The Bp. is Treasurer.
Llanbister	60	0	0	Lives.	2	6	8				Chancellorship.
Llandysilio	26	0	0	Years.	1	4	0				
Llangynllo	26	0	0	Lives.				2	5	8	
Llanvynydd	22	0	0	Years.	2	6	8				Precentorship.
Trallwng	20	0	0					1	4	0	
Llanarthne	16	0	0	Years.	2	6	8				
Clyro	15	6	8	Lives.	1	10	8				
St. Harmon	14	0	0	Years.				1	10	8	
Llanwrthwl	13	6	8	Lives.	2	6	8				
Llandygwydd	12	0	0	Ditto.	1	13	4				
Llandegle	11	0	0	Ditto.	2	6	8				
Garthbrengy	10	0	0	Years.	1	10	8				
Nant Gynllo	10	0	0	Lives.	1	4	0				
Llanddarog	10	0	0	Ditto.	1	10	8				
Llandeilo-Graban	9	15	4	Ditto.	1	10	8				
Mochdre*	8	0	0	Years.	1	11	8				
Llanelwedd	7	13	4	Lives.	1	4	0				
Lledrod	6	13	4	Years.	1	4	0				
Llan-y-Drindod	6	0	0	Lives.				0	9	0	
Boughrood, Llanbedr, Pain's Castle	2	0	0	Years.	1	10	8				
Llan St. Ffraid yn Elvael	1	6	8	Ditto.	1	4	0				
	387	2	0		30	18	4	21	9	4	

"* It must not be supposed, that the tithes attached to the Prebends are of little value, because the reserved rents are so insignificant. On referring to the remarks previously made on the parish of Mochdre, (see p. 128) the reader will be enabled to conjecture, that the intrinsic value of these tithes, may be very considerable indeed. The parish of Mochdre, here set down at £8, is worth £200 a-year; so that if we take the reserved rents as a criterion, many of the Prebends must be of seven times greater value than this sum (£200)."

SOUTH WALES.

N.B. In the first columns of the following Tables, the letters R.V. P.C. C. and Ch. closely adjoining the names of the Benefices, signify respectively, Rectories, Vicarages, Perpetual Curacies, Curacies, Chapelries.—The right hand column of letters indicates the Patronage to which the benefice is subject: B. signifies that it is in the gift of the Bishop; E. of some Ecclesiastical body or person; L. of a layman; K. and Cr. of the Crown; P.W. of the Prince of Wales; Ld. Ch. of the Lord Chancellor.

BRECKNOCKSHIRE.—Population in 1831—47,763.

[Parishes, &c.]	Value in King's Book.			Parish Rates in 1803.					Modern Value.		
	£	S.	D.	£	S.	D.	S.	D.	£	S.	D.
Aber Yscyr, V. . . . . E.	3	6	3	83	10	2	at 6	0	113	14	10
Allt Vawr, P.C.	2	17	10	14	13	6	4	0	55	11	6
Battle, P.C. . . . . . . L.	5	5	0	45	1	6½	5	3	47	5	0
Brecknock.—St. David's, V.	5	15	7½	120	12	2	7	3	135	5	0
				139	5	5	9	0			
St. John's, V.	6	13	4	424	16	4¼	12	0			
				66	8	9½	6	0			
St. Mary's, Ch.	4	6	2	374	1	5½	7	6			
Bryn Llys, V. . . . . . L.	4	16	0½	100	10	9	4	3	104	11	6
Buallt, P.C. . . . . . L.	10	0	0	189	19	3½	12	0	63	0	0
Cantrev, R. . . . . . . E.	9	10	7½	58	7	6					
Capel Coelbren, C. . . E.	1	0	0						57	9	0
Cathedine, R. . . . . . E.	5	2	11	65	1	10	5	0	105	11	0
Cell Wen, V.									42	13	0
Crûg Cadarn, V. . . . . E.	14	0	0	182	6	8	6	0			
Crûg Hywel, V. . . . . L.	3	17	8½	139	8	2	3	0	79	0	6¼
Devynog, V. . . . . . B.	14	14	4½	502	8	0¼					
Dyffryn Honddu, C. . . E.									60	7	0
Faenor, R. . . . . . King.	8	3	11¼	122	8	8	6	9	123	15	8¼
Garth Brengy, P.C. . . E.	10	0	0	81	16	8	7	1	34	10	0
Glasbury, V. . . . . . B.	10	0	0	403	10	10½					
Glyn Collwyn, P.C. . . E.									64	4	0
Gwen Ddwr, C. . . . . L.	6	0	0	192	8	9	5	6	65	5	0
Hay, V. . . . . L.	7	0	5	476	13	7½	3	0	112	0	0
Llan Avan Vawr, V. . B.	9	8	9	330	11	2½			103	12	1
Llan Avan Vechan, C. . B.	13	0	0	60	7	0			20	5	5
Llanaml-llech, R. . . . L.	6	1	8	268	1	7	6	0			
Llan Bedr, R. . . . . . L.	16	17	6	120	9	5½	3	0			
Llanddetty, R. . . . . L.	7	10	7½	109	9	1½	5	0			
Llanddewi, P.C.	6	0	0	121	14	0	5	6	42	5	0
Llanddewi Ab Gwesin, V. B.	18	0	0	7	7	6	1	0	24	16	8
Llanddewi 'r Cwm, C. . L.	5	0	0	91	12	2	6	9	58	0	0
Llandevaelog Vach, R. P.W.	13	0	0	62	16	8	6	0			
Llandevaelog Tre'r Graig, Ch. . . . E.	1	7	3½								
Llandevalle, V. . . . . E.	5	0	0	276	3	1½	5	6	Very Valuable.		
Llandeilo ar Vân, P.C. . L.	9	0	0	133	11	6	7	6	53	8	0
Llanelien, R. . . . . . L.	4	6	3	49	6	3	1	0	103	12	0
Llanelli, Ch. . . . . . L.				259	2	6	7	0			
Llanveugan, R. . . . . L.	20	10	0	294	6	0	8	4			
Ll Vihangel Ab Gwesin, C.B.				63	12	0	6	2	28	18	10
Ll. V. Bryn Pab Ieuan, C.B.	16	0	0	110	2	6			34	2	6

BRECKNOCKSHIRE CONTINUED.

Parishes, &c.	*Value in King's Book.*			*Parish Rates in 1803.*						*Modern Value.*		
	£	S.	D.	£	s.	d.		S.	D.	£	S.	D.
Ll. V. Cwm Du, R. & V. . L.	R. 19	15	2¼	536	10	7	at	5	6			
	V. 9	13	1¼									
Ll. V. Vechan, C.										78	10	0
Ll. V. Nant Brân, P.C. . . L.				192	2	6		7	9	58	13	3
Ll. V. Tal-y-Llyn, R. . . L.	4	12	3½	47	11	0		3	3	110	15	0
Llanvilo, R. . . . . L.	6	14	9½	148	2	3		6	0			
Llanvrynach, R. . . . . . L.	4	10	7¼	93	5	8½		3	6			
Llan Gammarch, V. . . . . B.	8	14	5	320	12	6		9	0	93	15	2¼
Llan Ganten, P. C. . . . . L.	5	0	0	78	3	4½		6	0	47	18	0
Llan Gasty, Tal-y-Llyn, R.. E.	4	18	9	64	7	7½		4	9			
Llan Gattwg, R. . . . . . L.	31	13	9	420	15	1		7	6			
Llan Geneu, Ch. . . . . . L.				90	5	4		2	9			
Llan Gors, V. . . . . E.	5	10	0	176	7	5		8	0			
Llan Gynog, C . . . . E.	2	12	9	19	5	9		5	0	46	12	0
Llan Gynydr, R. . . . . . L.	13	14	7	202	17	0		6	6			
Llan Igon, V. . . . . P. Ch.	7	12	8½	260	8	9½		6	0			
Llan Ilid, Ch.	See Devynog.									28	16	0
Llan Illtid, P. C. . . . . . E.	3	0	0.	See Devynog.						45	7	0
Llan Lleon Voel, P. C. . . L.	2	13	4	47	10	0		6	0	57	15	0
Llan St. Ffraid, R. . . . . L.	6	4	7	178	2	6		8	9			
Llan Yspyddad, V. . . . . L.	5	17	8½	315	0	10¼				78	17	6
Llan Wrthwl, V. . . . . . B.	9	12	11	185	9	10		8	4	57	1	10
Llan Wrtyd, C. . . . . . B.	14	7	10	122	3	11		9	6	49	17	1
Llan Ynys, R . . . . . . B.	7	0	7½	43	7	3		4	0	75	7	6
Llan y Wern, P, C. . . . . B.				72	6	5¾		4	3	52	8	0
Llys Wen, R. . . . . . . L.	3	14	7	66	9	3		1	0	96	9	0
Llywel, V. . . . . B.	9	10	5	495	5	1						
Maes Mynys, R. . . . . . B.	7	1	3	85	3	5		6	2			
Merthyr Cynog, V. . . . . E.	7	10	5	350	7	6½		7	1½	50	11	8
Nant Ddu, C. . . . . . . E.	2	0	0							52	10	0
Partrishow, Ch. . . . . . L.				60	13	2		3	3½			
Pen Daren, R. . . . . . . L.	9	3	11½	242	18	8½						
Pen-y-Bont, Ch. . . . . . L.	2	0	0							64	10	0
Rhyd-y-Briw, Ch..	2	0	0									
Tav Vechan, C. . . . . . E.	2	12	0							47	0	0
Tal-ach-Ddu, R. . . . . . E.	4	12	1	38	12	5½		4	0	130	19	0
Talgarth, V. . . . . E.				834	9	3						
Tir-yr-Abad, P. C. . . . . L.				28	10	7		7	6	35	0	0
Trallong, P. C. . . . . . E.	10	0	0	100	8	11		5	4	42	0	0
Tre'r Twr, P. C. . . . . . L.	2	10	0	See Ll. V. Cwm Du.						60	10	0
Ystrad Vellté, C. . . . . . L.	22	0	0	177	15	4		5	5			
Ystrad Gynlais, R. . . . . L.	9	10	7½	194	15	9½		7	0			
										£3133	12	1¾

CAERMARTHENSHIRE.—Population in 1801—100,655.

Parishes, &c.	Value in King's Book.			Parish Rates in 1803.				Modern Value.		
	£	s.	d.	£	s.	d.	s. d.	£	s.	d.
Aber Gorlech, P.C............E.								47	0	0
Aber Gwili, V..................B.	3	6	8	450	6	0 at 7	9	110	17	10
Aber Nant, V ....L.	7	13	4	76	18	8		61	8	10
Bettws, P.C ....B.	6	0	0	107	9	1	16 0	46	4	0
Brechva, R........................L.	8	5	0	13	14	0	7 6	85	6	0
Caermarthen, V...........King.	6	13	4	1008	16	0½		104	11	8
Cappel Bettws, P.C............B.								13	9	0
Cenarth, V ....B.	4	6	8	207	11	3½		62	15	0
Cil Rheiddyn, R........Ld. Ch.	8	12	8½	190	15	7½				
Cil y Cwm, V ....L.	5	0	0	284	9	11½	9 0	54	0	0
Cil y Maenllwyd, R......L. Ch.	6	10	0	86	10	9½				
Clare, St., V......................E.	4	17	1	202	14	0	10 4½	73	3	0
Cydweli, V ....King.	7	10	0	395	2	2½	8 0	109	19	6
Cyffic, Ch								40	13	6
Cynwyl, V ....L.				236	5	11	17 6			
Cynwyl Gaeo, V...........King.	5	0	0	401	10	7	7 9	63	15	4
Eglwys Cymyn, R.......Ld. Ch.	8	0	0	40	2	8	2 0	94	0	0
Eglwys Vair Achyrig, Ch.......				32	15	4	15 0			
Eglwys Glyn Tav, P.C. ....L.								29	18	0
Gwynve, P.C.								56	0	0
Henllan Amgoed, R. ....L.	6	10	5	70	10	1½		80	6	0
Ishmael, St., V.................K.	7	0	0	273	5	6½	8 6	89	10	0
Llacharn, V......................E.	6	0	0	431	13	6				
Llan Arthne, V..................B.	8	0	0	406	11	3	7 6	122	14	0
Llanbeudy, V. ....L.	8	0	0	420	0	0		59	14	8
Llandeuddwr, R. ....L.	6	0	0	116	3	9½				
Llandaug, R ....L.	7	10	0	3	6	0		32	0	0
Llanddarog, V ....B.	8	0	0	154	6	8	20 0	40	16	0
Llanddeusant, Donative......B.				117	11	11	7 6			
Llandeilo, Ab Cywyn, P.C..B.				16	15	0	7 0	31	10	0
Llandeilo Vawr, V.............B.	16	0	0	621	4	0				
Llandingad, V...................B.	7	0	0	243	7	2½		91	5	8
Llanddyvri, (in Llandingad)....										
Llan Ddowror										
Llan Dibie, V ....B.	4	0	0	194	17	0	8 0	93	8	0
Llandyvaelog, V.................L.	9	13	4	422	18	4		36	8	5
Llandyveisant, Donative......L.				31	11	4	5 0	52	3	0
Llandysilio, V....................B.	7	0	0	113	7	9		76	0	0
Llanedy, R ....K.	8	0	0	128	6	2	10 6			
Llanegwad, V ....B.	8	13	4	396	3	4	12 0			
Llanelli, V........................L.	6	6	8	688	17	10		71	11	10
Llan Vair ar y bryn, Ch.........				391	3	8		65	5	7
Llan Vallteg, R.. ....…...B.	4	0	0	43	1	4		82	4	0
Ll. Vihangel A. Bythych, Ch. L	15	0	0	152	3	1	5 1	69	12	4
Llan V. Aber Cywyn, Ch....B.				211	12	0				
Ll. V. Aber Arth, V............L.	6	6	8	246	0	5	10 4	90	10	0
Ll. V. Cil Vargen, R..........L.	1	6	8	4	15	6	1 0	55	6	4
Ll. V. Rhos y Corn, C.......B.				92	10	8	10 0	9	10	0
Ll. V. Uwch y Gwili, Ch....E.								44	19	0
Llanvynydd, V... ....B.	6	13	4	240	10	4	3 9	95	15	6
Llangadog Vawr, V ....B.	9	0	0	495	0	7	13 6			
Llan Gain, C.. ....L.				169	5	3	18 4	80	10	0

CAERMARTHENSHIRE CONTINUED.

Parishes, &c.	Value in King's Book.			Parish Rates in 1803.					Modern Value.		
	£	s.	D.	£	s.	D.	s.	D.	£	s.	D.
Llan Gan, V ....B.	3	0	0	179	12	3 at			50	0	0
Llangathan, V. Bp. of Chester	6	13	4	239	15	1	4	0	91	10	0
Llangeler, R. & V ....B.	R 12	18	9	270	12	3					
	v 6	13	4								
Llan Gennych, Ch........ ....L.	6	13	4	97	1	0	11	0	60	14	4
Llan Gledwyn, R..,.........P.W.	2	13	4	41	18	4	18	3	56	7	6
Llangyndeyrn, Ch.... ....L.	6	13	4	687	2	2			63	1	5
Llan Gynin, Ch.. ....L.				122	6	4			65	7	0
Llan Gynog,[C.................K.				163	9	0	13	3	25	0	0
Llan Gynyr, V .. ..B.	3	0	0	267	3	0	7	3			
Llan Llawddog, Ch...... ......E.	5	0	0	85	12	0	5	3	67	0	0
Llan Llwch, P. C............	0	10	0	See St. Peter.					65	5	0
Llan Llwny, V........... .. ... B.	5	0	0	115	12	9	9	0	89	10	0
Llan Non, Ch.................L.	6	13	4	172	11	4	8	6	39	13	0
Llan Sadwrn, V.................L.	6	10	0	167	10	5¼	7	6	60	0	10
Llan Sadwrnen, R.................	6	0	0	60	17	2	1	6			
Llan Sawyl, Ch.				137	5	5	4	0	62	8	9
Llan Stephan, V..............K.	8	13	4	443	15	3			24	0	0
Llan Winio, P. C............L.				157	15	6			35	13	0
Llan Wrda, Ch............L.				86	14	2	11	0	46	11	0
Llan' y Byddar, V..............K.				287	11	0	10	3	92	16	0
Llan y Crwys, P. C............L.				35	8	7¼	4	8	42	11	0
Llan y Pumsant, C......... ...E.	5	0	0	100	13	6	12	0	41	0	0
Marros, Ch..... .'........ ...				52	2	8	1	8	52	14	0
Merthyr, R. .... King	4	17	1	69	0	5	15	0	142	15	0
Myddvai, V. ....B.	6	6	8	166	1	8	11	0	3:!0	0	0
Mydrim, V................B.	7	10	0	293	10	5¼	9	6	73	16	0
Nant y Bai, P. C..................									43·15		10
New Castle in Emlyn, Ch....B.				In Parish of Cenarth					53	5	0
New Church, P.C..............L.	6	0	0	173	4	7			41	14	0
Penboyr, R... ....L.	9	9	4½	178	6	0					
Pen Bre, V..... ....L.	6	6	8	314	14	1½	15	0	39	6	8
Pen Carreg, V...... ....L.	4	0	0	115	10	0	6	0	73	18	10¼
Pen Dyn, R. ....' L.				17	16	2	2	0	48	0	0
Taliaris, P. C ....L.	10	0	0	See Ll. Deilo Vawr.					47	11	0
Tre' Lech ar Bettws, V.......B.	6	13	4	264	17	9½			42	2	2

£4561 9 5

CARDIGANSHIRE.—Population in 1131—64,780

Parishes.	Value in King's Book.			Parish Rates in 1803.				Mod. r.i Value.		
	£	s.	D.	£	s.	D.	s. D.	£	s.	D.
Aber Porth, R. ....B.	5	13	9	37	6	6	at 7 0	74	2	4
Aber Ystwyth, P.C. ....E.				329	3	7	3 0	86	2	0
Bettws Bleddrws, R. .... B.	4	7	8½	35	0	0	5 0	52	1	3
Bettws Ieuan, Ch.				69	3	0	12 5	92	0	0
Bettws Lleuci, P.C. .....·.........	0	13	4	134	19	0	4 9	58	10	6
Blaen Penial, P.C.	0	13	4	46	0	0	11 0	55	2	10
Blaen Porth, P.C. .... L.	5	0	0	129	7	4	15 8	61	17	0
Bryn Gwyn, Ch. ....B.				76	18	6	17 0			
Cardigan, V. ....Pr. W.	9	15	10	368	2	8	3 1	131	17	0
Caron, V. ....B.	8	0	0	481	1	0				
Cellan, R. .. ..B.	5	7	8½	47	12	3	5 0	101	13	7
Cil Cennin, V. ....B.	5	0	0	99	13	6	12 0	40	17	6
Ciliau Aeron, R. ....B.	5	0	0	50	6	5	10 0	88	10	0
Dihewid, P. C. ....L.	4	0	0	93	10	9	14 0	62	18	6
Eglwys Vach, Ch.								71	9	0
Eglwys Newydd, P. C.	5	0	0					27	17	8
Ferwig, V. ....Cr.	10	13	4	129	4	1	11 0	87	12	0
Gartheli, P.C.	0	13	4					87	9	6
Gwnnws, C. ....L.	5	0	0	123	8	7		36	0	4
Gwynvil, Ch.	0	13	4	See Llan Dewr, B.						
Henvynwy, P.C. ....E.				86	6	10	16 9¾	58	16	0
Henllan, R. ....B.				17	7	8		21	2	6
Llanavan, P.C. .... L.	3	6	8	56	5	9	6 7	80	3	8
Llanarth, V. ....B.	4	18	1	366	16	8	15 6	700	0	0
Llanbadarn Vawr, V ....R.	20	0	0	959	9	9		136	12	0
Llanbadarn Odwyn, Ch..........	5	0	0	52	8	0	5 0			
Llanbadarn Vach, V. ....B.	6	0	0	138	0	0	12 0	40	17	6
Llanbedr Pont Stephen, V...B.	6	13	4	217	5	0	10 0			
Llan Ddeiniol, P. C. ....L.	6	0	0	37	0	11	5 3	48	7	0
Llan Ddewi, A. Arth, P. C..E.	6	0	0	94	12	7	9 5	60	11	6
Llan Ddewi Brevi, P. C .....L.	6	0	0	287	19	3		110	10	6
Llan Dyvriog, V. ....B.	8	0	0	143	6	8				
Llandygwydd, P. C. ....E.	7	0	0	207	1	7	11 0	73	1	6
Llandysil, R. & V. ....B.	12	16	8	604	17	2	15 0	31	10	0
	10	0	0							
Llan Dysilio gogo, V. .... B.	3	18	1	224	11	5	15 0	4	0	0
Llanvair Clydogau, P. C. ....L.	4	0	0	50	14	0	6 1	83	14	6
Llan Vair Oer llwyn, R. ....B.	4	13	4	31	2	3	12 4			
Llan Vair Tre Lygon, R......B.				6	0	3	3 5			
Ll. Vingl. Geneu'r Glyn, V. B.	12	0	0	687	4	5				
Ll. V. Llethyr Troed, P.C..E.	4	0	0	120	13	9		88	0	0
Ll. V. y Creiddyn, V.........B.	8	0	0	311	9	2	9 6	118	4	3
Ll. V. Ystrad, V. ....B.	4	18	1	317	4	5	14 0	78	4	0
Llan Geitho, R. ....L.	6	0	0	75	18	0	12 2	72	11	0
Llan Goed mawr, R. ....Ld.Ch.	12	18	6	233	5	11	11 0			
Llan Granwg, V. ....B.				96	11	8	11 10	72	0	0
Llan Gybi, P.C. ....L.	2	0	0	24	3	0	4 6	76	8	0
Llan Gynvelyn, P.C. ....L.	6	13	4	128	13	0	12 0	29	9	4
Llan Gynllo, R. ....L.	6	13	4	114	14	11	15 6			
Llan Ilar, V. ....B.	6	13	4	169	0	5		102	19	0
Llan Ina, Ch. ....S. Llanarth.				43	10	10	14 0			
Llanllwchhaiarn, P.C. ....L.				185	0	6	11 7	62	15	0

CARDIGANSHIRE CONTINUED.

Parishes, &c.	Value in King's Book. £ s. d.	Parish Rates in 1803. £ s. d.	s. d.	Modern Value. £ s. d.
Llanllwchhaiarn, R.........B.	6 7 8½	148 3 8½	at 19 0	
Llan Rhystyd, V......... ......B.	6 13 4	193 4 7½	10 0	133 3 4
Llan St. Ffraid, V.............B.	6 13 4	153 6 0	9 6	94 15 10
Llan Wenog, V..................B.	8 0 0	222 13 4½	10 0	97 13 6½
Llan Wnen, V...................B.	3 4 9½	54 17 6	7 6	60 3 8
Llan Ych Aeron, P. C........L.	4 0 0	90 8 0	18 0	53 18 4
Llangwyryddon, P. C..........L.	6 13 4	72 0 0	8 0	45 1 4
Llech Rhyd, P. C..............E.		40 12 0	12 0	34 12 0
Mount, P. C....................E.	3 0 0	66 11 1½	16 0	54 14 0
Nant Cynllo, V.................B.	3 13 4	61 7 9	6 10	71 19 8†
Pen Bryn, V ....B.	15 0 0	256 6 7	13 6	
Rhos Ddu, R .... B.	1 6 8			88 13 0
Silian, V.......................B.		38 5 2	7 0	15 0 6
Strata Florida, Ch.............L.	8 0 0			72 5 8
Trev Ilan, R ... .B.	5 0 0	96 15 6	12 0	107 10 0
Tre' Maen, P.C................L.	10. 0 0	46 5 10	10 6	21 0 0
Troed-yr-Aur, R... .....Ld. Ch.	13 0 0	229 10 2	17 6	
Yspytty Cynvyn, P. C........L.		See Ll. Badarn Vawr		73 9 0
Yspytty Ystwyth, P. C......B.		44 13 11	7 0	83 18 0
Ystrad Meirig, Ch..............L.				

£5973 17 3

GLAMORGANSHIRE.—Population in 1831—126,612.

Aber Avan, V. ....L.	9 4 9	16 19 10	1 3	28 13 10
Aber Dâr, V......................E.		436 12 7	13 11¼	34 13 0
Andrew's, St. R...........King.	14 13 1	273 19 8	6 9	
Andrew's, Minor, C............L.	5 0 0			5 0 0
Athan, St. R..... ....L.	15 9 7	125 17 1	1 8	
Baglan, C. . . . . . . L.		121 19 2		52 0 0
Barry, R. . . . . . . L.	26 0 0	47 9 10		41 13 0
Bettws, C. . . . . The Crn.	37 0 0	180 19 10	4 0	
Bishopston, R. . . . . B.	9 6 8	102 18 9	7 10	134 18 11
Bonvilston, C. . . . . L.	6 9 2	67 14 0	1 6	32 11 3
Bride, St. R.		72 1 4	3 4½	
Bride, St. Major, V.. . . L.	9 16 5	352 11 0¾	2 2	
Bride, St. Minor, R. . . L.	5 3 6	90 3 3¼	5 3	134 14 7
Briton Ferry, C. . . . . L.		72 12 2	8 0	72 16 8
Cadoxton, V. . . . . . L.	5 11 10	1162 17 5		79 15 3
Cadoxton juxta Barry, R. . L.	5 2 1	55 7 7¼	9 9	69 10 7
Caerau, P. C. . . . . . E.	3 10 7	46 6 4	2 6	35 0 0
Cardiff, St. John's, V. . . E.	13 14 6	784 6 7	3 0	99 13 4
St. Mary's V. . . E.	4 5 10	331 17 5		
Cheriton, R. . . . Ld. Ch.	9 7 3	26 7 4¼	0 8	116 4 7
Cil Bebyll, R. . . . . . K.	4 6 8	39 7 5	5 0	54 17 4
Coychurch, R. . . . . . L.	21 1 8	352 13 6		
Cogan, V. . . . . . . L.		43 2 2	6 0	

† Two-thirds of the tithes belong to a Prebend in Brecon Church.

GLAMORGANSHIRE CONTINUED.

Parishes, &c.	Value in King's Book. £ s. d.	Parish Rates in 1803. £ s. d. e. d.	Modern Value. £ s. d.
Colwynston, V. . . . . . L.	6 6 8	101 6 10 at 1 6	111 18 0
Cowbridge, Ch. . . . . . E.		209 15 9 5 6	
Coyty, R. . . . . . . L.	21 12 3½	304 0 11½	
Cynvig, V. . . . . . .Cr.	4 8 11½	79 9 2 8 0	67 0 0
Donat's, St. V. . . . . . L.	3 14 4½	124 10 0	99 15 3
Do. Welsh, Ch. . . . . . E.	15 0 0	87 18 1 6 0	
Eglwys Brewis, R. . . . E.	3 18 6½	37 19 0 2 0	73 16 4
Eglwys Ilan, V. . . . . B.	6 13 1½	870 8 8½ 18 10	120 0 0
Ewenny, Donative. . . . L.			40 0 0
Fagan, St. R. . . . . . L.	14 9 7	385 14 7	400 0 0
Flemingston, R. . . . . L.	4 18 9	28 3 5	86 11 3
Gelli Gaer, R. . . . . . L.	20 7 11	391 13 5 7 0	260 0 0
George, St. R. . . . . . L.	7 5 7½	57 14 8	105 17 0
Gileston, R. . . . . . E.	5 13 6½	7 17 2½	63 15 2
Glyn Corwg, C. . . . . L.	10 0 0	89 6 10	59 8 4
Hilary, St. V. . . . . E.	5 14 4½	107 15 4 1 9	37 14 0
Ilston, R. . . . . Ld.Ch.	9 6 8	87 12 2 9 0	105 10 0
John's St. P.C. . . . . L.	5 0 0		27 0 0
Knelston, V. . . . . . E.		23 2 11 8 0	
Lalyston, C. . . . . . K.	17 0 0	124 2 0 4 0	
Lantwit Vaerdre, C. . . .		238 0 0	32 0 0
Lantwit Lower, Ch. . . . L.		393 18 0	
Llavernog, R.		46 15 2 6 9	
Llanbleiddan, V. . . . E.	10 3 4	166 18 6 1 9	
Llancarvan, V. . . . . E.	8 3 9	318 11 6 1 6	74 10 3
Llanddewi, V. . . . . B.	3 3 4	36 17 2 3 6	55 5 0
Llan Giwg, P.C. . . . . L.		121 12 3 13 0	51 10 0
Llandaff, V. . . . . . E.		621 4 9 10 0	61 16 8
			39 6 8
			V. Ch. £100.
Llandeilo Tal y bont, V. . L.	4 14 7	171 18 10 8 0	
Llan Doch, R. . . . . L.	8 8 4	67 7 7 8 6	136 8 3
Llan Doch, R. . . . . L.	4 18 9	44 14 2 1 5	
Llan Dwvr, R. . . . . E.	7 4 4½	14 2 0	
Llandyvodwg, V. . . . L.	8 13 4	155 9 0 5 6	63 0 0
Llan Edeyrn, V. . . . . E.	5 1 11¼	271 9 7¼ 4 3	
Llan Vabon, Ch. . . .		191 14 5 8 0	
Ll. Vihangel Bont Vaen, R. L.		34 9 6 1 3	72 11 3
Llan Ganna, R. . . . . L.	12 16 0	88 14 4 5 0	
Llangevelach, V. . . . B.	9 14 9	982 10 0	
Llan Geinwyr, P.C. . . . L.	10 0 0	103 3 0 8 6	29 13 0
Llangenydd, V. . . . . E.	5 16 8	87 16 0 3 0	60 16 8
Llan Gynwyd Vawr, V. . L.	19 5 0	438 7 2	149 13 11
Llan Haran, C.		77 18 0 6 0	
Llan Hary, R. . . . . L.	5 12 8	122 0 1 6 7	94 19 0
Llan Ilid, R. . . . Ld.Ch.	7 15 7	66 17 8 4 0	92 17 8
Llan Illtrwm, Ch. . . . L.		61 0 3	
Llan Illtid Vawr, V. . . E.	14 13 9	362 17 5 2 0	
Llan Isan, P. C. L. . . L.	10 0 0	269 1 0 11 0	46 0 0
Llan Vadoc, R. . . P.W.	9 0 0	21 12 4 2 2	124 4 6
Llan Vaes, R. . . . . L.	10 2 3	84 19 9 1 6	305 12 0
Llan Rhidian, V. . . . L.	12 13 4	848 3 10	40 0 0
Llan Samled, C. . . . B.	12 0 0	525 2 3	
Llan Sannwr, R. . . . L.	7 15 7	63 5 3 3 0	82 10 6

GLAMORGANSHIRE CONTINUED.

Parishes, &c.	Value in King's Book. £ s. d.	Parish Rates in 1803. £ s. d. s. d.	Modern Value. £ s. d.
Llan Trisant, V............E	24 14 2	1268 16 9 at	
Llan Tryddyd, R............L.	8 13 4	65 13 8 3 0	
Llan Wyno, C.............E.		362 9 9 9 6	18 0 0
Llechwedd, R..........L.		70 10 10 3 9	
Lloughor, R............Ld.Ch.	9 10 5	124 15 4	105 18 0
Llys Vaen, P.C............L.	10 0 0	55 5 6 8 6	18 0 0
Llys Werni, V.............E.	4 7 3	83 1 3¼	
Lythian, St. V............L.	6 1 3	54 0 8	115 16 4
Marcrees, R. ....B.	9 10 10	15 3 7	
Margam, C...............C.	40 0 0	780 19 9 10 0	40 0 0
Martin, St. Ch...........E.			81 0 0
Mary, St. on the Hill, R...L	5 11 3	53 6 10 5 0	
Mary, St. P.C...........L.	5 6 8	69 18 3 2 3	110 0 0
Merthyr Dyvan, R........L.	4 17 3	105 4 5¾	64 16 8
Merthyr Mawr, P.C.......E.	13 6 8	80 11 0 3 7	42 16 4
Merthyr Tudvyl, R........L.	20 5 7	1453 17 10 6 6	
Michaelston, Le Pit, R....L.	4 10 7	35 16 0 5 0	53 11 3
Mich. super Avan, P.C....L.		74 9 6	60 0 0
Mich. super Elay, R.....L.	8 6 8	13 15 1 1 1	117 7 6
Monk Nash, C............L.	15 0 0	46 10 0 ·7 3	48 0 0
Neath, R................L.	16 2 3	919 15 1 5 6	
New Castle, V.........King.	7 7 3	249 18 7	
Newton Nottage, R........L.		171 12 8 10 6	
Nicholas, St. R............L.	11 0 0	140 7 7 1 7	
Nicholaston, R............L.		15 4 5 4 0	43 14 4
Oxwich, R................L.	9 9 2	18 7 3 4 6	120 7 11
Oystermouth, P.C........L.	10 0 0	132 13 10 5 6	35 14 0
Penarth, V...............L.	4 17 11	41 13 7¾ 5 0	119 6 4
Penarth, V.............E.	3 16 8	79 13 0 5 9	54 0 0
Pen Deulwyn, V............E.	8 13 4	221 5 5 5 0	143 13 11
Pen Llyn, V...............L.	4 15 2	89 4 3 4 6	35 14 10
Pen Maen, R........Ld.Ch.	4 10 0	7 7 9	143 10 0
Pen Marc, V ....E.	8 13 4	309 15 3 2 11	140 19 10
Pen Rhys, P.C ....L.	5 0 0	63 7 4 5 6	37 0 0
Pentyrch, V... ......E.	8 3 1	324 17 6¼ 17 4	94 0 0
Peterstone, R. ....!.	71 2 8	155 1 6¼ 2 1	
Porth Ceri, R. ....L.	7 8 1	25 6 2 0 8	138 19 8
P -th Einion, R ......Ld. Ch.	9 5 10	42 19 3 6 4	139 3 0
Pyle, Ch........ .....Cr.		126 7 11 7 6	
Reynoldston, R............L.	5 11 0	39 3 3 1 2	79 13 11
Rhaiadr, V. ....L.	15 0 0	135 2 4¾ 6 6	79 0 0
Rhos Sili, R....... Ld.Ch.	9 6 8	31 16 4¼ 2 11¼	102 15 0
Rhudd Dre, Ch........B.		157 12 3	
Roath, V.................L.	7 0 0	264 12 2 8 0	49 0 0
Sully, R·................L.	11 9 9	105 13 3 5 0	133 9 6
Swansea, V. ....L.	7 14 4	1630· 9 11	50 0 0
Tythegston, C... ......King.		107 19 8¼	
Wenvoe, R..............L.	13 7 1	178 10 11 1 10	350 0 0
Whitchurch, Ch..........E.		370 10 6 13 4	
Wick, Cu....	14 0 0	67 18 6	
Ystrad Dyvodwg, P.C.....E.		222 19 1	44 0 0
Ystrad Owain, P.C........E.		49 3 1 2 6	9 0 0

£7382 15 2½

PEMBROKESHIRE.—Population in 1831—81,424.

Parishes, &c.	*Value in King's Book.*			*Parish Rates in 1803.*					*Modern Value.*		
	£	s.	d.	£	s.	d.	s.	d.	£	s.	d.
Ambleston, V .... . Ld. Ch.	3	19	4½	164	8	9 at			56	11	5
Amroth, V................L.	3	18	6¼	112	5	11½	7	6	88	14	6
Angle, R.& V........Ld. Ch.	14	9	2	123	19	4			48	15	0
Bayvill, V............Ld. Ch.	5	0	0	17	11	6	14	4½	133	14	6
Bugeli, R........Ld. Milford.	12	19	2	91	18	5					
Bletherston, Ch				145	0	11	4	0			
Bosheston, R...... ....L.	11	6	8	79	2	2	1	0	128	18	0
Boulston, C ....L.				42	16	2¼					
Brawdy, V................B.	3	18	9	123	3	5½			22	3	8
Briddell, R................L.	9	0	0	54	17	8			112	9	3
Bride, St. R...............L.	15	12	11	111	0	1	2	0			
Burton, R.................L.	15	12	11	85	4	0	3	0			
Camrhos, V........... .. L.	6	10	5	371	15	1			89	0	0
Carew, V..................B.				404	18	7			74	15	3
Castle Beith, R.........Ld.Ch.	6	0	0	69	17	9¼			98	10	3
Castle Martin, V...........L.	7	17	6	233	11	2½			53	14	8
Cil Garan, R..... .... King.	9	0	0	177	18	7			149	0	0
Cil Gwyn, Ch.... See Nevern.									0	12	0
Clarbeston, P.C	5	15	0	40	10	0			29	10	0
Clydau, Preb. & V ....B.	12	0	0	156	13	3			70	10	0
	6	0	0								
Coed Camlas, C......				31	6	3¼					
Colman, P.C...... .... L.				35	3	7			32	2	6
Cosheston, R............. L.	11	12	11	111	17	6¾	2	4	131	0	0
Crinow, R........... Ld.Ch.				12	8	2	2	0	46	14	3
Cronwear, R...............Do	6	16	10½	63	13	5	12	0	110	0	0
Dale, P.C ....L.	6	0	0	175	17	7	3	9	59	18	0
David's, St. V........... E.				667	13	11			59	11	6
Dinas, R.. ....L.	8	0	0	76	11	11	6	0	101	6	0
Dogvael, St. V............E.	4	16	0½	106	4	4½			71	0	0
Dogmael, St. V..... Ld.Ch.	4	13	4	400	0	0			67	4	4
Edeyrn, St. P.C..... .....E.	4	0	0	37	13	4			35	16	8
Eglwys Wrw, V. ..... Ld.Ch.	3	13	4	119	2	6			85	15	0
Egremont, Cu...............L.	3	0	0	29	12	6	18	0	32	12	0
Elvis, St. R.............Ld.Ch.	2	10	10	7	3	3			59	18	6
Fishguard, V.............Do.	4	0	5	287	0	7¾			61	1	0
Florence, St. R. & V.......E.	R 16	12	1	94	18	2	1	0	59	14	3
E.	V 4	18	4								
Ford, Ch	2	0	0						35	0	0
Freystrop, R...........Ld.Ch.	5	13	9	94	9	9¼					
Grandston, V....... ......B.	6	8	11½	52	7	0			29	18	7
Gumfreston, R ....L.	9	12	3½	39	12	6	1	0	117	4	3
Haroldston, East, P.C.........L.	5	0	0	47	5	4½	1	0	33	2	6
Ditto, West, do........E.				46	6	2			100	17	0
Haverfordwest.											
St. Martin's, R.......L.				404	9	7	5	6	47	0	0
St. Mary's, V..........L.				539	6	11	6	6	101	13	0
St. Thomas's R.......K.				287	6	6	5	3			
Hay's Castle, V...............B.				62	4	7			20	0	3
Haysguard, R. ...... Ld.Ch.	18	6	6	68	7	1	2	8	115	6	3
Henry's Moat, R.. ....L.	5	6	8	93	18	6			66	2	6
Herbrandston, R.......Ld.Ch.				132	13	9½	3	6			

PEMBROKESHIRE CONTINUED.

Parishes, &c.	*Value in King's Book.*			*Parish Rates in 1803.*					*Modern Value.*		
	£	S.	D.	£	S.	D.	S.	D.	£	S.	D.
Hodgeston, R..............L.	7	13	4	27	17	3 at			100	13	10
Hubberston, R..........Ld.Ch.	6	2	8½	235	0	0	6	0			
Ishmael, St. V............Do.	6	12	8½	177	6	0½	4	8	62	19	4½
Issell's, St. V.............E.	3	17	6	274	14	11½			91	1	0
Jeffreyston, V ....E.	4	17	6	146	2	8			47	19	0½
Johnston, R ... .Ld.Ch.	2	0	5	28	0	0					
Jordanston, R ....L.	6	3	9	57	14	7			57	13	0
Lambston, P.C ....E.	5	0	0	53	0	0	1	2	108	9	0
Laurence, St. R.......Ld.Ch.	3	18	9	31	15	8			111	0	0
Lamphey, V..............B.	5	8	11½	75	0	1	1	0	69	10	8
Letterston, R...............B.	12	11	0½	47	12	0					
Llanbedr Velvrey, R...Ld.Ch.	10	0	0	276	12	8					
Ll. Ddewi Velvrey, R.&V. Do.	8	0	0	141	7	3					
	7	9	4½								
Llandeilo, V... ....L.				3	8	7	16	10			
Llan Dylwyv, V..........E.	5	0	0	60	12	11			29	18	9
Llanvair Nant Gwyn, C....L.	3	0	0	48	18	7½			77	17	6
Llanvernach, R ....Ld.Ch.	10	0	0	131	4	0			138	12	0
Ll. Vihangel Penbedw, R..K.	6	0	0	61	2	4			70	10	0
Llan Golman, C .... L.				41	12	10½					
Llan Gwm, R...............L.	7	12	11	184	3	4½			110	11	1½
Llan Hauaden, V...........B.	8	18	6½	161	14	8	1	5½	128	12	8
Llan Hywel, V.............				40	8	3			26	18	7
Llan Llawen, R.............				47	12	7			53	6	3
Llan Rhiain, V... ....B.	6	11	3	2[illegible]2	14	11½			69	10	6½
Llan Rhidian, P.C........E.				68	15	0			48	0	4
Llan Stadwel, V.... .....L.	7	17	0	189	15	7½	0	6	93	16	9
Llan Stinan, P.C. ....L.	4	0	0	89	5	3½			56	11	0
Llan Tyd, V..........Ld.Ch.	5	0	0	49	18	1			23	2	0
Llan Wnda, V...... .....E.	3	5	2½	178	18	10½			71	10	0
Llan y Cevn, P.C..........L.				59	14	1	1	6¼	35	0	0
Llan y Chaer, R..........L.	3	6	8	23	1	5			57	1	0
Llan ych Llwydog, R.... ..L.	8	0	0	46	1	8	3	6	75	5	0
Llaw Rynni, R ....L.	13	0	0	164	11	4					
Llys y Vran, R..... ......L.	3	0	5	46	7	3½	2	1¼	102	5	6
Loveston, R............ ..L.	4	5	5	61	11	2	3	4	81	4	3
Ludchurch, R.........Ld.Ch.	3	14	4½	42	14	7			82	18	3
Maen Clochog, V ....L.	3	18	9	51	7	10¾			21	1	0
Manachlog Ddu, P.C.... .L.	5	0	0	65	8	11½			133	11	11
Maenor Byrr, V........ E.	8	0	0	273	13	2	1	0	31	4	11
Maenor Dewi, R.........King.	9	0	0	114	2	9½	18	0¼	200	0	0
Maenor Owain, C. ...... .E.	4	0	0	52	2	2¾			44	2	6
Marloes, V ....Ld.Ch.	5	0	0	130	4	11	3	4	67	5	0
Martletwy, V........ ..... L.	4	0	0	149	2	7½			61	4	0
Melinau, R.................L.	10	0	0	96	4	0			109	6	0
Morthyr, V ....B.	4	7	6	237	3	11			118	8	9
Minwear, V.. ....L.	7	0	0	46	5	7	3	0	49	5	0
Monington, V ....Ld.Ch.	3	0	0	56	13	9			12	2	0
Morvil, R ....L.	2	0	0	17	15	6					
Mounton, Ch...............E.				11	2	1	1	7½			
Mor'grove, V.........Ld.Ch.				73	7	9½	12	0			
Narberth, R.............King.	25	10	10	406	10	6½					

PEMBROKESHIRE CONTINUED.

Parishes, &c.	*Value in King's Book.*			*Parish Rates in 1803.*					*Modern Value.*		
	£	S.	D.	£	S.	D.	S.	D.	£	S.	D.
Nash, R....................E.	6	12	8½	27	6	4 at			78	15	3
Nevern, V............Ld.Ch.	8	0	0	373	6	2					
New Castle, (Little) P.C. .L.	5	0	0	39	9	8	6	8	37	0	0
New Moat, R...............L.	2	4	7	112	4	5½	2	1½			
Newport, R....... ....L.	16	0	0	159	11	2			93	14	0
Newton North, P.C .... ..L.				22	15	3			57	7	0
Nicholas, St. V.......... ..B.				59	6	11			17	5	7½
Nolton, R .. .. .. .Ld.Ch.	4	2	11	62	16	4			95	6	6
Pembroke, Mary, St. V.. L.				512	12	6	0	6			
Michael, St. V..L.	4	0	0	215	10	7					
Nicholas, St ...L.				329	7	0¼	0	6			
Penaley, V........... ....B.				110	6	0	1	0	81	10	5
Pen Rhydd, R ....Ld.Ch.	4	0	0	57	6	0			58	3	6
Petrox, R.... ....Do.	7	3	9	42	16	5			113	0	8
Pont Vaen, R...	3	6	8	16	8	0½					
Pendregast, R..... ...Ld.Ch.	9	14	9	202	11	5	8	9	100	0	6
Puncheston, R ....L.	5	6	8	38	11	0			110	9	0
Pwll-y-Crochan, R.....Ld.Ch.	9	12	11	94	2	7			115	1	4
Redbert, Ch....................B.	2	5	0	13	2	9	4	0	27	9	0
Reynoldston, Donative.....L.				35	6	7½			39	1	0
Rhos Gylyddwr, R....Ld.Ch.	15	12	11	94	19	1½					
Rhos Market, V...........L.	4	0	0	123	9	2½	3	0	77	14	0
Robeston, Wathan, Ch				82	18	5	2	0			
Robeston, West, R....Ld.Ch.	6	6	8	78	6	0	0	6	104	19	11
Roch, V....................Do.	4	13	9	122	12	0			84	3	9
Rudbaxton, R...... .... Do.	15	4	2	198	1	8					
Slebech, P.C...............L.	5	0	0	199	2	11			55	15	0
Spittal, C....................L.	5	10	0	56	13	7	6	1	44	8	0
Stackpool, R. & V...........L.	R 15	12	11	97	5	6			63	13	8
	V 3	18	4								
Stainton, V............Ld.Ch.	9	17	3½	426	3	6	4	6			
Talbenny, R..................L.	9	12	6	57	7	3	2	6			
Tal-y-llechau, P.C. ....E.	8	0	0	168	3	9	5	6	54	4	0
Tenby, R. & V.........King.	R 26	10	10	371	5	4					
	V 13	6	8								
Trev Garn, R...............E.	14	0	0	25	16	4	2	0	47	13	0
Twynell's, St. V............E.				80	6	0			82	3	6
Usmaston, P.C........ ....E.	5	10	0	116	13	6			35	0	0
Walton, East, C...........L.	10	0	0	56	18	9			50	2	6
Walton, West, R............L.	6	13	4	62	14	10			141	15	6
Walwyn's Castle, R..Ld.Ch.	7	13	4	129	15	10					
Warren, V..................B.	4	8	1½	72	12	3			49	12	11
Whitchurch, or Eglwys Wen, R....L.	6	0	0	66	4	9					
Whitchurch, or Tre 'r Croes, V.....E.	5	15	7½	169	14	5			79	7	9
Williamston, Ch				60	11	5					
Wiston, C...................L.	9	0	0	320	14	7			131	15	0
Yerbeston, R...............L.	5	3	9	46	19	7			100	9	2
									£6678	7	11

RADNORSHIRE.*—Population in 1831—24,651.

Parishes.	Patron.	Incumbent.	His Income.		Incumbent's Residence.	Extent, &c.
Aber Edw. R	Archdeacon of Cardigan	J. Williams			Abercamlais, near Brecon	8000 acres, very valuable
Llanvaredd, Ch						
Bleddva, R	Bishop of St. David's	E. Halliday			Portsmouth, Hampshire	
Boughrood, V	Ditto ditto	W. Wilkins			Hay, Breconshire	
Bryn Gwyn, R	Ditto ditto	J. Davies			Glamorganshire	4000 acres
Bugeildy, V	Ditto ditto	J. Evans	143 9 6		Harrow, near London	
Cascob, R	Ditto ditto	J. Rees	143 6 8		Resides	
Cevn Llys, R	Ditto ditto	— Barker			Whitton	5000 acres
Clyrow, V	Ditto ditto	Dr. Venables			Clyrow	
Bettws Clyrow, Ch						
Cregrina, R	Ditto ditto	— Powel	80 14 0		Resident	
Llanbadarn y Gareg, Ch			40 14 0			
Cwm Dauddwr, V		— Evans	59 4 7		Rhaiadr	
Diserth, R	Ditto ditto	C. Griffith			Brecon	4000 acres
Bettws	Ditto ditto					
Glasbury, V	Ditto of Gloucester	— Bradley			In England	
Gladestry, R	The Crown	Under Sequestration				
Glascwm, V	Bishop of St. David's	— Jones	62 2 5		Glascwm	
Colva, Ch			24 19 0			
Rulen, Ch			16 10 6			
Harmon, St. V	Ditto ditto	— Thorsby	97 10 2		Brecknockshire	
Heyop, R	Ditto ditto	W. J. Rees	103 6 0		Cascob	
Knighton, P.C	Warden of Clun Hospital	— Morris			Resides	Tithes belong to Clun Hospital
Llan Anno, P.C	Chancellor of Brecon	— Foley	33 1 6		Ditto	
Llanbadarn, Vawr, R	Bishop of St. David's	C. Griffith	136 12 0		Brecon	
Llanba:larn Vynydd, P.C	Chancellor of Brecknock	— Foley	50 3 0		Llan Anno	
Llanbedr, Pain's Castle, P.C.	Prebendary	E. Lewis	50 0 0		Crug Hywel, Brecknockshire	

Parish	Patron	Incumbent	£ s. d.	Notes
Llanbister, V.	Bishop of St. David's.	E. Lloyd.	46 6 0	Resident.
Cwm Hir, Ch.	}		35 15 0	
Llanddewi Ystradenni, P.C.	Prebendary of Llanbister	A. Barker.		
Llandegla, V.	Bishop of St. David's.	Jones.	76 10 6	Ditto.
Llandeilo Graban, P.C.	J. Mayberry, Esq.	Powel.	69 0 0	Ditto.
Llandrindod, P.C.	J. Dale, Esq.	Jones.	35 0 0	Ditto.
Llanelwedd, C.	The Prebendary.	Powel.	45 18 0	Ditto.
Llan Vihangel Helygen, P.C.	Vicar of Nantmel.	Wood.	85 0 0	Lancashire.
Llan V. Nant Melyn, V.	The Crown.	W. P. Williams.	112 13 6	New Radnor.
Llan V. Rhyd Ithon, P.C.	Prebendary of Llanbister	A. Barker.	36 10 0	
Llangynllo, V.	Bishop of St. David's.	M. Evans.	83 2 5	Resident.
Llan St. Ffraid, V.	Ditto ditto.	Davies.	128 11 11	Ditto.
Llan Stephen, P.C.	Prebendary.	Powel.	45 10 0	Llandeilo Graban.
Llowes, V.	Ditto.	J. Williams.		Abercamlais, near Brecon.
Llundewi Vach, Ch.	}			
Michaelchurch, Ch. to Kings'n	Bishop of Hereford.	Wall.		Kingston.
Nantmel, V.	Ditto of St. David's.	Venables, D.D.	71 10 0	
Llanhir			112 0 0	Clyrow.
New Church, R.	Ditto ditto.	Byers.		Pembrokeshire.
Norton, V.	The Crown.	Jenkins.		Neighbourhood.
Pilleth, V.	Bishop of St. David's.	M. Evans.	21 1 7	Llangynllo.
Presteign, R.	Lord Oxford.	Beebee.		Resides.
Radnor, Old, V.	Dn. & Ch. of Worcester.	T. Powel.		Herefordshire.
Radnor, New, R.	The Crown.	Merreweather.		London.
Rhaiadr, P.C.	Vicar of Nantmel.	Evans.	49 19 0	Resident.
Whitton, R.	Bishop of St. David's.	Brigstock.	125 11 1	Pembrokeshire.

Worth £1000 a year.

* 'In many parts of South Wales, all the tithes belong to laymen, who pay but little to the Church. In such cases, though no fixed stipend was prescribed at the Reformation, it was, undoubtedly, meant, that the curate should be maintained by the lay rector. At present, many lay rectors do not pay enough to *keep the veriest pauper from starvation*: they leave the clergyman to fees and Queen Anne's Bounty, thus shifting on the people those charges to which even Henry the Eighth had subjected them!

NORTH WALES.

The valuation of the Benefices in North Wales, as stated in the following Table, is the result of a correspondence carried on by the Author, with gentlemen well acquainted with the present condition of the various parishes, and on whose intelligence he can rely. To his informants, he takes this opportunity of expressing his acknowledgments, for the great and laborious exertions that they have made on his behalf, and for the kindness and confidence they have extended to him.

ANGLESEY.—POPULATION IN 1831—48,325.—DIOCESE OF BANGOR.

Parish.	Patron.	Lay Impropriator.	His Tithe	Ecclesiastical Impropriator.	His Tithe	Incumbent.	His Tithe &c.	Residence & its Distance from Parish.	N
			£		£		£		
Aberffraw, R	The Crown.					H. Wynne Jones.	700	His own property in Bodedeyrn parish	8
Amlwch, P.C. Llanwenllwyvo. Bodedeyrn, P.C.	Jesus College, Oxon.	Lord Boston.	150	Bishop of Bangor, annexed in 1685. Jesus College, Oxon, with Holyhead.	700	Mr. Johnson.	180	Partly fees.	
Bodwrog, P.C. Llandrygarn. Bodewyrd, P.C. Hen Eglwys, R. Gwalchmai.	Sir J. Stanley. Bishop.				1450	Mr. Hughes. H. Griffith.	105 100	Llechgynfarwy. Caernarvonshire.	2
						J. Owen. T. Evans.	110 400	Llaneilian. Beaumaris.	6 13
Holyhead, P.C	Jesus College, Oxon.			Jesus College, Oxon, see Bodedeyrn.		J. Jones, mostly fees	145		
Llanbadrig	Lord Chancellor.	H. D. Griffith, Esq. Caerhun.	900			J. Ellis	250	Llanveehell	

Parish	Patron	Farms Tithe free	Incumbent		Residence	
Llanbeulan, R	Bishop		W. Roberts	700	Beaumaris	28
Llanvaelog						
Llechylched						
Ceirchiog						
Ll'erchymedd						
Tal-y-llyn						
Llandegvan, R	Sir R. Bulkeley	Sir J. Stanley	J. Vincent	100	Caernarvonshire	12
Beaumaris		Lord Boston	R. Howard, D.D.	380		
		750	H. Rowland	300		
Llanidar, V						
Llaredwen						
Llanddeiniol						
Llanvair-y-Cwm-mwd						
Llanddeusant, R	Bishop	Lord Boston	J. Williams	680		
Llanvair yn nghornwy		200				
Llanbabo						
Llanddona	Lord Boston		W. Lewis	110	Llangoed	4
Llaneilian, R	Bishop		M. Lewis	400	Beaumaris	15
Coed-ana						
Rhos-beirio						
Llaneigrad, R	Bishop		R. Davies	180		
Llanallgo						
Penrhos llugwy						
Llanddyvnan, P.C	Bishop	Bishop of Bangor in commendam	B. Williams. Made up chiefly of Fees paid by the people	100		
Pentraeth		700	E. Williams			
Llanbedr				100		
Ll'avair Math avarn eithav						
Llanddwyvdog, R	Bishop		Dr. R. Williams	520	Trevdraeth	3
Llanvihangel Tre'r Beirdd						

ANGLESEY, DIOCESE OF BANGOR, CONTINUED.

Parish.	Patron.	Lay Impropriator.	His Tithe	Ecclesiastical Impropriator.	His Tithe	Incumbent.	His Tithe &c.	Residence & its Distance from Parish.	MHM
			£		£		£		
Llanddwynwen.	In ruins.								
Llanvachreth, R...	Bishop.					T. Ellis.	480	Bangor	20
Llanvugail.									
Llanynghenedl.									
Llanvaes, P. C.		Sir R. Bulkeley.	180			J. Williams.	100	Beaumaris	
Penmon.									
Llanvacthlu, R.....	Bishop.					Lloyd.	440		
Llanvrog.									
Llanvechell, R.....	Bishop.					J. Lewis.	280		
Llanddygwel.									
Llanvair Pwll-gwyngyll, R.	Bishop.					— Prichard.	254	Llangaffo	5
Llandysilio (in the Sea).				Rev. J. Warren, Dean of Bangor.	400	W. Warren.	110	Bangor	7
Llan V. Ysgeir-iog Llaufihnan.	Lord Chancellor.					J. Williams.	200		
Llangadwaladr, R.	Mrs. Hughes.					W. Williams.	600	Caernarvon	3
Llanveirion.									
Llangeinwen.......	Bishop.					E. Williams.	400		
Llangaffo.									
Llangevni, R.......	— Hughes, Esq.	— Hughes, Esq.	380			J. Williams.	100	Beaumaris	4
Tregaian									
Llangoed, P. C....									
Llaniestyn									
Ll. V. Din Sulwy									

Parish	Patron		Value	Incumbent	Value	Residence	Notes
Llangristiolus, P.C. / Cerig Ceinwen.							
Llaugwyllog, P.C.	Sir R. Bulkeley.	Sir R. Bulkeley.					150
Llanrhuddlad, R. / Llanfflewyn. / Llaurhwydrus.	Bishop.		300	J. Roberts, made up in a great measure of Fees paid by the people.	500		120
Llansadwrn, R.	Bishop.			O. G. Williams.	75	Pentraeth.	2
Llantrisant, R.	Ditto.			S. Majendie.	550	Lichfield.	8
				W. Thomas.	380	Pentraeth.	
Llechcynvarwy. / Llanllibio. / Gwaredog. / Ceidio.				H. W. Jones.	500	Bodedeyrn.	
Newborough, R.	Lord Chancellor.						
Penmynydd, P.C. Pre	Prebend.			H. Rowlands.	250	Llanedwen.	6
Peurhos, P.C.	Lord Boston.	Lord Boston.	100	Davies Owen.	90	Beaumaris.	4
Rhos-colyn, R.	Bishop.		550	O. G. Williams.	55	Pentraeth.	7
Llanvihangel-yn-nbywyn. / Llanvair-yn-neu-bwll.				E. Williams.	400	Llanbeulan.	Preb. H. Majendie; resides in England.
Trevdraeth, R. / Llangwyven.	Bishop.			R. Williams, D.D.	500		

SUMMARY.

ABSENTEEISM.—Anglesey contains 75 parishes, (chapelries included); 62 of these are in the hands of non-resident incumbents; 55 have no resident minister whatever. Total number of incumbents, 40; non-residents, 22. Benefices without either incumbent or curate, 19.

CURATES.—19 parishes are served by six ministers. The curate of Llanrhuddlad and three other parishes travels 14 miles every Sunday. The Curate of Ceirchiog and of two others has to travel 10 miles along a wretched road. The Curate of Llanvachreth and of two others has to travel eight miles.

OPULENT CLERGY.—The following incumbents have two or more parishes, and reside on neither :—H. W. Jones has six parishes (two benefices), £1200; W. Roberts, six parishes (one benefice), £700; W. Williams, two parishes (one benefice), £600; T. Ellis, three parishes, (one benefice), £480, also Llanvihangel, in Merionethshire, and resides at Bangor, but he is very old; T. Evans, two parishes (one benefice), £400; Morris Lewis, three parishes (one benefice), £400; Evan Williams, three parishes (one benefice), £400.—The following pluralists reside on one of their benefices :— Dr. Williams has four parishes (two benefices), £1020; H. Rowland has five parishes (two benefices), £550.—J. Vincent, £100; resides in Caernarvonshire, but is not possessed of any valuable Church preferment.— S. Majendie has three parishes (one benefice), which he owes to his father, Bishop Majendie, £550 and resides near Lichfield, at Longdon, which living he also enjoys.

The total amount enjoyed by all the above incumbents, who are either absentees from the county, or living without performing any parochial duty whatever	£4450
Dr. Williams £520. Rev. H. Rowland £250—benefices from which they are absentees	770
Bishop's livings £1,900 Dean Warren £400 Prebendary H. Majendie £500	2850
Jesus College, Oxford	1450
Total as above above, deducting £620 for salaries of the Curates of absentees	8900
Total enjoyed by resident clergy, including curates' salaries paid by absentees, &c. £880, and exclusive of Queen Anne's Bounty and Fees, £1300	5179

Of all abuses in the Church the grossest is the system of relieving Bishops and sinecurists from the maintenance of their own curates, by grants out of Queen Anne's Bounty!! Penmynydd—curate's salary £90 of which only £30 (!) is paid by Prebendary H. Majendie; the rest consists of "bounty" and fees paid by the people. Llanvihangel Ysceiviog—curate's salary £110 of which £36 (!!) only is paid by the incumbent, Dean Warren; the rest is "bounty" land and "fees." The curate himself, a relative of the Dean, is resident in another county! Amlwch—curate's income £180, of which only £45 is paid by the Bishop, who enjoys the benefice. Llanddyvnan—curate £100, of which only £51 is paid by the Bishop. Llangristiolus—curate's salary £120, of which only £30 is paid by the Bishop. Similar remarks are applicable to the livings belonging to Jesus College, Oxford.

Lay impropriators* possess (independently of a few farms which are tithe free) £1890

In every point of view, the state of the Church in this county is indescribably disgraceful. The toil and privations which the poorer clergy have to endure are equal to those of the ministers of South Wales, though here the wealth of the Church is as remarkable as its poverty in that district. There are scarcely any gradations of rank between the sinecurist with a thousand a year, who lives at his ease on his own paternal acres, and the curate of two or three parishes—the serf of the sanctuary!˙ Dissenters are in possession of the whole county.

* The bounty fund has also been applied with a very unsparing hand, in relieving lay impropriators from the burden of supporting their curates; but the responsibilities of a lay impropriator are not of quite so high an order as those of an ecclesiastical sinecurist, who is bound as strictly as an ordinary absentee incumbent, to provide his parish with an officiating minister.

CAERNARVONSHIRE.—POPULATION IN 1831—65,753.—DIOCESE OF BANGOR.

Parish.	Patron.	Lay Impropriator.	His Tithe	Ecclesiastical Impropriator.	His Tithe	Incumbent.	His Tithe &c	Residence & its Distance from Parish	
			£		£		£		
Aberpwyngregin, R.	Sir R. Bulkeley					R. Williams	400	Cheltenham	150
Aberdaron, V.	St. John's College, Cambridge.			St. John's College, Cambridge; added in time of Charles I.	320	— Roes	104		
Llanvaelrhys, C.									
Abererch, V.	Lord Newborough.	Lord Newborough.	350			R. Richards	85	Pwllheli	2
Penrhôs, C.									
Bangor, V.	Bishop.					1st Vicar, J. Cotton	235		
Llangedol, C.						2nd Vicar, J. Hamer	235		
Bedd-Gelert, P.C.	S. Priestley, Esq.	S. Priestley, Esq.	58			H. Pugh	65	Llanvrothen in Merionethshire	7
Bettws Garm'n, P.C.	Bishop.	Lord Newborough.	300			G. A. Williams	150	Caernarvon	5
Ll'nv'r-is-ga'r, P.C.						James Vincent	73		
Bettws-y-coed, P.C.	Lord Willoughby.	Lord Willoughby.	120			E. Evans	100	Llanrwst	3
Bodvaen, R.	Bishop.					J. Owen	230	Conway	37
Bryn croes, P.C.	— Wynne, Esq.	— Wynne, Esq.	450			— Roberts	70	Bottwnog	3
Caernarvon (see Llanbeblig)									
Caer Rhun, V.	Bishop.					J. Hamer	500	Bangor	17
Llanbedr, R									
Ceidio, P.C.	— Wynne, Esq.	— Wynne, Esq.	50			J. Parry	40	Edeyrn	3
Clynnog Vawr, V.	Bishop.			Jesus Col. Oxford.	900	— Williams	220		
Conwy, V.	Sir D. Erskine.	The Poor.	200			J. Owen	127		
Cricineth, R	Bishop.					J. Jones	300		
Ynys Cynhaiarn, C									
Trevlys, C.									
Dolbenmaen, R.	Ditto.					Jeffrey Holland	300		
Pen-morva, R.									
Dolwyddelan, P.C.	Lord Willoughby.	Lord Willoughby.	250			M. Hughes	100	Llanrwst	6

Place					Incumbent		Location	
Dwygyvylchi, C.	Rev. H. Eyton.	H. Eyton.						
Edeyrn, R.	Bishop.		100		J. Eaton.	150	Llangollen, Denbighshire.	40
Pistyll, C.					J. Parry.	350		
Carnguwch, C.								
Gyffin, C.	Dean of Bangor.			J. Warren, Dean of Bangor.	J Owen.	70	Conway.	
Llanaelhaiarn, R.	Bishop.				— Ellis.	200	Abererch.	2
Llanarmon, R.	Ditto.				T. Roberts.	360		
Llangybi, R.								
Llanbeblig, V.	Bishop of Chester.			Bishop of Chester.	J. Trevor.	300		
Caernarvon, C.								
Llanberis, R.	Bishop.				P. B. Williams.	100	Llanrhug.	5
Llanrhug, R.	Ditto.				Ditto.	200		
Llanbedrog, R.	Ditto.				P. Williams, D.D.	580		
Llangian, C.								
Ll.V.bachellethC								
Llanddeiniolen, R.	Chancellor.				T. W. Roberts.	350	Lleyn.	30
Llandegai, V.	Bishop.			Bishop of Bangor, annexed 1865.	E. Jones.	108	Bangor, 2nd master of its school.	2
Capel-Curig, P.C					R. Hughes.	140		
Llandudno, P.C.	Lord W. D. Eresby.				R. Williams.	68		
Llandwrog, R.	Bishop.			J. Jones, Archdeacon	W. Griffith.	540		
Llanengan, R.	Ditto.				W. Jones.	500		
Llangwynodl, P.C.	Ditto.		125		— Evans.	47		2
Llaniestyn, R.	C. Wynne, Esq.	C. Wynne, Esq.			Robert Jones.	500	Bottwnog.	
Bodverin, C.	Bishop.							
Penllech, C.								
Llanvairvechan, R.	Bishop.				R. Thomas.	250	Bangor.	7
Llangelynin, R.	Ditto.				H. Price.	300	Bangor.	3
Llanllechyd, R.	Ditto.				J. H. Cotton.	450		
Llanllyvni, R.	Ditto.				J. Jones.	230		

CAERNARVONSHIRE, DIOCESE OF BANGOR, CONTINUED.

Parish	Patron	Lay Impropriator.	His Tithe	Ecclesiastical Impropriator.	His Tithe	Incumbent.	His Tithe &c.	Residence & its Distance from Parish.	
			£		£		£		M
Llannor, V.	Bishop.					W. Williams	250		
Dineio, C.									
Ll. V. y Pennant, R.	Ditto.					J. Jones.	120	Cricaeth.	2
Llanystumdwy, R.	Ditto.					J. Kyffin.	400		
Llanwnda, V. }	Ditto.			Jesus Col. Oxford.	500	— Hughes.	180		
Llanvaglan, C.						Rev. G. Jones.	250	Rhuthin, Denbighshire.	50
Mellteyrn, R.	Ditto.								
Bottwnog, C.						T. Owen.	95	Bodvaen.	2
Nevyn, V.	C. Wynne, Esq.	C. Wynne, Esq.	210			P. Titley.	92	Llanrwst.	6
Penmachno	Sir R. W. Vaughan.	Sir R. W. Vaughan.	140			J. Ellis.	130		
Rhiw, R. }	Bishop.								
Llandudwen, C.						M. Hughes.	275		
St. Anne's, P.C.	G. D. Pennant, Esq. Penrhyn Castle.					L. Hughes.	200	Bettws y Coed.	
Trefriw, R. }	Bishop.								
Llanrhychwyn.									
Tydweiliog, P. C.	Sir J. Salisbury.	Sir J. Salisbury.	154			J. Evans.	64		

DIOCESE OF ST. ASAPH.

Parish	Patron	Lay Impropriator.	His Tithe	Ecclesiastical Impropriator.	His Tithe	Incumbent.	His Tithe &c.
Eglwys Rhos, V.	Bishop.	Hon. E. Ll. Mostyn.	300	Bishop, added in 1573	300	J. Hughes.	180
Llangwstenin, V	Ditto.	The Poor.	100	Ditto.			
Llyzvaen, R.	Ditto.				35	J. Parry.	250

ABSENTEEISM.—Exclusive of chapels of ease, this county contains 48 benefices, the incumbents of 28 of which are non-resident. Most of the absentees live in an adjoining parish ; but the incumbents of six live, severally, 15 miles off, 50 miles, 40 miles, 37 miles, 30 miles, and 17 miles. One of them is master of Bangor school ; two others vicars choral of Bangor.

CATHEDRAL OF BANGOR.—The Rev. James Cotton, one of the vicars, is a pluralist ; he enjoys one-half of the tithes of Bangor, £235 ; also Llanllechid, £450 ; also a considerable sum from the parishes of Lladdinam comportion, in Montgomeryshire. When preferred to Bangor, he was unacquainted with the Welsh language, and he owes all his preferments to his connection with the late Dr. Majendie, Bishop of Bangor. At the same time, it must be added, that great praise is due to the Reverend gentleman for his zeal in establishing Sunday Schools, and in other good works ; a short time since, he sustained a very considerable pecuniary loss, in consequence of a failure of a savings' bank, at Bangor, for the solvency of which he had pledged himself. On the whole, he is entitled to the gratitude of the people.—The Rev. J. Hamer, the other vicar of Bangor, is also a pluralist, and enjoys the two parishes of Llanbedr and Caerhun, £500 ; but he keeps a curate in each of them, which reduces his clear emoluments from all his preferments to a sum not exceeding those of one good benefice. This, however, cannot and ought not to be deemed any defence of abuses of this description, though it may remove all odium from the individual. The Church is for the people, and not the people for the Church ; and the claims of her ministers are not to be made paramount to the interests and rights of individual parishes. It has been before stated, that the aggregate amount of the income enjoyed by the resident clergy of a whole Hundred in Montgomeryshire falls short of the emoluments of these two vicars choral.

Resident clergy of Llanidloes Hundred . . . . £835.

Two vicars of Bangor (exclusive of curates' salaries) . . . 880.

The ill-fated Hundred alluded to is bound to contribute annually the immense sum of £1305 for the benefit of this single parish,—for the *support of its Cathedral*, which, judging from the immense sums annually required for its repair, must be as unstable in its foundations, as the stone of Sisyphus,—whose ill fate bears but too strong a resemblance to that of the ill-starred inhabitants of the hundred of Llanidloes !

QUEEN ANNE'S BOUNTY.—But the most flagrant abuses in this county arise from a misapplication of Queen Anne's Bounty. To enable the general reader fully to understand the nature of those abuses, a brief history of the origin of that fund may be necessary.* Before the Reformation, the Pope was entitled to the full first year's revenues of every spiritual preferment in England, and to a clear tenth of the revenues of each ensuing year. These charges, which were called the "First fruits" and "Tenths," were annexed to the Crown by an Act passed in the reign of Henry the Eighth. By this statute, it was expressly provided, that the payments due from the Church on account of "First fruits" and "Tenths," should be raised in proportion to the improved value of Church property, and the Sovereign was enabled to issue a commission from time to time, for the purpose of ascertaining the rate of such improvement. One of these commissions was issued in the time of Elizabeth, and a valuation taken under it, which is believed to have been an accurate one for the time. But, from a variety of causes, no further enquiry was instituted down to the reign of Queen Anne, and the sums exacted from the clergy still continued to be regulated by the Standard of Queen Elizabeth's reign, though that valuation had, in the interval, become manifestly insufficient, owing to the improved state of agriculture on the one hand, and the diminished value of the currency on the other. The only effect of this indifference to its rights on the part of the Crown, was to enrich the most opulent clergy at the expense of its hereditary income,—to transfer an immense treasure to those, to whom it in no sense belonged—any more than the tithes of the tithe-owner, or the rents of the landlord, can be said to belong to the farmer. I am not aware that any blame is imputable to the clergy in these transactions, I merely wish to draw the reader's attention to their effect, as the history of these revenues, beyond all question, developes one source of the great wealth of the higher clergy of the Church of England,—and contributes to prove, that those striking inequalities in her preferments, which are by some supposed to have the sanction of high antiquity, are in reality the growth of comparatively modern times. Finally, in the time of Queen Anne, a statute was passed, by which the "First fruits" and "Tenths" were alienated from the Crown altogether, and formed into the fund for the purpose of augmenting poor benefices—still known under the appellation of Queen Anne's Bounty.

If ever there was a time at which a strict exercise of the royal prerogative would have been an act of grace and equity, it was on this occasion ; and the reader will naturally expect to find, that, previously to this statute, a Royal commision was once more issued for the purpose of accommodating these taxes to the actual value of them. Whatever might have been said of this measure, if resorted to for the benefit of the Crown, not even the shadow of a just objec-

* A great part of the remarks in this paragraph are abridged from an able article in the *Edinburgh Review* for February, 1823.

tion could have been raised against it, when intended solely for the purposes of charity—for the benefit of the Church itself! The reader, however, will be much deceived, if he imagines that any such steps were taken. On the contrary, the sum transferred to the bounty fund consisted simply of the old and most inadequate payments of Queen Elizabeth's time ; not only were the opulent clergy left free from all additional demand but the insufficient valuation of Queen Elizabeth, which hitherto had existed only by the mere sufferance of the Crown, was ratified by a positive Act of the legislature, and *declared irrevocable and perpetual!* Thus, though a considerable fund was no doubt given to the poorer clergy, an incalculably larger addition was made to the wealth of the opulent ! Of the proportions received by each party, an idea may be formed from the following remarks :—"If," says the Edinburgh Reviewer, "The 'First fruits' and 'Tenths' had been paid subsequently to the gift of Queen Anne, according to the rates which the law provided for, and as they had been paid "without grief and contradiction," i. e. according to the real value of the benefices, instead of a million and a half at *least thirty millions* would have been received from those taxes ; a sum not only quite sufficient to have removed the poverty of all the poor livings in the kingdom (in 1809,) but to have established schools in every parish of England, and to have left a large surplus for other useful purposes."

The foregoing narrative is intended to convey to the reader some idea of the nature of the fund which constitutes Queen Anne's Bounty. I shall now proceed to examine into its application,—I mean as far as North Wales is concerned. After the immense revenue which was lost to the bounty—and gained by the dignified clergy—(by the circumstances just narrated), the reader is doubtless, prepared to expect, that the scanty residue still left has been employed most frugally—most conscientiously—in bettering the condition of the inferior orders of clergy,—and that, however corruption and nepotism might prevail in other branches of the revenues of the Church, this charitable donation has been held peculiarly sacred from all encroachment. Alas! how different is the real fact from the natural anticipations of every ingenuous mind. What will be thought, when it is stated, that a vast portion of these revenues have been added to the wealth of the highest dignitaries of the land,—I say added to their wealth, for such is practically the effect of relieving them, in whole or in part, from the charge of paying their own curates ! Anglesey, as it has already appeared, is full of instances of this most repulsive practice. I shall now proceed to enumerate those which occur in this county, which will evince, not only that the bounty fund has been occasionally drained for the benefit of the most overpaid members of their profession,—but that *every benefice* in this county possessed by the Bishops and sinecurists has been augmented out of it !

Llandegai belongs to the Bishop of Bangor—(was not annexed to the see till 1685). Curate, £118. Of this £30 consists of fees, £80 of "bounty," and *only £8 is paid by the Bishop* !

Llangwstenin belongs to the Bishop of St. Asaph—(was not annexed till 1573). Curate, £180. Of which £30 only is paid by the Bishop. The rest consists of "bounty," and stipend from a lay impropriator of the parish of Eglwys Rhos !

Gyffin belongs to the Dean of Bangor ; and here, as in Anglesey, he does not keep any resident minister. Officiating minister, £70. Of which £10 *only is paid by the Dean.*

Llandudno belongs to Archdeacon Jones. Curate's salary, £68. Of which only £20 is paid by the Archdeacon. The remainder is from Queen Anne's Bounty ! Population, 1000. The Curate has resided for 37 years, and is a very old man.

Now, be it observed, these are not individual instances of abuse ; but the above include *all the parishes in the county of Caernarvon* which belong to the Bishops, the Dean, and the Archdeacon.*

Amount enjoyed by Welsh Bishops, £985.—Bishop of Chester, £560. —Dean, £600.—Archdeacon, £250 (£74 being deducted for curates' salaries, the curates' income being made up chiefly of Queen Anne's Bounty) £2271

Absentees, living more than seven miles' distance from their benefices, (£530 being deducted for curates' salaries) 1650

Colleges 1720

Total as above 5641

Total enjoyed by the general body of the clergy (including £630 the salaries of curates of absentees, &c., and exclusive of Queen Anne's Bounty and Fees, £1503) 7803

Lay Impropriators 2307

The Poor 300

---

* Of course, we are not to consider the present possessors of these benefices as the authors of the abuses alluded to, which were the acts of the government. But what are we to think of the vigilance and integrity of our representatives, when it is added, that the Bounty Fund has been augmented by immense parliamentary grants, within the last twenty years, unaccompanied, too, by any restriction providing against future mal-administration, though nothing could be more notorious at the time those grants were made, than the prevalence of abuses such as those enumerated.

DENBIGHSHIRE.—Population in 1831–83,167.—DIOCESE OF BANGOR.

Parish.	Patron.	Lay Impropriator.	Ecclesiastical Impropriator.	His Tithe	Incumbent.	His Tithe &c.	Residence.	Curate's Salary.
Clocaenog, R.	Bishop				R. Newcome	320	Rhuthin	80
Derwen, R.	Ditto				R. Jones	400		
Evenechtyd, R.	Ditto				E. Thelwall	250		
Llanbedr, R.	Ditto				J. Jones	380		
Llandyrnog, C.	Ditto		Bp. in commendam, added some time since 1685 Rhuthin School	600 400				110
Llanelidan, V.	Ditto				R. Roberts	400		
Llanhychan, R.	Ditto				— Davies	200		
Llangynhaval, R.	Ditto				J. Jones	400		
Llangwyven, R.	Ditto				L. Roberts	300		
Llanrhaiadr Dyffryn Clwyd, V.	Ditto		Bp. added in 1685	1200	E. Williams	1200		
Llanrhydd, R.	Dean and Chapter of Hospital Westminster				R. Newcome	340		70
Rhuthin, C.					Lecturer, F. Owen	20		80
Ll'vair D. Clwyd, V. & Jesus Chapel.	Bishop		W. Warren, Preb	600	J. Jones	300	Bangor, (Warren)	
					R. Roberts	45	Llanelidan	
Llanvwrog, V.	Ditto				R. Newcome	450	Rhuthin	70
Llanynys, R.	Ditto		Bp. added in 1713.	550	E. Roberts	550		
Cyfylliog, C.				200	Ditto	100		

DIOCESE OF ST. ASAPH.

Parish.	Patron.	Lay Impropriator.	Ecclesiastical Impropriator.	His Tithe	Incumbent.	His Tithe &c.	Residence.	Curate's Salary.
Abergele, V.	Bishop		Bishop	1150	R. Jackson	380		
Bettws, V.	Ditto		Ditto	120	R. Phillips	350		
Bryn Eglwys, P.C.	Sir W. Wynne				E. Williams	88	Wrexham	
Cerig y Drudion, R.	Bishop				J. Ellis	450		
Chirk, V.	Ditto	Lord Dungannon.		60	G. Robson	600	Erbistock	65

DIOCESE OF ST. ASAPH CONTINUED.

Parish.	Patron.	Lay Impropriator.	His Tithe	Ecclesiastical Impropriator.	His Tithe	Incumbent.	His Tithe &c.	Residence.	Curate's Salary.
Denbigh, R.	Bishop.					R. Howard, D.D.	400	Anglesey.	120
Eglwys Vach, V.	Ditto.					D. Owen.	220		
Erbistock, R.	Ditto.	Left to School and Alms-house.	650			G. Robson.	350	Edinburgh.	120
Gresford, V.	Ditto.			Dn. and Ch. of Winchester; lands inclusive — Gresford and Wrexham.	2400	H. Horseley.	450		
Gwythcrin R.	Ditto.			Dean of St. Asaph, C. S Luxmoore.	1500	— Rowland.	150	Montgomeryshire.	90
Henllan, C.	Dean of St. Asaph			Bishop.	300			Herefordshire.	
	Bishop.			J. M. Luxmoore, sinecure Rector.					
Llanarmon yn Ial, V.	Ditto.				500	E. Evans.	320	Marchwiail. — J. M. Luxmoore.	
Ll.armon D. Ceiriog R.	Ditto.					W. Griffith.	200	
Ll.armon M. MawrCh.	Ditto.					G. Steele.	45	Llaurhaiadr.	
Llandegle, R.	Ditto.					E. Williams.	108	Wrexham.	
Llandidoged, R.	Ditto.					J. Davies.	200		
Llandidulas, R.	Ditto.			Bishop of St. Asaph.	320	L. Roberts.	100		
Llaudrillo yn Rhos, V.	Ditto.					T. Alban, sen.	320		
Llaudysilio, P.C.	Sir W. W. Wynn.					— Hughes.	100		
Llanelian, V.	Bishop.			Ditto.	130	T. Alban, jun.	200		
LlanvairT. Haiarn, C	The Dean and Prebends.			C. S. Luxmoore, D. H. Horseley, P. G. Robson, P.	150 400 400			Herefordshire. Edinburgh. Erbistock.	115
Llanveres, R.	Bishop.					C. B. Clough.	300	Mold.	120
Llanvihangel, R.	Ditto.					— Pritchard.	220	England.	
Llangadwaladr, P.C.	Ditto.			D. & C. of St. Asaph.	40	W. Griffith.	35	Ll. Armon D. Ceiriog.	

Parish	Patron	Patron		Office		Incumbent		Location	
Llangedwyn, P.C.	Sir W. W. Wynn					J. Daniel	100	St. Asaph	
Llangernyw, V.	Bishop		300	W. Cleaver, centor of Asaph.					120
Llangollen, V.	Sir W. W. Wynn	Sir W. W. Wynn			250	E. Williams.	260		
Trevor, P.C.	R. Thomas, Esq			S. Holland, sinecure Rector.		H. Eaton.	350		
Llangwm, V.	Bishop					— Hughes.	80	England	
Llan Nerydd, R.	Ditto				260	J. Jones.	200		
Llanrwst, R.	Ditto					R. Chambers.	400		
CapelGarmon,PC	Ditto			Bishop.		J. Roberts.	750		
Llan St. Ffraid, V.	Ditto					T. Lewis.	120		
Ll. St. Ff. G. Cerriog P.C.					300	H. Pughe.	300		
						G. Steele.	128		
Llansannan, V.	Ditto			R. Clough, sinecure Rector.					
Llansilin, V.	Ditto			Bishop.	200	G. Strong.	280	Chester. Dysserth.	80
Llanyblodwel, V.	Ditto			Dean and Chaptor.	130	W. Jones.	270		
Marchwiail, R.	Ditto			Bishop.	670	Dr. Donne.	170	Oswestry.	
Nantglyn, V.	Ditto			Bishop. Vicars Choral.	150	J. M. Luxmoore.	720		
Pontre'r Voel-las,PC	C. Wynne, Esq.				14s.	E. Roberts.	200		
Rhiwabon, V.	Sir W. W. Wynn	Sir W. Wynn & oths	1100	W. Cleaver, Precentor.	1l.7s.	P. Price.	200		
St. George's, V.	The Crown			J. M. Luxmoore, Preb. of Meivod.	30	R. Wingfield.	700		80
			2700		60	J. Jones.	160	St. Asaph. Marchwiail. St. Asaph.	
Wrexham, V.	Bishop	Ditto ditto				G. Cunliffe.	900		
Berse Drelincourt P.C.	Ditto					T. Jones.	100		
Minera, P.C.	Vicar of Wrexham					Ditto.	100		
Yclbytty, P.C.	Lord Mostyn	Ld. Mostyn & others	140			W. Davies.	110	Montgomeryshire.	

DENBIGHSHIRE CONTINUED—DIOCESE OF CHESTER.

Parish.	Patron.	Lay Impropriator.	His Tithe	Ecclesiastical Impropriator.	His Tithe	Incumbent.	His Tithe &c.	Residence.	Curate's Salary.
Holt, P.C.	Dean and Chapter of Winchester.			Dean and Chapter of Winchester.	900	T. Edwards.	120		
Iscoed, P.C.						.. Reynolds.	120		

S U M M A R Y.

BANGOR DIOCESE.—The total amount of Church property in these 17 parishes is............£8805
Of this the Bishops of Bangor enjoy.. 2550

The whole of which has been added since the Restoration.

Prebendary Warren owes to his affinity to a prelate of that name.............(a sinecure) 600
Of the remainder, the Rev. R. Newcome, Warden of Rhuthin, possesses.................... 1110

Such, however, is the Christianlike,—the munificent disposition of the excellent Warden, that what would have been a crying abuse in other hands, is felt by all to be a public blessing in his. Many of the clergy of this district are much beloved ; and here I may mention, that both the Warden of Rhuthin and the Rev. E. Thelwall, Rector of Evenechtyd, were presented some time ago, by their respective parishioners, with handsome pieces of plate, in token of their sense of their high professional merits.

ST. ASAPH DIOCESE.—The clergy in the diocese of Bangor are generally natives of that district, a great part of them possessed of good private fortunes, and almost all men who have received a good education at the English Universities. In the diocese of St. Asaph, very few indeed of the clergy are connected with the North Welsh gentry ; and it is a singular fact, that more than half of the officiating ministers of this diocese are not even *natives* of North Wales ; the majority consisting of Englishmen and natives of South Wales. This difference may be thus accounted for : the diocese of Bangor extending over those parts of Wales where the English language is least understood, and where the introduction of English Incumbents would be a more palpable breach of trust,—nepotism has less prevailed ; and hence, the gentry of the country have been encouarged to bring up their children to the Church. But in St. Asaph, English being the prevailing language in some parishes, and partially uuderstood in others, a pretext has been found—and most amply employed—for thrusting the English relatives of our Bishops into almost every valuable benefice : the consequence has been, that the gentry of the country have become disgusted with the system, and in very few instances devote their sons to the profession. The vacancy thus left is supplied by clergymen brought up in the grammar schools of South Wales, which render education peculiarly accessible in that district ; being, for the most part, men of a more humble rank in life, they are prepared by previous habits, to rest satisfied with the inferior preferments, to which by the present system in North Wales, the native clergy are generally confined. Such are the causes of the difference alluded to. As to its effects, I believe it is generally found, that clergymen who have been educated in Wales, are more popular, and animated preachers, than their countrymen who have been educated at the Universities ; whose learning, as I have elsewhere remarked, is often alloyed with cold and formal manners in general life,—and with a tame and insipid style of oratory in the pulpit. Hence, whilst there are perhaps more decidedly useful clergymen in St. Asaph diocese, than in that of Bangor, there are more gross abuses, and more instances of men whose notorious ignorance of the language of the country is a prominent disgrace to the Church ; and it needs hardly be remarked, that nothing can be more glaringly unjust, than the system by which the natives of the diocese of St. Asaph are excluded even from an equal participation in the emoluments of their own Church.

DENBIGH, £400.—The most populous town in the county is in the hands of Dr. Howard, who is also incumbent of Beaumaris, the county town of Anglesea. The gross income of the individual is not excessive ; but this must be pronounced a gross abuse of patronage.

LLANSANNAN, £480.—One portion is a sinecure, held by the Rev. R. Clough, a clergyman resident in Chester, who has, I believe, no other preferment and is far advanced in life. The vicarage belongs to the Rev. G. Strong, who resides at Dyserth, in Flintshire, a parish belonging to the Bishop, by whom he is there employed as his curate. Though an absentee, Mr. Strong's emolu ments, both as a vicar and a curate, are certainly not exorbitant ; nor do I think that any stigma attaches to him ; but what are we to think of a diocesan, who directly sanctions the nonresidence of his clergy by employing them as his curates? Of all persons, a Bishop should be the last to forget the golden rule, "Vicarius non habet vicarium." Mr. Strong, I have been given to understand, supports a very good school here at his own expense.

DEANERY—HENLLAN.—From this great tract of country £1500 is enjoyed by the Rev. C. S. Luxmoore, the Dean of St. Asaph, who is also Chancellor of this diocese, incumbent of seven livings, and lessee of two! Doubtless, the Reverend gentleman has such views of the sacred responsibilities of his profession, that he feels no difficulty in reconciling them with the researches of a civil lawyer, and the speculation of a tithe proctor.* Yet, I can tell that Reverend gentleman, that however much his immense possessions may be a subject of pride to himself,—the exorbitant wealth which has been wrung from this very diocese by himself and his connections, is at this moment the greatest humiliation to the friends of the Church of England—the bitterest of all satires on the lips of her enemies!

LLANARMON-YN-IAL.—Rector, the Rev. J. M. Luxmoore, a brother of the last, incumbent of four parishes, and registrar of Hereford.

Such are a few of the many advantages possessed by one single family in the Church and soil of the Principality; and however high we may place the doctrine of prescriptive rights, I trust, that when this subject comes before the legislature, it will be remembered, that the strongest prescriptive claim in the property of the Church, is that of the people, to have it applied for their religious benefit; and that the immediate removal of abuses such as these,—violations as they are of the spirit even of our most technical laws,—is not likely to involve the security of the property of the gentlemen of England! When we consider the ages of certain individuals, one thing is quite clear, that to the present generation in Wales, prospective laws would in this case be little better than a mere mockery, as their whole effect would be to ensure a reform after the lapse of half a century!

It is well for the Church of England, in these critical times, that examples are not wanting of a far different spirit, amongst her more highly favoured sons. And here I may advert to two instances of pious generosity and conscientious

---

* I shall take occasion by and by, to enumerate the parishes belonging to the bishopric of which the very Rev. gentleman has received leases from his father, the late Bishop Luxmoore. These leases are so beneficial, that the lessee, in two instances, enjoys at least *two-thirds* of the profits, at the expense of the see! It is with the greatest pain and reluctance, that I feel myself compelled, by a sense of justice to my country to notice transactions such as these.

self-denial, which do not require the aid of contrast to ensure to them the gratitude of every well-wisher to his Church and his country.

The Rev. Wm. Cleaver having been presented to the valuable living of Denbigh, and not feeling himself adequately acquainted with the language of his flock, with equal delicacy and disinterestedness, resigned it upon the death of the patron who had conferred it. The Rev. Holland Edwards, on being made Prebendary of Westminster, resigned the living of Llanrwst, the most valuable in the diocese of St. Asaph, because he could no longer reside on it ; and at the same time, gave £100 towards building a parsonage-house, there not being one at that time fit for the residence of the clergyman.

SINECURE APPROPRIATIONS. — What is technically termed "Appropriation," that is, the system of taking the tithes of a parish from the officiating clergymen and other parochial purposes, and making them a perquisite of some sinecure office—a system to which the county of Denbigh is most signally a prey — was one of the bitter fruits of the Norman Conquest. Its origin is thus narrated by Dr. Burn, (*Ecclesiastical Law*, p. 64, vol I.) :—

"The way of strictly appropriating parish churches to religious houses or giving them in full right to the monks' absolute property and use, was an engine of oppression which came in with the Norman Conquest ; when the greater prelates being Normans, did trample upon the inferior clergy, who were generally English ; increased the pensions which the clergy were to pay them, or else withdrew their stipends ; and yet loaded them with new services, and in every way oppressed them without mercy. And to complete the servile dependence, an artifice was contrived, to obtain indulgence from the Pope, that whatever churches they held in advowson, they should commit them to be served by clerks, who, as to the cure of souls, should be responsible to the Bishop, but as to the profits, should be accountable to the abbot or prior and his brethren.

"And this was, indeed, effectual appropriation ; a badge of slavery unknown to the Saxon Churches, brought over by the Norman lords, and imperiously put upon the English clergy by the authority of the Pope. And this practice, which crept in with William the Conquerer, in a few reigns, became the custom of the land ; and the infection spread until within the space of 300 years, above a third part, and those generally the richest benefices in England, became appropriated.

"The next injury to parochial churches came from the surrendering of their right of patronage to collegiate bodies.

"From corporations aggregate of many, this example went on to *single persons;* not only to deans, chaunters, treasurers, chancellors, and separate officers, but at last to the parish priests themselves, who, in populous or rich places, obtained a vicar to be endowed, and casting upon him the cure of souls, they had the rectory appropriated to them and their successors as a *sinecure* for ever."

Such is the origin of the system of appropriations, —a system of which the general effects have for ages continued well worthy of the tyranny in which it arose. Of late years, indeed, it has been discovered, that her sinecures have been the very cradle of all that is good and great in the Church of England ; though it is, at the same time, admitted, that learning and piety have declined since that period at which it can be proved, that these abuses were far less prevalent! Undoubtedly, the sinecures of the Church, like every other absurd and anomalous institution, have occasionally furnished a reward to merit,— and literary repose to piety and learning ; but it is equally certain, that their general application has been far more in accordance with the usual frailty of human nature, than with the romantic speculations of their advocates, whose confidence in human nature is so chivalrous and unbounded, as far as the possessors of irresponsible power are concerned,—yet so restricted as far as regards those who are exposed to its exercise.* How far the Principality of Wales has been benefitted by the system of appropriations we have a singular example in this county.

EGLWYS VACH.—The rectorial tithes, £650, were given by Sir John Wynne, of Gwydyr, to support a school and alms' house at Llanrwst. Their present application can hardly be said to realize the aspirations of the donor.

LLAVAIR-TAL-HAIARN, £950—Is shared between three sinecurists ; the Rev. C. S. Luxmoore, son of Bishop Luxmoore; the Rev. H. Horseley, son of Bishop Horseley ; and the Rev. G. Robson, a gentleman connected with the last mentioned prelate by circumstances which it is unnecessary to detail. In 1809, when the two latter gentlemen were already in possession, the curate's salary was £34 only, though it now amounts to £115.

GRESFORD—Is thus divided—Dean and Chapter of Winchester, £2400, the Rev. H. Horseley, £450. Of all the evils to which a country can be exposed, exactions such as those to which this district is subjected, for the benefit of the Dean and Chapter of Winchester, are the most degrading and oppressive. It would be assuredly most unjust to throw upon the remote glens of the Principality the support even of those institutions which are the very keystone of English greatness—of institutions of which the benefit is equally diffused through every province of the British empire ; but that such a dis-

* *Theological Quarterly Review*, for January, 1832, which contains some excellent remarks on this branch of Church patronage. The Author of this Essay does not mean to enter into the question, whether the revenues attached to sinecures might not be beneficially employed in the support of certain ecclesiastical offices, involving positive and arduous duties.

trict as this should be made an appendage to the sinecures of a single and most remote English Cathedral, is a species of injustice, which to name is to expose!

t cannot be too often remembered, that appropriations of this kind are the very bane of the Principality; they are more permanently injurious than the savage wars to which she was, in ancient times, a prey; the calamities of war arrest, indeed, the progress of society for a time; but grievances of this kind grow with the growth and strengthen with the strength of a country; only drain its resources more deeply as it advances in wealth and prosperity! The vicar, the Rev. H. Horseley, resides in Edinburgh—was promoted to this benefice in extreme youth—has enjoyed it nearly 30 years, during the whole of which time, the care of this extensive parish, containing 3000 souls, has devolved upon a curate whose salary has not amounted till very lately to more than £30 (!) a year, and who is now so far advanced in life, that he is obliged, by his growing infirmities, to expend his scanty stipend in obtaining the aid of another curate!

ERBISTOCK, £350.—Belongs to the Rev. G. Robson, the other comportionist of Llanvair-Tal-Haiarn, together with

CHIRK, £600.—Population, 1500. Curate's salary, £65.

HOLT AND ISCOED—Like Gresford, are in the hands of the Dean and Chapter of Winchester, who derive from them £900 per annum. Not only are these two parishes lavished on the sinecurists of one of the most distant provinces of England—but here also abuse is added to abuse—and their emoluments are eked out by liberal grants from Queen Anne's Bounty! The Curate of Holt has an income of £120 of which only £20 is paid by the Dean and Chapter—the rest is from the bounty fund! The Curate of Iscoed has an income of £120 of which no part whatever is paid by the Dean and Chapter—it consists entirely of bounty money!! In point of fact it will be found, that the *most liberal grants of Queen Anne's Bounty are those which have been made to parishes in the hands of Bishops and sinecurists!* But to conclude. Strange as it may appear, it is, nevertheless, a most literal truth, that the abuses of Church patronage in this county far surpass even those which have just been described as a result of the Conquest of England by the Normans; appropriations are carried to as great an extent—and in favour of persons possessing no better claims on Wales than those of her Norman oppressors on the soil of England—and to the evil of appropriations, are added abuses of a different description.

Denbighshire contains 55 parishes (exclusive of 10 small livings, which consist chiefly of Queen Anne's Bounty, or private donations, and which are all either chapels of ease, or in the gift of laymen.) Of these 55, no fewer than 31 belong, in whole or in part—1st. To the Bishop of Bangor, £2550 and the

Bishop of St. Asaph £2600. 2nd. To their relatives* £6330 (including Llansilin parish, which belongs to the Chapter, which consists chiefly of the relatives of Bishops). 3rd. To the Dean and Chapter of Winchester, £3300. 4th. To pluralists possessed of other high Church preferment—and sinecurists and absentees resident at more than seven miles' distance from their benefices, £2070. 5th. To schools at Llanrwst, not properly applied, £650. 6th. Cathedral of St. Asaph, £40.

Total held as above, deducting £1820 for salaries of curates of absentees, &c. 15,780

Total enjoyed by the general body of the clergy, including £400 belonging to Rhuthin School, (and properly applied,) and curates' sala.ies, £1320—but exclusive of Queen Anne's Bounty and Fees, £1500......13,849

Lay Impropriators.. 4300

Alms' House 160

---

* Besides the preferments already enumerated as enjoyed by relatives and connect'ons of the Bishops of Wales, who are non-residents,—the following benefices belong to clergymen of the same class, who are, however, resident upon them : - Erbistock. Marchwiail Rhiwabon. It is not my intention to contend that every appointment of this description is in itself reprehensible: it is only when regarded in the mass, that they evince that shameful abuse of Episcopal patronage, which is the very bane of the Principality.

** The Author has found, on further inquiry, that the following is a more accurate representation of the condition of certain parishes in this county, than that which is contained in the foregoing table :—Llan Nevydd, C. S. Luxmoore, Chancellor, £300 R. Chambers, £300.—Llanvair Talhaiarn, C. S. Luxmoore, Dean, £220 the two Prebendaries, £440 equally divided. The curate is paid in part by Queen Anne's Bounty. The Bishop has a manor at Llandegle, value £80 per annum. These alterations slightly increase the proportion en. enjoyed by absentees, &c.

FLINTSHIRE.—POPULATION IN 1831—6,012.—DIOCESE OF ST. ASAPH.

Parish.	Patron.	Lay Improprietor.	His Tithe. £	Ecclesiastical Improprietor.	His Tithe. £	Incumbent.	His Tithe.	Residence.	Curates' Salary. £
Aberchwiler	A Township in Bodvary.			Bishop of St. Asaph.	400				
Bodvary, E.	Bishop.					E. Hughes.	300	England.	
Caerwys, R.	Ditto.					R. Richards.	300	Holywell.	
Cwm, V.	Ditto.								
Dinmeirchion, V.	Ditto.			R. D. Finch, sinecure Rector.	210	J. Jones.	210	St. Asaph.	
Dyserth, P. C.	Ditto.			Precentor of St. Asaph, W. Cleaver.	300	W. Owen.	300	St. Asaph.	
East Hope, V.	Ditto.	St John's Hospital, Chester.	375	Rev. — Thurlow, sinecure Rector.	400	G. Strong.	80	England.	
Flint, V.	Ditto.			Bishop.	600	T. Moulsdale.	225		
Gwaunysger, R.	Ditto.				60	M. Williams.	180		
Halkin, R.	Ditto.					R. Davies.	180	Liverpool.	80
Holywell, V.	Ditto.					E. Roberts.	300		
Kilkain, V.	Ditto.	D. Pennant, Esq. and others.	903			J. Jones.	250		
Ll'elwy,(see St.As'ph				F. Corie, D. D. sinecure Rect. Head of Emmanuel Col.	400	J. Hughes.	200	Cambridge.	
Llanasaph, V.	Ditto.			Bishop.	600	H. Parry.	300		
Mold, V.	Ditto.	P. Davies, Esq., and D. Cooke, Esq.	2400	Ditto.	—5	C. Clough.	280		
Nerquis, P. C.	Ditto.					— Evans.	95		
Meliden, P. C.	Treas. of S. Asaph.			H. Milner, Treasurer of St. Asaph.	300	E. Jones.	90	Doncaster.	
Nannerch, R.	Bishop.					Ll. Lloyd.	250		

FLINTSHIRE CONTINUED.

Parishes.	Patron.	Lay Impropriator.	Ecclesiastical Impropriator.	His Tithe.	Incumbent.	His Tithe &c.	Residence.	Curates' Salary.
Newmarket, C........	Bishop.		Bishop.	250	No Incumbent.	400		80
Northop, V.........	Ditto.		Ditto.	800	H. Jones.	250		
Rhuddlan, V.........	Ditto.	Mrs. Young.	Ditto.	12	T. W. Edwards.			
			Dean and Chapter.	60				
St. Asaph*..........	Ditto.		Bishop of Bangor.	5				
			Bishop.	30	4 Vicars Choral.	200	St. Asaph.	
			W. Cleaver as Precentor.	500				
			C. S. Luxmore, as Dean.	213			Herefordshire.	
			As Chancellor.	213				
Treuddyn, P. C.....	Ditto.				J. Williams.	80		
Whitford V.........	Ditto.		J. M. Luxmore, sinecure Rector.	1000	E. Roberts.	360	Marchwiail.	
Yscelving, R.	Ditto.				W. Williams.	750		

HAWARDEN PECULIAR.

Hawarden, R.......	Sir S. Glynne.				Hon. and Rev. N. Grenville, Head of Magdalen.	2800		130
Broughton, C.......								120
Buckley, C.........								120

A DETACHED PART OF FLINTSHIRE, IN CHESTER DIOCESE.

Bangor, R........ }	Mrqs. W'stminst'r				Dr. Wynne.	1800		
Overton, C. ..... }								
Hanmer, V........	Sir J. Hanmer.	Sir J. Hanmer.			J. Hanmer.	Value unknown.		
Worthenbury, R.....	Sir Rich. Puleston.				H. Matthie.	400		

* The Bishop of St. Asaph has in this parish, lands, manors, &c., worth £1600. The Dean has lands, &c., worth £40. The Precentor has lands, &c., worth £6. The Chancellor of the Church has lands worth £15 (per annum).

SUMMARY.

ST. ASAPH DIOCESE.—*Leases enjoyed by the Dean of St. Asaph.*—The emoluments he derives from leases granted to him by his father, the late Bishop Luxmoore, are immense.—Llanasaph.—From this he gains about £400 and pays the Bishop about £100.

As to the extent to which the system of appropriation is carried, I need only refer the reader to the table; all the benefices in the district, except seven, belong, either in whole or in part, to the Bishop of St. Asaph, or to sinecurists. Nor is even the portion left to the vicars reserved for the officiating clergy. For instance in the parish of Cwm, the sinecure rectory falls to the lot of an Englishman, the Rev. D. Finch, who never officiated in this diocese, and the vicarage belongs to the vicar of Holywell. The income of the latter, deducting curates' salaries, does not amount, after all, to more than £280—anything but a liberal revenue for a minister of a populous town: nor do I think any stigma attaches to him; the blame rests with those who bestow the sinecure rectories on persons who have no claim on the diocese,— and, thus, having deprived themselves of the legitimate fund for augmenting the income of ministers of populous parishes—attempt to cure one injustice by another—and squander the vicarial tithes also on non-residents!

GWAUNYSGOR—Belongs to the minister of the Welsh Church in Liverpool, a deserving man, and to whose support a sinecure might, without impropriety, have been applied; but for sinecures, as has before been observed, a different application has been found.

NEWMARKET—Belongs to the Bishop, who does not keep a resident curate, but employs the curate of the last mentioned parish to do the duty.

NORTHOP, £850—Belongs to the bishopric. This immense parish was added to the see in 1687, in lieu of mortuaries,—a kind of tax due to the Bishops of St. Asaph on the decease of every clergyman. Of the value of these mortuaries, thus generally relinquished for a living of £850 a year, some idea may be formed from the following specimen. " His" (i.e. the clergyman's) "best cloak—item, his best coat, jerkin, doublet, and breeches—item, his hose or nether stockings, shoes, and garters—item, his hat and cap—item, his falchion!! &c., &c.—B. Willis, vol. II. p. 161.

ST. ASAPH CATHEDRAL.—Of the immense sums expended in its repair, something has already been said; its congregation generally consists of about thirty individuals! The revenues of the Church in the parish of St. Asaph amount to nearly £3000; £1000 more are annually levied on a single parish of Montgomeryshire, for the use of its Cathedral; £280 more are taken from a poor parish in Merionethshire, for the benefit of its Vicars; and there is only one resident Minister in the parish, the Rev. W. Owen, who derives from St. Asaph tithes £50 per annum.

MELIDEN—Belongs to a gentleman resident in Yorkshire. The curate is paid chiefly out of Queen Anne's Bounty.

Amount belonging to the bishopric of St Asaph, £4202.—To the Bishop of Bangor, £5.—The Rev. C S. Luxmoore, as Dean and Chancellor, £466 an absentee from the county. — To other sinecurists, absentees from the county, £2565.—Sinecurists resident in the county, £866.—Absentees from the county, £180.— St. John's Hospital, Chester, £375.

Total as above, deducting salaries of curates of Bishops and absentees, £330.. £8329

Total enjoyed by the general body of the clergy, including £330 the salaries of curates of Bishops and absentees, and exclusive of Queen Anne's Bounty and fees, £330....................... 5320

Lay Impropriators 3825

HAWARDEN.—Is a Peculiar, exempt from episcopal jurisdiction. The interest of the inhabitants obviously requires, that this immense district should be divided into several benefices.

CHESTER DIOCESE.—BANGOR.—The same remark may be extended to this parish; but as the three benefices in this diocese are in lay patronage, and separated from the other districts of Wales, they can hardly be said to come within the scope of this Essay.

MERIONETHSHIRE.—POPULATION IN 1831–35,609.—DIOCESE OF BANGOR.

Parish.	Patron.	Lay Impropriators.	His Tithe.	Ecclesiastical Impropriator.	Hd. Tithe	Incumbent.	His Tithe.	Residence & its Distance from Parish.	
Dolgellau, R.	The Crown.					H. White.	400		
Ffestiniog, R.	Bishop.					— Jones.	290		
Maen Twrog, R.									
Llanaber, R.	Lord Chancellor.					J. Jones.	215		
Llandanwg, V.	Bishop.					D. Evans.	160		
Llanbedr, C.									
Llanvachraith, C.	Sir R. W. Vaughan.	Sir R. W. Vaughan.	100			H. Pritchard.	150	Dolgellau	2
Llanelltyd, C.	Colonel Vaughan.	Colonel Vaughan.	100						
Llanegryn, P.C.	Rev. J. Titley.	Rev. T. Titley.	150			F. Jones.	70	Llangelynin	4
Llanddwywe, C.	Bishop.					E. Anwyl (Owen	250		
Llanenddwyn, R									
Llanvair, R.	Ditto.			Treasurer of Bangor, T. Ellis.	100	W. Pugh.	200		
Llandecwyn, V.	Ditto.								
Ll. V. y traethau, C.	Ditto.					J. Pugh.	100	Bangor	40
Llanvrothen, R.	Ditto.					— Pugh.	103	Llanvrothen	3
Llanuwchllyn, P.C.	Sir W. W. Wynn.	Sir W. W. Wynn.				H. Jones.	70	Llangywar	2
Tywyn, V.	Bishop of Lichfield and Coventry.			Bp. of Lichfield.	1100	J. Edwards.	150	Bala	44
Llan Vihangel- y-Pennant.						D. Davies.	80		6
Tal-y-llyn.									
Trawsvynydd, R.						T. Evans.	100	Llangelynin	
Llangelynin, C.	Jones Parry, Esq.					P. Williams.	230		
						J. Parry.	350	Caernarvonshire	40

MERIONETHSHIRE CONTINUED, DIOCESE OF ST. ASAPH.

Parish.	Patron.	Lay Impropriator.	His Tithe	Ecclesiastical Impropriator.	His Tithe	Incumbent.	His Tithe &c.	Residence & its distance from parish.	Distance.
Btt's Girvyl Goch R.	Bishop.		£		£	E. Edwards.	£ 120		
Corwen, V.	Ditto.			Rev. J. Cleaver, sinecure Rector.	300	— Hughes.	250	St. Asaph.	
Gwyddelwern, V.	Ditto.			4 Vicars Choral of St. Asaph, £70. each.		D. Jones.	120	Corwen.	3
Llandrillo-yn-Edeyrnion, V.	Ditto.			S. Thurlow, sinecure Rector.	280			St. Asaph. England.	
Llanddervel, R.	Ditto.					J. Wynn.	200		
Llanvawr, V.	Ditto.			W. Cleaver, sinecure Rector.	350	J. Jones.	400		
Llangar, R.	Ditto.				340	H. Lloyd.	110	St. Asaph.	
Llangywar, R.	Ditto.					— Williams.	200		
Llan St. Ffraid, Glyn Dyvrdwy, R.	Ditto.					H. Jones.	150		
Ll'yn-Mowddwy, R.	Ditto.					J. Hughea.	90		
Llanycil, R.	Ditto.					W. W. Owen.	180		
Mallwyd.	Ditto.					J. Lloyd.	250		
						— Pugh.	400		

SUMMARY.

BISHOPRIC OF LICHFIELD. — The prominent abuse of this county is the sacrifice of four of its parishes (£1100) to the support of the see of Lichfield! The origin of this appropriation deserves to be borne in mind. Prior to the Reformation, it belonged to an English Nunnery in Essex, to which it had been given by the pious rapacity of the Anglo-Norman oppressors of North Wales. At the Reformation, it was taken away from the English Nunnery, with much virtuous indignation, and given to an English bishopric!! To restore it to the people from whom it had been taken, on whom it is still--and ever must be—a most unjust—a most ignominious burden, was a plain and obvious measure of equity—a common place axiom of justice, for which the speculations of English Church Reformers, from that time to the present, have soared far too high! Yet, it is not too much to affirm, that a Protestant Church is not very likely to become popular in a country by a mere renunciation of those superstitions, of which she copies the spirit and preserves the fruits; that it is not enough for the Church of England to renounce the Popish dogma, that the sins of the oppressor may be effaced by the spoils of the oppressed—she must relinquish those spoils, if she would possess the hearts of a free people. If there be one species of public trust, which ought, above all others, to be regulated with an anxious regard to justice, with a nice, a delicate, nay even a fastidious respect to the feelings of the people,—assuredly, it is that trust which exists only for the maintenance of religion and charity and peace among men. Is it wise, then, to base the religious institutions of England on a galling system of absenteeism,—to associate her noble hierarchy with an impoverishing tax on the very poorest county in North Wales—an exaction which is literally a record and a repetition of the wrongs of other days, and which must ever be as repugnant to every patriotic and generous feeling, as the toll of the curfew bell?

In this county, also, the Bishop's curates are paid chiefly out of Queen Anne's Bounty. The Rev. Thomas Evans, curate of Tal-y-llyn and Llanvihangel, £100, of which £40 only is paid by the Bishop. Mr. Evans is seventy years of age. Curate of Penal, £80, of which £40 is from the bounty fund. Nonresidence is not so common in this county as in some others; but the sums drawn out of it, by the Bishop of Lichfield and sinecurists, are exorbitant indeed.

Amount enjoyed by the Bishop of Litchfield, £1100—vicars choral, £280
—treasurer of Bangor, £100--sinecure rectors, £990—incumbent of
Llangelynin, resident forty miles from his benefice, £380.

Total as above, deducting salaries of curates of Bishops and absentees,
£140 .... £2710

Total enjoyed by resident clergy, including £140 the salaries of curates
of Bishops, absentees, &c., and deducting £300 for Queen Anne's
Bounty and fees 4860

Lay Impropriators, about.. 600

MONTGOMERYSHIRE.—Population in 1831—66,485.   DIOCESE OF BANGOR.

Parish.	Patron.	Lay Impropriator.	His Tithe.	Ecclesiastical Impropriator.	His Tithe.	Incumbent.	His Tithes &c.	Residence.	Curates' Salary	C'hn.
			£		£		£		L	
Carno, V.	Bishop.	— Farr, Esq.	45	Dean and Chapter.	90	″ ″.....	100	Herefordshire.	40	4
Llanwynog, V.	Ditto.			Ditto.	410	R. Davies.	205	Leicestershire.	55	4
Llanddinam, V.	Ditto.			Ditto.	560	J. Davies.	290	Llanidloes.	120	2
Llangurig, V.	Ditto.	Sir W. W. Wynn	250			— Anwyl.	200			3
Llanidloes, V.	Ditto.	Ditto.	230			J. Davies.	180			5
Trev-eglwys, V.	Lord Mostyn.	Ditto and others.	295			G. Lloyd.	110	Cheshire.	70	4

DIOCESE OF ST. ASAPH.

Parish.	Patron.	Lay Impropriator.	His Tithe.	Ecclesiastical Impropriator.	His Tithe.	Incumbent.	His Tithes &c.	Residence.	Curates' Salary	C'hn.
Aberhavesp, R.	Bishop.					R. Davi.	250			2
Berriew, V.	Ditto.					C. Luxm. ...	450	Shropshire.	150	3
Buttington, P. C.	Vicar of W. Pool.	C. H. Tracey, Esq.	750	Christ Church, Oxford.	200	C. Williams.	100	Welsh Pool.		2
Bettws, R.	Bishop.					J. Pryce.	250		70	1
Castell Caereinion, R	Ditto.					H. Horsley.	600	Edinburgh.		4
Cemaes, It ...	Ditto.					J. Hughes.	350	Herefordshire.		6
Darowain, V.	Ditto.									
Garthbeibio.	Ditto.					R. Richards.	120	Caermarthenshire.	60	2
Guilsfield, V.	Ditto.					100				5
Hirnant, R.	Ditto.			C. Luxmoore, sinecure Rector. — Evans.	900	C. Luxmoore.	300			1
Llan St. Ffraid, V.	Ditto.			Christ Church, Ox.		D. Williams.	180			
Llanwyddelan, R.	Ditto.			C. R. Thoroton.	500	H. Neve.	250	Cambridgeshire.	90	4
Llanbryn Mair, V.	Ditto.					M. Hughes.	300	Bedfordshire. Denbighshire. London.	70	2
Llanvechain, R.	Ditto.			— Gibson, sinecure Rector	300	R. Lewis. — Price.	300 750	Denbighshire.	70	3

Parish	Patron		Incumbent	Value		Notes
Llandrinio, C.	Bishop.			120		3
Llandysilio, C.	Ditto.			120		5
Deuddwr, P.C.	Ormsby Gore, Esq.					12
Llanerryl, R.	Bishop.					3
Llanvair, V.	Ditto.					5
						4
						2
						2
						1
Llanvihangel, R.	Ditto.	Sir W. W. Wynn.		400	Bishop.	3
Llanvyllin, R.	Ditto.	C. Jones, Esq.		400	Ditto.	5
Llangadvan, R.	Ditto.					2
Llangynyw, R.	Ditto.					2
Llangynog, P.C.	Freeholders.	Freeholders.		Tithe free.		7
Llanllugan, P.C.	Bishop.					2
Llanllwchhaiarn, R.	Ditto.					9
Llanmerewig, R.	Ditto.					5
Llanrhaiadr, V.	Earl of Powys.	Earl of Powys.		60		5
Llanwddyn, C.	Bishop.					1
Llanwrin, R.	Ditto.					
Llandysul, R.	Ditto.					4
Machynllaeth, R.	Ditto.					1
Manavon, R.	Ditto.					3
Meivod, V.	Ditto.					
Newtown, R.	Ditto.					
Pool, V	Ditto.					
Pennant, V	Ditto.					
Penegoes, R.	Ditto.	.H. Tracey, Esq.		300		
Pen-y-strowed, R.	Ditto.					
Tregynon, P.C.	Ditto.					

			Value		
			550	J. Russell.	100
			450	J. Lloyd.	330
				D. Williams.	400
				— Pugh.	350
				D. Hughes.	500
				G. Howel.	300
				T. Richards.	350
				J. Jones.	120
				— Williams.	50	Llanvair.
				— Wynnfield.	400
				J. Parker.	100
				— Steele.	100
	Dean and Chapter of St. Asaph.		1000	J. Richards.	450
				J. Bonsel.	100
				D. Myrton.	400
				W. Venables.	450
				W. Davies.	400
	Christ Church, Ox.		500	R. Williams.	300
				— Foxton.	500
	Christ Church, Ox.		900	W. Clive.	400
	Bishop of St. Asaph incommendam, recently taken.		300	M. Davies.	300	120
				— Hughes.	300
				— Evans.	140
				J. Price.	8	Bettws.

DIOCESE OF ST. DAVID'S.

Parish	Patron		Incumbent	Value		Notes
Kerry, V	Bishop.		— Jackson, Preb.	660	— Mo...	;30	Cambridge
Mochdre, V.	Ditto.				— Pe...	100
						3
						2

MONTGOMERYSHIRE CONTINUED, DIOCESE OF HEREFORD.

Parish.	Patron.	Lay Impropriator.	His Tithe.	Ecclesiastical Impropriator.	His Tithe.	Incumbent.	His Tithe, &c.	Residence.	Curate's Salary.
			£		£		£		
Churchstoke, P. C.	Warden of Clun Hospital.	Clun Hospital.	900			R. Ambler.	200		
Forden, P. C.	Grocers' Company.	Grocers' Company.	250			D. Nihil.	100	Montgomery.	
Hissington, P. C	R. Owen, Clerk.	J. Clayton, &c.	170			R. Owen.	160		
Montgomery, R	Chancellor.					M. Lloyd.	400		
Snead, P.C.	P. Morris, Esq.					T. Alban.	90		1

SUMMARY.

Amount enjoyed by Bishops, £1960.—Prebendary, £200.—Absentees from the county, £4185.—Cathedrals, £2305.—Colleges, £2500.—Clun Hospital, £900.—Incumbents ignorant of the Welsh language, £850.—Relatives of the Bishops, £1030.

Total as above, deducting curates' salaries, £1115 .... £12,815
Total enjoyed by the general body of resident clergy, including £1115 the salaries of curates of Bishops,
    absentees, &c., and exclusive of Queen Anne's Bounty and fees, £600 9026
Lay Impropriators 2900
Grocers' Company 250

Number of Churches belonging to the Establishment 53
Number of Dissenting Chapels 155

Enormous as is the number of Dissenting Chapels in this county, they are equally numerous in all the other North Welsh counties, in proportion to their extent and population—in many, more so. The comparison here drawn is perhaps a more accurate one than that adopted in the body of the work.

** For further remarks on this county, see pages 118-134.

N.B.—All the incumbents whose residence is not mentioned in the preceeding tables are residents.

SUMMARY OF THE STATE OF THE CHURCH IN SOUTH WALES.

Though I am not furnished with the same minute details respecting this district as I possess respecting North Wales, the following list of sinecures in South Wales, combined with the valuation of its smaller benefices previously given, will evince, I believe, that the same process has been going on in both districts. In both instances, the bishoprics have been enriched with new appropriations; in both, the stipends paid by ecclesiastical sinecurists to their curates have been allowed to continue the same that they were centuries ago, at the same time that the tithes attached to their sinecures have been continually improving. Thus, the property of the Church has been insensibly accumulating into the hands of the higher orders of the clergy.

APPROPRIATIONS AND SINECURES IN SOUTH WALES.

BISHOPRICS AND SINECURES IN ENGLAND.

	Brecknockshire.	Caermarthenshire.	Cardiganshire.	Glamorganshire.	Pembrokeshire.	Radnorshire.
See of Gloucester......	Dovynog, a third.			Cardiff. Llancarvan. Roath. Llanbleiddian. Llanilltyd. Llyswerni.		
Chapter of Ditto........						
See of Chester.........		Llan Gathan. Llanllwni.		Llantrisant.		
See of Lincoln..........	Llan Gors					
Canons of Windsor....		Abergwili. St. Clare.	Llandysil.			
Dn. and Ch. of Ditto...						
Colleges of Oxford.....						
Christ Ch. Cambridge..					Maenor-byr. St. Florence.	
St. John's College, Do..						

BISHOPRICS AND SINECURES IN WALES.

	Brecknockshire.	Caermarthenshire.	Cardiganshire.	Glamorganshire.	Pembrokeshire.	Radnorshire.
Bishop of St. David's.	Llan Gamarch, settled on Bishop in lieu of Mortuaries, about a century and a half ago.	Myddvai, £300. Mydrim.	Llanarth, 700l. (takn lately into comdm) Llanddyvriog, (Archdeacon, Cardigan.) Llanwnen.			Glascwm.
Chapter and Prebends of St. David's.	Llywel.	Llandybie. Llanbeudy. Llangan. Llanarthne. Llanddarog. Llanddingad. Llanvynydd (Pentr.)	Llandysilio-gogo. Llanbedr. Llanddewi Aberarth. Llanrhystyd. Llan St. Ffraid. Henvynwy. Llangranwg. Silian.		Clydan. Llan Hauaden (Chancellor.) Spittle, (Precentor.) Usmaston. Jeffreyston. Edeyrn. Llanrhiain. Whitchurch. Another Ditto. Llanwynda. Merthyr. St. David's. Maenor Owain. Llanrhidian.	
Bp. and Ch. of Llandaff				Eglwys Ilan. St. Hilary. Llan Edeyrn. St. Lythian. Pen-deulwyn. Ystrad Owain. Llandaff. Caerau, (Prebend.)		

Prebs. &c. of Brecon College.	Brecknockshire.	Caermarthenshire.	Cardiganshire.	Glamorganshire.	Pembrokeshire.	Radnorshire.
	Garthbrengy. Trallong. Llanwrthwl. Llan Gauten. Llan Avan Vawr. St. David's Brecknock, (belongs to Archdeacon.)	Llandysilio.	Llandygwydd. Nantcwnlle. Lledrod. Llanbadarn Treveglwys. Dihewid.			Clyro.—St Harmon's Llanbedr Pain's Castle. Llanbister. Llandegle. Llangynllo. Llanelwedd. Nantmel. Llan St. Ffraid. Llowes, (Archd.)
Sinecures.	Crug Howel. Cwm Du.		Llangeler.		Llanddewi Velvrey.	

The above parishes are most of them exceedingly extensive and opulent, as the reader may find, by the description of them in Carlile's *Topographical Dictionary*. But, of late years, our prelates have acted, nevertheless, on the maxim, that appropriation ought to be carried still further in this devoted country; and judging from the havoc they have made in the benefices of Cardiganshire—the most meanly endowed district even in South Wales,—we may prognosticate, that the working clergy of that county may shortly be left without any provision whatever !

In Cardiganshire, the benefices, with cure of souls, above the annual value of £150, are only eight in number, and only two of these are held by the parochial clergy resident in that county! viz., Llanvihangel Geneu yr Glyn, and Troed yr Aur; whilst the remaining six are shared amongst the following clergymen, viz., the Bishop, Llanarth, £700, which has been taken into commendam in recent times; the professors of Lampeter College, Bettws Ieuan, £200, Bryngwyn, £400, Llangoedmor, £300, Penbryn, £300, to which institution they have all been annexed within the last two years! the Rev. John Williams, Master of the High School, Edinburgh, Llanbedr, £200, also the small living of Strata Florida, £75 5s. 8d.; the Rev. D. Jenkins, resident in England, Llanllwchhaiarn, £200.

Besides the above, two small livings, Llanilar and Lledrod, belong to the Rev. P. Felix, a gentleman resident on a rich benefice in Northamptonshire; two others, Trev Ilan and Ystrad, to the Rev. T. M. Davies, a gentleman resident chiefly at Chester; two other small livings, Ferwig and Tremaen, to the Rev. T. James resident in England. It redounds but little to the credit of the Bishops of St. David's, that every one of the above are benefices in their gift; instead, therefore, of having set a good example to the lay patrons,* they have shown even less regard than that body to the interests of the Church and the country! Nothing could have been more unjustifiable than the annexation of the livings just enumerated to the College of Lampeter; for in this very county, there are no fewer than nine sinecures, most of them above the annual value of £200, and which might have been thus applied, without depriving whole districts of a resident ministry. As for the remainder of the parishes in Cardiganshire, none are above the annual value of £150—two-thirds are below that of £90.

Never was the system of appropriation carried to so fearful an extent in so short a time, even in the very darkest ages of Popery. In this county, Methodism first gained a firm footing, and it is still the stronghold of Dissent.

It would be a measure both of justice and sound policy to apply some of these sinecures to the religious and general education of the Welsh people, more particularly those endowments which are attached to the bishoprics and sinecures of England, and which are not only a gangrene on our Church, but a most incessant drain on the scanty capital of our country. Hitherto, Wales has received but few benefits of this description, and, undoubtedly, she has suffered much in consequence. Yet, notwithstanding her disadvantages, she has not been so entirely destitute of illustrious individuals as is sometimes imagined. A few names may be enumerated. Inigo Jones, the Architect; Dr. Donne, Poet and Divine; Sir Hugh Middleton, who supplied London with water, by the formation of "the new river;" Archbishop Williams; Sir William Jones, Justice Powel, and Baron Price, three Judges celebrated for their great patriotism and inflexible integrity; Dr. Rees, the Encyclopædist; Sir William Jones oriental and general scholar, and a man of extraordinary general attainments; Wilson, the Painter;—in our own times, Dr. W. Owen Pughe, Philologist and Celtic Scholar; Dr. Meyrick, Author of the Essay on Ancient Armour; the Rev. Walter Davies, Celtic Scholar; the Rev. John Williams, Author of the Life of Alexander the Great; Mrs. Hemans. I have reason to believe that an Essay will shortly be published on this subject, by — Williams, Esq., to whom the prize of the Cymmrodorion was awarded in 1831, for a Biographical Sketch of the eminent Men Wales had produced since the Reformation.

* In Pembrokeshire, which is also in the diocese of St. David's, I am informed that absenteeism is comparatively uncommon. Not above fifteen of the parishes are in the gift of the Bishop; the rest are in the patronage of the Crown, laymen, &c.

SUMMARY OF THE STATE OF THE CHURCH IN NORTH WALES.

Amount of Church Property enjoyed by the Higher Orders of the Church, compared with the Amount possessed by the Working Clergy.—Progressive Increase of the Wealth of the Bishoprics.

The increase that has taken place within the last two centuries in the wealth of the North Welsh bishoprics, and in the proportion which it bears to that of the inferior clergy, has been enormous indeed, and is ascribable to a variety of causes. 1. To the improved value of agricultural produce, and, consequently, of tithes and church lands. 2. The annexation of new benefices to the bishoprics, either by Act of Parliament, or a commendam from the Crown. 3. The exemption of the possessions of the wealthier clergy from the payment of "First fruits" and "Tenths," according to the strict ancient proportions. 4. The salaries paid by Bishops to curates employed by them in parishes annexed to their sees being allowed to remain stationary— instead of advancing in proportion to, the increased value and population of such parishes. 5. The practice adopted by the Governors of Queen Anne's Bounty, of applying the Bounty fund in relieving Bishops from the charge of supporting their own curates. Many of these causes have also operated in favour of cathedrals, lay impropriators, &c.

BANGOR DIOCESE.

BISHOPRIC OF BANGOR.—Dr. Bethel, Bishop.—Manor of Edeyrn in Lleyn, (which was leased by a former Bishop for a long period, and has never since been recovered). Manor of Llanelidan, county of Denbigh. House in London. By an Act passed in 1685, wherein it is stated that the certain revenues of the see did not exceed £200 the following parishes were annexed to the bishopric :—Llanrhaiadr-yn-Nghinmerch, £12 0. Amlwch, £700. Llangrustiolus, £500. Llandegai, £600. Since that time (1685), Llandyrnog, £600, and Llanddyvnan, £700, have been taken into commendam. In 1813, Llanynys, £550, and Cyffylliog, £200

Total revenues of the Bishopric, allowing £350 for manors &c............ £5400
Bishop of Lichfield, Tywyn, &c ....:...... 1100
Bishop of Chester, Llanbeblig........:.. 560
Dean of Bangor, son of Bishop Warren, Llanvihangel Ysceiviog, £400:
    Gyffin, £600.—as Chancellor, £3 0 1300
H. Majendie, son of Bishop Majendie, Pen-mynydd Prebend 550
W. Warren, relative of Bishop Warren, Llanvair Prebend 600
S. Majendie, son of Bishop Majendie, Rectory of Llanrhuddlad............ 550
Total enjoyed by Bishops and their connections 10,060
Cathedral and Choir of Bangor, added in 1685..... 2305
Colleges, Bodedeyrn and Holyhead, £1450.—Llanwynda, £500.—Clynnog, £900.—Aberdaron, £320 added in the time of Charles I......... 3170
Archdeacon of Merioneth, J. Jones.................... 250
Absentees, living more than seven miles from their livings, in Anglesea, £4470.—Caernarvonshire, £2240.—Merionethshire, £560.—Montgomeryshire, £415.—Denbighshire, Llanvwrog, held by incumbent of two other rich benefices, £450....... ....:..............................,,....... 8135

Total as above, deducting for salaries paid by Bishops, absentees, &c.,
to their curates, £1715... 22,205
Amount enjoyed by the general body of the clergy in this diocese, including salaries* of curates of Bishops, absentees, &c., £1715,
and deducting Queen Anne's Bounty and fees, £3253. 20,295

ST. ASAPH DIOCESE.

BISHOPRIC OF ST. ASAPH.—Dr. Carey, Bishop.—Manors and lands in Flintshire, £1600 Manor of St. Martin's, £200. Ditto at Llandeglo, £8⁰. The above Manors produce little emolument to the present Bishop, in consequence of their having been almost all leased on very advantageous terms, by Bishops Shipley and Luxmoore, and in most instances to their relatives. The Rev. C. S. Luxmoore, is lessee of Llandeglo, Mrs. Shipley, of one half of St. Martin's, &c. Pensions, spiritualia and lactualia, £400.—Rectories of Llanasaph, £600.—Llan-y-Blodwel, £150.—St. Asaph. £30.—Rhuddlan, £12. Tithes of Aberchwiler, £400.—Henllan, £300.—Llansilin, £130. In 1567, the following Rectories were annexed :—Newmarket, £250. Abergele, £1150.—Llangwstenin, £300.—Llysvaen, £35.—Llanelian, £130.—Bettws, £120.—Dyserth, £400.—Llan St. Ffraid, £300. In 1662, taken into commendam, Llandrinio, £550.—Llandysilio, £450.—Melverley, £200. Added in 1687, Northop £800. —Flint £60. Added in 1759, Llandrillo, £320. In 1810, Pennant taken into commendam, £300. Some of the preceding parishes are leased. Aberchwiler is leased to Mrs. Shipley—Llanasaph to the Very Rev. C. S. Luxmoore.

Total amount of the revenues of the Bishopric.. ....£9267

From the above details, it is clear, that, for some time after the Reformation, the revenues of the Welsh bishoprics were trivial compared to what they now are ; or rather, that their possessions were scanty in number and extent, compared to what they now are ; for, in estimating the increase in their revenues, we must also take into consideration the prodigious increase in the value of agricultural produce. It has, I trust, been sufficiently proved, in a former part of this Essay, that the episcopal duties were more satisfactorily performed when the income of the Welsh sees were more proportioned to the wants and resources of the country, than they have been in modern times. There can be no doubt, that the great wealth of our bishoprics has been the temptation by which the Ministers of the Crown have been led to fill them with improper persons. Certain it is, however, that when the Welsh sees were on their ancient simple footing, they were filled by men who, though well versed in the language of the people, were quite as learned—quite as upright—and quite

* These items, in the statement of which there has been some slight variance, are here reckoned at the highest amount.

as pious, as the prelates we have had in modern days; and what by some will be thought a matter of no slight importance, they were quite as often men of high birth—members of "the most respectable families in Wales."*

RELATIVES OF THE BISHOPS OF ST. ASAPH.

RELATIVES OF BISHOP LUXMOORE.—C. S. Luxmoore, Dean and Chancellor. —House, &c., belonging to the Deanery, £40.—Parishes of Henllan, £1500.— St. Asaph, £426.—LlanNevydd, £300.—Llanvair-Tal-Haiarn, £220.—Darowain, £120.--Chancellorship, (from fees,) £400..£3006

Besides the above, the reverend gentleman enjoys at least £600 in this diocese, as lessee under certain leases granted to him by his father, Bishop Luxmoore, of tithes and manors belonging to the see. He also owes to the same patron the following preferments in Hereford Diocese. Cradley, R. £1200.—Bromyard, V. £500.—Prebend of Hereford, £50. Portion of Bromyard £50 at present; but on the expiration of a lease, dependent on a very old life, this preferment will be worth £1400. Thus, the Reverend gentleman is possessed of no less than eleven sources of emolument !

The total value of all his Church preferments may be estimated at
least at.............. ....£6356!!

J. M. Luxmoore, brother of the Rev. C. S. Luxmoore.—Marchwiail, R. £720.—Llanarmon-yn-Iâl, £500.—Prebend of Meivod, in St George's parish £60.—Morton Chapelry,† £800 (from land purchased with Queen Anne's Bounty !)—Whitford, £1000......... .... £3020

Besides the above, the Reverend gentleman enjoys £200 as joint Registrar of Hereford; but the tithes of Whitford being on lease, they are not at present of any great value to him. The total actual value of his Church preferments may be stated at about £3000.

C. Luxmoore.—Berriew, £450.—Llanymynach, £450, conferred when the Reverend gentleman was only twenty-four years of age......... ....£900

Coryn Luxmoore..., ...£300

Total enjoyed by relatives of Bishop Luxmoore, in the diocese of St.
Asaph alone £7226

* Catherall's North Wales—Bangor.

† MORTON CHAPEL IS IN SHROPSHIRE,—A small portion of which county lies in this Diocese. Five parishes of the Shropshire district thus situated are included in this comparison; the remainder, being the gift of laymen, have been excluded from it, inasmuch as the object is to compare the extent to which the Bishops of Wales have consulted the welfare of the church, on the one hand, and their own personal interests on the other, in the disposal of those benefices of which they are themselves the Patrons.

The value, however, of Church property belonging to the relatives of Bishop Luxmoore, in Hereford and St. Asaph, is £10,776! Such is the amount *at present* in the hands of this single family. In the time of the late Bishop Luxmoore the case stood thus :—such was the prosperity of the times, that the revenues of the see of St. Asaph were worth at least £12,000, and the parishes, &c. belonging to his relatives were worth at least £15,000, so that the country has had to pay £27,000 per annum! for the services of one prelate!!

RELATIVES AND CONNECTIONS OF BISHOP HORSELEY.—H. Horseley.—Gresford, V. £450.—Castell Caereinion, V. £600.—Llanvair-Tal-Haiarn, Preb. £220.

G. Robson, Prebendary of Ditto, £220.—Chirk, V. £600.—Erbistock, R. £350.

H. Neve.—Llan Saint Ffraid, V. £250.

Total enjoyed by connections of Bishop Horseley............................... £2690

RELATIVES AND CONNECTIONS OF BISHOP CLEAVER.—J. Cleaver.— Corwen, £300.—Newtown, £400, exchanged with G. Foxton, for a living in England.

W. Cleaver, as Precentor of St. Asaph, Lands, £6.—Llangernyw, £250.—St. George's, £30.—St. Asaph, £500.—Dinmeirchion, £300 as sinecure Rector.—Llanvawr, £340. The Rev. W. Cleaver is a most charitable and excellent man. Many of the above parishes are in lease, by which his actual revenues are somewhat reduced. Total enjoyed by the relatives of Bishop Cleaver.. £2126

RELATIVES OF BISHOP BAGOT.—R. Wingfield.—Rhiwabon, £700.

C. Wingfield.—Llanllwchhaiarn, £400.

Total enjoyed by relatives of Bishop Bagot 1100

DEAN AND CHAPTER—Consisting chiefly of the relatives and connections of Bishops—Llansilin, R. 670

SINECURISTS,—Who owe their preferments to mere influence and personal favour, and who are unconnected with the country, have never done any duty in this diocese, and are all resident in remote parts of England!

S. Thurlow, son of Lord Chancellor Thurlow, Hope, £600.—Llandrillo-in-Edeyrnion, £350.—Gibson, Llanbryn-Mair, £300.—R. Finch, Cwm, £210.—F. Corie, Kilcain, £400.—H. Milner, Treasurer of St. Asaph, Meliden, £300.—J. Drake, Chancellor of St. Asaph, £15.— C. Thoroton, Llan St. Ffraid, £500. 2675

Dean and Chapter of Winchester, Gresford and Wrexham. 2400

SINECURISTS AND ABSENTEES, but connected with the Diocese.—S. Holland, Llangwm, £260.—R. Clough, Llansanan, £200	460
CATHEDRAL OF ST. ASAPH.—£1040 added in the reign of Charles the Second.	1040
COLLEGES.—Guilsfield, £900.—Pool, £900.—Buttington. £200.—Meivod, £500,—all added since the time of Henry the Eighth	2500
To schools at Llanrwst, not properly applied.—Eglwys Fach	860
Incumbents ignorant of the Welsh language.—Llanrhaiadr, £450.—Machynllaeth, £400.	850
Absentees from the county in which their benefices are situated, and residing remote from them.	3185
Total employed as above, deducting salaries of curates of Bishops, absentees, &c., £2680.	34,369
Total enjoyed by the general body of the resident clergy, including the salaries of the curates of Bishops, absentees, &c., £2680, and exclusive of Queen Anne's Bounty and fees, £2230.	18,391

The amount enjoyed from this diocese, by the Bishop and the relatives of former Bishops alone, amounts to £23,679,—and thus, on the most liberal calculation, exceeds the whole amount enjoyed by all the other resident clergy put together!

Such is a picture of the Church in North Wales in the nineteenth century! I shall abstain from all comment; for, I can little hope to add anything to the plain force of facts, by any comment of mine; facts, indeed, which it is equally impossible to strengthen, to paliate, or to deny! The future prospects of the Principality are in the hands of our present rulers; and though her hopes and fears may appear of little moment amidst the interests of a mighty empire, yet, I trust, that they will not be altogether disregarded. The preceding enquiry has, I trust, been conducted in the spirit of fairness, and not in the spirit of party; and I may conclude with a sentiment in which the good and patriotic of all parties will, I believe, unite. *In redressing the wrongs of a people conspicuous alike for their bravery in the field, and their patience under domestic misrule,—our present rulers may earn from the lips of all, the noblest praise that can be awarded to statesmen—the glory of having acted—not under the pressure of existing dangers, but under the guidance of the still small voice of wisdom and justice.*

*NOW READY, in One Handsome 8vo. Volume of nearly 800 Pages, in
Elegant Cloth Binding, Gilt Lettered, and Red Burnished Edges,
Price 15s., Postage 1s.*

CAMBRIAN BIBLIOGRAPHY:

CONTAINING

AN ACCOUNT OF THE BOOKS PRINTED IN THE WELSH
LANGUAGE, OR RELATING TO WALES, FROM THE YEAR 1546 TO THE END
OF THE EIGHTEENTH CENTURY; WITH BIOGRAPHICAL NOTICES.

BY THE LATE

Rev. William Rowlands

(GWILYM LLEYN).

EDITED AND ENLARGED

BY THE REV. D SILVAN EVANS, B.D.

Rector of Llan ym Mawd lwy, Merioneth.

LLANIDLOES:
PRINTED AND PUBLISHED BY JOHN PRYSE.
1869.

Opinions & Notices of "Llyfryddiaeth y Cymry."

It is most interesting and very valuable.—Rev. D. R. Thomas, M.A., Rector of Cefn, St. Asaph.

The Rev. W. Watkins, M.A., Warden of Llandovery College, says:—"I like it much, and think that you as well as the editor deserve much gratitude from lovers of the language and its literature."

From *The South Wales Press*.

Few pursuits have met with the persistent ridicule that has bestowed upon book collecting; and the very term "Bibliomania" seems to have been given it in order to express the contempt its professors are held in. Novelists and dramatists have made their readers and hearers merry with the wittily exaggerated portraits they have drawn of the poor, awkward, ill-dressed, and often half-starved bibliomaniac. And yet we venture to say that of all the manias which have at different times taken hold of men, this is by far the most intelligent, and the one most likely to reach its climax in the highest cultured people. It does, no doubt, appear strange to the ordinary man that any one should not only profess, but evidently have such rapturous pleasure in becoming the owner of a dingy old volume, more fitted it would appear for the waste basket than the library cabinet. But they, and they alone, who have experienced the inexpressible delight, the overwhelming sense of joy with which every leaf—from title page to colophon of a new found treasure in the shape of such a book, is tenderly turned over, the creases carefully taken out, the pagination examined and checked by reference to the catch words, together with numerous other delightful tasks, can appreciate in the smallest degree the thrill with which the despised "hunter" seizes upon the wished-for work. In this handsome volume of "Cambrian Bibliography" we have a proof that the mania or whatever it may be called, has found cultivators in Wales. The enterprising publisher, Mr. Pryse, in a short address to the reader, explains that the book owes its existence to the following circumstances:—"Upwards of forty years ago the Rev. William Rowlands, a Wesleyan minister stationed in Wales, began the compilation of a register of books published in the Principality, or having reference thereto. After many years of labour and diligent research, a prospectus was issued proposing to publish the work in one volume, at fifteen shillings. Although an energetic canvass was made throughout the Principality, the number of orders obtained was not sufficient to encourage Mr. Rowlands to place his MSS. in the hands of a printer. Some portions of the work were, however, published in the *Traethodydd*, and of their value a reviewer in the *Athenæum* wrote thus:—'It yields the fruit of well-directed research, comprises a large amount of interesting matter, and furnishes the best possible aid to collectors of books, and to historians who may desire to treat either of the general or particular history of the period: with respect to Welsh affairs, as well as to Welsh literature, it is absolutely invaluable. We hope that the author will continue his labour, and render his catalogue and commentaries complete to this third century.' All that the author lived to complete, but it was not until some time after his death that steps were taken to ensure its publication."—After this comes the preface in Welsh by the editor, and it is followed by the preface of the compiler, the Rev. William Rowlands. In a work of this description it is, of course, impossible to do more th   speak of the general completeness of the various notices, and we can say that .   , careful perusal, there is nothing appertaining to the subject which will be :   d for in vain. Of the influence of the compilation on the spread of a knowledge of Welsh literature in England, as well as its certain tendency to keep alive the native interest in the language, we cannot make adequate mention otherwise than in terms which would seem greatly exaggerated. The style in which it is got up with regard to the binding and whole external appearance would do credit to any London publishing house, and Mr. Pryse deserves the highest praise for this addition to the Literature of Wales.

OPINIONS AND NOTICES.—Continued.

The author's trustee (T. G. Jones, Esq.) after inspecting a complete copy of the work, has written these kind and encouraging words to its publisher:—"I am more than pleased that it fell into your hands, and that you have turned out such a really handsome volume. Poor Gwilym Lleyn, could he but have had a look at it before he went."

One gentleman (J. Joseph, Esq., F.S.A., Brecon), whose acquaintance with the literature of Wales is most extensive, after inspecting the work and the way it has been got up, writes as follows:—"Mr. Rowlands must have been diligent beyond measure in compiling so large and interesting a volume; and I must confess that the manner in which it has been printed reflects no ordinary amount of credit upon you as printer and publisher."

The Rev. Dr. James, of Panteg, Pontypool, says:—"Your *Llyfryddiaeth y Cymry* is a very well got up volume, and well bound, which is seldom the case with Welsh books. The arrangement of the books chronologically, and the numbering of them 1, 2, 3, &c., under each year, is the best mode of presenting the gradual growth of Welsh literature since the Reformation, and one which offers great facility for reference. I admire your public spirit in bringing out so large a volume at a small town like Llanidloes."

Rowlands's Cambrian Bibliography is a bulky and handsomely got-up volume, long-promised to Welsh scholars, but the appearance of which has been delayed by various circumstances until now. The work is not a mere register of the titles of the great number of books, the publication of which it records, but it includes also descriptions of the rarer books, with short biographies of the authors of some of them; and these portions of the book are interesting as well as curious. This remark applies especially to the satirical and other pamphlets about Welsh affairs which were rather plentiful in the stormy 17th century. The review begins, however, in the early part of the 16th century, when the first book printed in Welsh made its appearance. Many other interesting facts might be cited, but we need add no more to justify our remark that the "Cambrian Bibliography" is a work full of curious matter, altogether unique, and well deserving of a place in the library of every gentleman connected with Wales, or interested with Welsh history or literature.—From *The Hereford Times*.

From *The Academy*, written by H. Gaidoz, editor of the *Revue Celtique*.

Although the present work is written in Welsh, we consider it worth bringing under the notice of our readers. To a few who are engaged in bibliographical researches, it may prove useful as a book of reference; and to others it is an eloquent demonstration that Welsh literature does exist. It was originally compiled by the Rev. William Rowlands, and occupied 40 years of his life. Portions of it were published during his lifetime in a Welsh magazine, *Y Traethodydd*. After the author's death one of the best authors of the Principality, the Rev. D. Silvan Evans was entrusted with the MS. Mr. Evans revised and greatly enlarged the work. As it is presented to us, it contains the title and the full bibliographical description of every work written in Welsh, or relating to Wales, published from the year 1546 to the year 1800, and besides, carefully written notices of the authors (original writers or translators), printers, and publishers. The English works of the chief Welsh writers have also being added. We have here, in a fragmentary form a complete history of Welsh literature during the last three centuries. The task of compiling such a work was all the more difficult from the fact that Welsh having been neglected for a long time many books had become very scarce. On the other hand there are very few public or private collections of Welsh books. Even the collection in the British Museum is very scanty. Nevertheless such has been the industry of the two compilers, that we may say with full confidence that very few works have escaped their attention. We dare not blame the authors for publishing this book in Welsh. When the *Times*, and the more prosaic part of the English public are scorning *Eisteddfodau* and every expression of Welsh nationality, it is not the moment for Welsh scholars to desert their language, and to betray the cause of their country.

OPINIONS AND NOTICES.—Continued.

O'r Traethodydd.

Prif orchestwaith llenyddol oes ein hen gyfaill Gwilym Lleyn ydoedd ei LYFR-YDDIAETH. Yr ydoedd erioed yn llyfrwr mawr; ac yr oedd ei hoffder at hen lyfrau Cymraeg yn nwyd angerddol yn ei natur. Bu yn chwilio, yn gohebu, yn ymholi, ac yn trefnu defnyddiau y gwaith mawr hwn ar hyd ei oes. Nid gwaith yw hwn ag y gallai gyfansoddi rhag ei flaen yn ei lyfyrgell; ond gwaith ag oedd yn gofyn llafur dybryd am flynyddoedd lawer, i chwilio llyfrgelloedd, gohebu â henafiaethwyr a llenorion, argraffwyr, awdwyr, cyhoeddwyr, llyfrwerthwyr, &c. Yn mharatoad defnyddiau y Llyfryddiaeth teithiodd gannoedd, os nad miloedd o fil'diroedd, yn benaf ar ei draed, ddydd a nos, haf a gauaf, am lawer o flynyddau. Ysgrifenodd gannoedd o lythyrau, a gwariodd lawer o'i arian yn gystal a'i amser. Mae o'n blaen gofnodiad yn ei lawysgrifen ei hun o'i gostau gyda'r gwaith diflas o geisio casglu enwau tanysgrifwyr at ei waith hyd Mehefin 28ain, 1859. Yr oedd costau llythyrau ac argraffu, hyd yr amser hwnw yn 7p. 2s. 4c.; ac mae yn debyg iddo wario llawer mwy na byny cyn ei farwolaeth, yn 1865. Ymysg items traul y gohebu, yr ydym yn cael un fel hyn,—Llythyrau at Weinidogion Wesleyaidd yn Lloegr yn deall Cymraeg, 2p. Yr ydym yn nodi yr item hon fel engraifft hefyd o'i aflwyddiant wrth bygoutu am danynt ymysg y Cymru yn Lloegr. Ond ni ddigalonid ef gan unrhyw siomedigaeth. Llwyddodd gyda'r gorchwyl o siorhâu tanysgrifwyr mor bell ag a gallesid dysgwyl at lyfr o gymeriad a phris y Llyfryddiaeth. Llawer o chwys a dagrau a gostiodd y Llyfryddiaeth iddo; a bu farw cyn gweled ei lafur wedi ei goroni â llwyddiant llawn. Pe cawsai ond golwg cyn marw ar y gyfrol hardd ag y mae Mr. Pryse, o Lanidloes newydd ei dwyn allan, diau y buasai ei lawenydd yn ddifesur. Mawr fyddai ei bleser pan, ymysg pentwr llechlyd o lyfrau yn y bwthyn pell, y deuai o hyd i hen lyfr pwdr, -hen almanac, fe allai, ag yr oedd mewn ymchwil am dano. Byddai yn cael mwynhad dirfawr ar y fath achlysur, fel un wedi cael ysglyfaeth lawer. A beth a fuasai y boddlonrwydd teimlad a gawsai ef wrth weled y gyfrol brydferth hon, ag yr aberthodd ef esmwythyd, ei gysuron, ei iechyd, os nad ei fywyd, i gasglu a threfnu ei defnyddiau, ac i wneyd i fyny restr ei thanysgrifwyr?

Heblaw y desgrifiad a rydd o wahanol lyfrau, mae y cofnodau bywgraffyddol am eu hawduron, cyfieithwyr, cyhoeddwyr, ac argraffyddion; yr hanesynau a'r nodiadau eglurhaol, yn peri fod y tudalenau yn ddifyrus ac addysgiadol i'r darllenydd. Nid llechres sychllyd a llom, fel rhestr rhyw lyfrwerthwr yn *Paternoster Row*, *Ave Maria Lane*, neu *Amen Corner*, Llundain, yw LLYFRYDDIAETH Y CYMRY, ond hanes llenyddiaeth ein gwlad, am yr yspaid a nodwyd, yn dangos yn ffyddlawn ei gwerth a'i rhagoriaeth, ar un llaw, a pha beth sydd yn wael a diffygiol ynddi, ar y llaw arall. Nis gall neb, er craffed a synwyroled y byddo, feddu syniad cywir am answdd a helaethder ein llenyddiaeth, ac am y llafur a gymerwyd, dan anfanteision a gwrthwynebiadau dirfawr, i daenu goleuni gwybodaeth yn mysg ein henafiaid, yn yr unfed ganrif ar bymtheg, yr eilfed ar bymtheg, a'r ddeunawfed, a bod yn ddyeithr i gynnwysiad y gyfrol werthfawr hon. Mae yn ddiau yn rhoddi achos diolch i bob Cymro ystyriol a gwladgarol wrth weled y cynydd a wnaed, a chynnyrch toreithiog y llafur a gymerwyd; er hyny, dylem gofio yn ostyngedig ein bod ni, erbyn hyn, ar lawer ystyr, "yn medi yr hyn ni lafuriason; ereill a lafuriasant, a ninau a aethom i mewn i'w llafur hwynt."

Byddai yn beth anesgusodol ynom beidio hysbysu fod y "Chwanegion a'r Cyweiriadau" gan y golygydd yn ychwanegiad mawr at werth y gyfrol. Ymgymerodd Mr. Silvan Evans â'r gorchwyl ar ddymuniad neillduol yr awdwr yn ei fywyd, ac oddiar awydd i weled y gwaith yn argraffedig. Nis gallasai yr olygiaeth ddisgyn i ddwylaw neb mwy cymhwys, o ran dysg a gwybodaeth, i wneyd cyfiawnder a'r gwaith, gan ei fod hefyd, er pan yn ieuanc, wedi gwneyd llenyddiaeth Gymreig yn un gangen arbenig o'i efrydiaeth; ac nid oes ond ychydig, yn maes ei lafurwaith ef, wedi gwneuthur cymaint erddi. Mae yn gweddi i ni gydnabod y gwasanaeth a wnaeth i'w genedl trwy y gofal mawr a gymerodd i ddwyn allan waith yr awdwr mor rydd oddiwrth gamsyniadau ag ydoedd modd, trwy ddefnyddio pob mantais o fewn ei gyraedd, ac nid llafur bychan, yn ddiau, ydoedd hyny. A pha ddiffygion neu wallau bynag a ddichon fod eto yn aros yn y gwaith, y mae yn addaw gwneyd hyd ci allu tuag at eu cyflawni a'u diwygio.

Gwnaeth yr argraffydd, yr hwn hefyd yw y cyhoeddwr, ei ran yntau yn hardd a destlus iawn. Mae y gwaith wedi ei gyhoeddi mewn un gyfrol wythplyg, yn cynnwys 784 o dudalenau, o argraffwaith glân, ar bapyr da, mewn rhwymiad prydferth a chryf, gydag ymylau cochion. Nid yn fynych y mae gwell gwaith yn cael ei droi allan o un argraffdy na swyddfa yn ein gwlad, er y canfyddir ynddi rai gwallau wedi dianc heb eu cywiro. Mae anturiaeth y cyhoeddwr yn fawr a chostus, ac yn teilyngu cefnogaeth arbenig dysgedigion a llenorion Cymru ; ac yr ydym yn gobeithio na fydd neb o honynt, na chamaint ag un Cymro gwladgarol yn unlle, a fyddo mewn modd i dalu am dano, heb roddi derbyniad parod a chalonog iddo. Ai tybed y rhaid i'r cyhoeddwr, wedi y cwbl, fod yn golledwr? A raid i ni gredu fod rhai o'r tanysgrifwyr yn gwrthod derbyn y gyfrol, gan ei dychwelyd yn ol heb gymaint a'i hagor, ac yn eu plith rai boneddigion a chlerigwyr, mewn sefyllfaoedd da a bywiolaethau breision? Os gwir hyn, fel yr ydym yn ofni, mae y cyfryw yn gwaradwyddo eu hunan yn fawr, er mwyn arbed ychydig arian ! Yn wyneb hyn, yr ydym yn galw ar lanciau y gweithydd mawrion, yn y Dê a'r Gogledd, i ddyfod allan i roddi ymwared. Ymunent yn gyfeillachau lliosog, a thrwy ragdaliadau wythnosol, ysgeifn, gallai pob aelod roi heibio yn fuan ddigon i dalu am y llyfr, a'i gael yn feddiant iddo ei hun. Ychydig ymarbediad oddiwrth gwrw, tybaco, a phethau diles o'r fath, a'u galluogai i wneyd i fyny 500, neu fwy, o danysgrifwyr newyddion, ffyddlawn,—nifer digonol i gadw y cyhoeddwr yn ddigolled ac i gywilyddio pob tanysgrifiwr anffyddlawn, fel na feiddio mwy ddangos ei wyneb. Lanciau Cymru, meddyliwch am hyn !

Mae y gyfrol yn gyflwynedig gan y cyhoeddwr i nawdd *llenorion* Cymru yn benodol, i ba rai y bydd yn dra dyddorol, ac o wasanaeth mawr. A oes rhai yn eu mysg yn caru chwilio i henafiaethau eu gwlad a'u cenedl? Cant yma hysbysrwydd am bob llwf= argraffedig sydd yn dwyn perthynas â'r gangen hon o wybodaeth, a chyfarwy.: yd hylaw at yr awdwyr sydd wedi ysgrifenu ar hanes gwlad eu genedigaeth, yn wladol ac eglwysig.

Preparing for Publication, in one handsome demy 8vo. volume,
elegantly bound in cloth, Price 6s. 6d.,

THE WELSHMAN'S CANDLE,

By VICAR PRITCHARD, of Llandovery,

Translated from the Welsh by the REV. W. EVANS, with an Introductory Essay by the REV. J. R. KILSBY JONES.

John Pryse, Printer and Publisher, Llanidloes, will feel much obliged if intending purchasers will kindly forward him their orders per post. This volume will form one of the most interesting and attractive table books published in Wales during the present century.

PRYSE'S
Welsh Interpreter,

CONTAINING AN EASY
INTRODUCTION TO THE WELSH LANGUAGE; COPIOUS
LISTS OF WORDS AND PHRASES IN COMMON USE; FAMILIAR
DIALOGUES; PARABLES, PROVERBS, AND POETRY;
USEFUL RECIPES, TABLES OF DISTANCES FOR
THE USE OF TRAVELLERS IN NORTH
AND SOUTH WALES.

ALSO AN ESSAY ON

The Literature of Wales.
&c., &c., &c.

"Fu Ner a folant; eu hiaith a gadwant; ei tir a gollant ond gwyllt Walia"—Their god they'l adore; their language they'll keep; their country they'll lose except wild Walia.—*Taliesin*.

Llanidloes:
PRINTED AND PUBLISHED BY JOHN PRYSE, AT THE "TELE-
GRAPH" AND "OBSERVER" OFFICE; AND SOLD BY ALL
BOOKSELLERS IN THE PRINCIPALITY.

PRICE 9d. IN PAPER COVERS; IN CLOTH, 1s.

www.ingramcontent.com/pod-product-compliance
Lightning Source LLC
Chambersburg PA
CBHW031727230426
43669CB00007B/278